Labour, Environment and Industrial Change

The International Geographical Union's Commission on Industrial Change was appointed in August 1984. Its work focuses on improving the understanding of the processes leading to industrial change at all spatial scales. It is concerned with the implications of such influences as technological change, the supply of and demand for labour, the organisation of work, the internationalisation of economic activities, and the roles of the various 'actors' involved such as firms, financial institutions, governments and trade unions. Emphasis is also placed on the cross-cultural applicability of the processes and impacts not only to improve theoretical constructs but also to try to narrow the gap between academic research and the development by agencies operating within various economic and social systems of appropriate planning policies and their implementation.

This publication is an outcome of its third annual conference, held at Rabka near Kraków in September 1987.

Also published on behalf of the IGU Commission on Industrial Change

New Technology and Regional Development
Bert van der Knaap and Egbert Wever (editors)

Peripheralisation and Industrial Change: Impacts on Nations, Regions, Firms and People
G.J.R. Linge (editor)

LABOUR, ENVIRONMENT AND INDUSTRIAL CHANGE

Edited by

G.J.R. LINGE

and

G.A. van der KNAAP

ROUTLEDGE
London and New York

First published 1989
by Routledge
11 New Fetter Lane, London EC4P 4EE
29 West 35th Street, New York, NY 10001

© 1989 IGU Commission on Industrial Change

Printed and bound in Great Britain by
Biddles Ltd, Guildford and King's Lynn

British Library Cataloguing in Publication Data

Labour, environment and industrial change
    Great Britain. Labour market
    I. Linge, G.J.R. (Godfrey J.R.). II.
    Knaap, G.A. van der
    331.12'0941

    ISBN 0-415-00928-6

Library of Congress Cataloging in Publication Data

Labour, environment, and industrial change / edited by G.J.R. Linge
and G.A. van der Knaap.
        p. cm.
    Papers from the 3rd annual conference held by the International
Geographic Union's Commission on Industrial Change, at Rabka near
Kraków, Sept. 1987.
    Bibliography: p.
    Includes index.
    1. Industry – Location – Social aspects – Congresses. 2. Industrial
organization – Congresses. 3. Organizational change – Congresses.
4. Labor supply – Effect of technological innovations on – Congresses.
I. Linge, G.J.R. II. Knaap, G.A. van der. III. International
Geographic Union. Commission on Industrial Change.
HD58.L235 1989
338.6'042–dc19   88-30767
                                                          CIP

Contents

List of contributors   vii

Acknowledgements   ix

Preface   xi

1. Labour, Environment and Industrial Change
   G.A. van der Knaap and G.J.R. Linge   1

2. Labour Market Models in their Spatial Expression
   Sergio Conti   20

3. Industrial Change in Poland and the Working and
   Living Environment
   Bronisław Kortus   39

4. Attitudes to Industrial Development and Quality of
   Life in Poland
   Bolesław Domański   50

5. Gender, Employment and Territory in Metropolitan
   Environments
   Paul Villeneuve   67

6. New Production Technologies, Labour and the North
   American Auto Industry
   John Holmes   87

7. Conceptualising Processes of Skill Change: A Local
   Labour Market Approach
   Jamie A. Peck and Peter E. Lloyd   107

Contents

8. The Changing Organisation of Labour and its
   Impacts on Daily Activities
   Roman Matykowski and Tadeusz Stryjakiewicz   128

9. Spatial Implications of Unionisation, Employment
   and Labour Activism
   G.A. van der Knaap and L. van der Laan   144

10. Strategies in Local Communities to Cope with
    Industrial Restructuring
    John Bradbury   167

References   185

Index   216

vi

Contributors

John BRADBURY, B.A. (Hons), M.A. (Wellington, New Zealand), Ph.D. (Simon Fraser, Canada), is an Associate Professor in the Geography Department at McGill University in Montreal, Quebec, Canada.

Sergio CONTI, Ph.D. (London), is Professor of Economic Geography, University of Turin.

Bolesław DOMAŃSKI, M.A. (Kraków), is Lecturer, Institute of Geography, The Jagiellonian University, Kraków, Poland.

John HOLMES, B.Sc., M.A. (Sheffield), Ph.D. (Ohio State), is Associate Professor, Department of Geography, Queen's University at Kingston, Canada.

G.A. van der KNAAP, drs (Geography, Utrecht), doctorate (Economics, Rotterdam), is Professor of Economic and Social Geography at the Economic Geography Institute, Erasmus University, Rotterdam. He is research adviser of the National Physical Planning Agency, The Hague, and Vice-Chairman of the IGU Commission on Industrial Change.

Bronisław KORTUS, M.A. (Warsaw), Ph.D. (Kraków), is Professor of Geography, Institute of Geography, The Jagiellonian University, Kraków, Poland.

L. van der LAAN, drs (Geography, Groningen), is Lecturer in Economic and Social Geography at the Economic Geography

Institute, Erasmus University, Rotterdam. He is also associated with Teachers' Training Colleges in Utrecht and Tilburg.

G.J.R. LINGE, B.Sc. (Econ.), Ph.D., is Professorial Fellow, Department of Human Geography, Research School of Pacific Studies, The Australian National University, and is Chairman of the IGU Commission on Industrial Change and Fellow of the Academy of the Social Sciences in Australia.

Peter E. LLOYD, M.A. (Birmingham), is Reader in Geography and Director of the Centre for Urban and Regional Industrial Development, Department of Geography, University of Manchester.

Roman MATYKOWSKI, Ph.D. (Poznań), is Adiunkt, Institute of Socio-Economic Geography and Spatial Planning, Adam Mickiewicz University, Poznań.

Jamie A. PECK, Ph.D. (Manchester), is a Research Associate at the Centre for Urban and Regional Industrial Development, Department of Geography, University of Manchester.

Tadeusz STRYJAKIEWICZ, Ph.D. (Poznań), is Adiunkt, Institute of Socio-Economic Geography and Spatial Planning, Adam Mickiewicz University, Poznań.

Paul VILLENEUVE, Ph.D. (University of Washington, Seattle) is Professor of Human Geography, Laval University, Quebec City, Canada.

Acknowledgements

John Bradbury wishes to acknowledge the financial support provided by the Fonds pour la Formation de Chercheurs et l'Aide à la Recherche, 1976-77, EQ 2944; the comments of Damaris Rose of the Institut National de la Recherche Scientifique-urbanisation (INRS) on an earlier draft of his text; and the help given by Jacques Critchley, Jean-François Marchand, Sophie Martin and Monique Tessier who collected data, undertook fieldwork, and made helpful comments for the chapter.

John Holmes gratefully acknowledges the support for the research and presentation of his paper by the Social Sciences and Humanities Research Council of Canada and the Queen's University Advisory Research Committee and School of Graduate Studies and Research. Table 6.2, p. 103, is reproduced by kind permission of the Canadian Automobile Workers Union.

G.J.R. Linge and G.A. van der Knaap warmly appreciate the practical assistance of Karen Manning, Christine Tabart and Mervyn Commons of the Department of Human Geography, ANU; Keith Mitchell and Ian Heyward of the Cartographic Unit, RSPacS, ANU; and Jan Linge for her scholarly and editorial contributions to this volume.

Roman Matykowski and Tadeusz Stryjakiewicz thank Maria Kawińska (Adam Mickiewicz University, Poznań) for translation assistance.

Jamie A. Peck and Peter E. Lloyd would like to thank Graham Haughton of the Centre for Urban and Regional Industrial

Acknowledgements

Development, University of Manchester, for his helpful comments on earlier drafts. The research they report here formed part of a larger project, funded by the Economic and Social Research Council (Grant No. FOO232350), entitled 'Skill needs and the effectiveness of training supply: case studies from the North West'. This support is gratefully acknowledged.

Paul Villeneuve wishes to thank Damaris Rose, Anne-Marie Séguin, Marc Miller, Reñe Morency and Gilles Viaud for their comments on drafts of his chapter, and to the Canadian Social Science Research Council and the Fonds pour la Formation de Chercheurs et l'Aide à la Recherche of Quebec for their financial support.

Preface

The rapid transformation of production processes in different parts of the world is having a considerable impact on the spatial organisation of industry and its related environments. This theme was studied at the 1987 conference of the IGU Commission on Industrial Change at Rabka near Kraków. Several important developments were discussed on the basis of the papers presented, a selection of which are brought together in this book. They focus on the ways in which people create different environments, adjust themselves to alterations in these environments brought about by external change, and on the spatial implications of these processes.

In the introductory chapter, van der Knaap and Linge discuss the nature of the complex relationships between the various themes. The labour market until now has been studied predominantly from the demand side using several paradigms. Conti (Chapter 2) compares these approaches and argues that segmentation theory appears to be an effective tool to gain an understanding of the changing relationships in the labour market. Using this theory he demonstrates for the area of the 'third' Italy that it can accommodate the increasing spatial variation and spatial differentiation which is emerging as a consequence of the process of industrial change. This is a worldwide process but in different environments the spatial impacts and institutional reactions may not be the same.

A clear example of this is the way in which government and households handle the increased awareness of environmental pollution in Poland. The nature of the problem is sketched by Kortus in Chapter 3, while Domański in Chapter 4 points up the difficulties of achieving spatial reorganisation in a labour-scarce economy. Important in this context is the role that the household plays in decision making. The provision and availability of basic amenities are here of crucial importance. The same set of constraints and decision processes operates in entirely different spatial and socio-economic situations. Villeneuve (Chapter 5) argues that the study of relations between individuals or, more generally, the study of governance structures is a powerful tool for understanding the nature of the changing relations between cities and suburbs, firms and households, and men and women. In his analysis of the Montreal labour market he takes the household and its internal and external relations as the focus to demonstrate this view.

A distinction can also be made between internal and external labour markets. One aspect of the former is the occupational mobility of persons having specific job functions. Another is the role skills play in the type and range of the task which belongs to a specific function. Holmes (Chapter 6) discusses the nature of change in the organisation of work in the large North American car manufacturing industry. Because of these changes functional flexibility has increased. This has led to a greater range of tasks and increased numerical flexibility. However, this applies only to the external labour market: the internal labour market remains very rigid because of the arrangements made in the past with the labour unions which were focused on the protection of the individual workplace and job function. Skills, their availability and qualities are becoming an increasingly important element for understanding the dynamics of the labour market. Peck and Lloyd (Chapter 7) argue that the study of skills has been rather neglected but that it has now become a corner-stone in the distribution of power in the labour market. This leads to reconsideration of the existing approaches to skill analysis. The unilinear, often unidirectional, model of skill change is no longer sufficient to cope with the increasing complexity of the dynamics of skill change so that a new analytical tool — the 'skill pool' — is being proposed. Skills and technology are closely related. In recent debates technology is often considered to be the main or dominant causal factor of change but this represents a rather narrow view of the various factors which contribute to the present process of socio-economic restructuring. The change in the numbers and variety of systems of technology is embedded within the information economy, the growth of which — along with the associated explosion of end-user computer applications — has improved the competitiveness of firms and regions. It also provides new and effective resources for future growth while, at the same time, affecting the organisation of both national and internal labour markets within the firm.

Various authors have pointed to the increased importance of the locality as a basis for the several processes at work. In this volume, too, Conti, and Peck and Lloyd, among others, argue — albeit from different points of view — along the same line. Matykowski and Stryjakiewicz in Chapter 8 provide a case study which examines ways in which constraints and incentives shape the organisation of labour at the local level. The problems of labour managements and how they cope with changes in the supply of labour is only one aspect. The position of the household and the decision where to locate appears to be a rather intricate problem. Not only the reaction of the household but also the reaction of the firm vis-à-vis changing conditions is of importance. The study of labour activism, such as strikes and factory occupations, by van der Knaap and van der Laan in Chapter 9 is one example of the complex relationships between place of work, nature of work, and households and their economic well-being. This point is taken up by Bradbury (Chapter 10) who examines the reaction within local communities to the closure of plants. The three case studies he presents provide valuable insights into the different strategies developed to cope with the sudden change in economic prospects. There is very little experience about how one should plan in a situation of decline. The problems are numerous and affect the community as a whole as well as individual households: the coping strategies vary for each of these groups.

Taken together, these chapters indicate that industrial geographers are widening their horizons and addressing some of the social issues raised by the processes of industrialisation. It is a recognition that what happens inside a factory affects society outside and what society does affects what happens within a factory. Hopefully, studies of this kind will help to reunite economic and social approaches to spatial analysis.

The contributions, we must emphasise, represent the views of the author(s) concerned: all have been subjected to searching editorial questioning but the opinions expressed may not necessarily be shared by us or by the referees to whom we turned for advice.

G. J. R. Linge   **G.A. van der Knaap**
Canberra, Australia   **Rotterdam, The Netherlands**

John Bradbury

It is with profound sadness that we have to record the death of John Bradbury, one of the contributors to this volume, on 20 June 1988. On behalf of all the authors in this book and the other participants at the Rabka Conference of the Commission from which it stemmed, we wish to acknowledge his contributions to the field of industrial geography and his interest in the work of the International Geographical Union (eds).

1

Labour, Environment and Industrial Change

G. A. van der Knaap and G. J. R. Linge

In recent discussions of the growth and development of the more industrialised economies, Kondratiev's formulation (dating from the 1920s) of the long-wave theory of trade has become rather prominent. Following the recession which started in Western Europe and the US in the mid-1970s, this theory gained in importance, especially because the length of the fourth cycle is estimated to be about fifty years (see van Duijn, 1977) and because of the coincidence of an economic downturn with the postulated crisis period during this latest cycle. According to Rothwell and Zegveld (1985), each of the Kondratiev waves or cycles can be associated with a particular cluster of innovations and characteristic products: the move from one period or cycle to the next also represents a related advance in technology (Table 1.1).

Technology encompasses the total body of knowledge that is necessary for the production of a good (van der Knaap et al., 1987). Technological change therefore refers to both institutional and social change and is reflected in the organisation of production as well as in the nature of production itself. It can be hypothesised that a change in production techniques and the associated organisational adjustments are an anti-cyclical phenomenon like the occurrence of major innovation waves. Such a change is thus most likely to start during a recession, a view that corresponds with Blauner's (1964) identification of three stages in the development of production techniques.

The first stage was dominated by manual labour and unsophisticated tools, with the occupational structure being closely associated with a wide product range. Traditional crafts were employed and little division of labour took place during the actual

1

Table 1.1: Main features of Kondratiev waves

Period		Characteristic product
1.	1782 - 1845	Steam power and textiles
2.	1846 - 1892	Railways, iron and steel
3.	1893 - 1948	Electric power, cars, chemicals
4.	1949 - (1998?)	Petrochemicals, synthetic materials, electronics
5.	(1998?) - ?	New materials, bio-technology

Source: after Rothwell and Zegveld, 1985:29.

production process: the organisation of the tasks needed was done freely and independently by the workers themselves. The second stage was characterised by the mechanisation of manual tasks that were still controlled by individual workers. At the same time the organisational structure of the production process was developing and this led to a division of the work process into preparatory and performance tasks. This was followed by a further division of labour, a greater standardisation of tasks and a more hierarchical structure of work supervision, which resulted in the considerable de-skilling necessary to enlarge the scale of production. The general introduction of scientific management techniques (Taylor, 1911), based on the principles of the division of labour and the standardisation of products (the Ford system), dehumanised labour and resulted in the dominance of the machine. The third (and current) stage is the automation of the production process by developing very advanced tools which themselves can be described as self-regulating systems. When these are combined with automated control systems people become less and less directly involved in the production process itself. The speed of this development has been closely associated in recent years with the introduction and incorporation of micro-electronics, although this revolution has taken place much more slowly than was predicated in the 1960s (cf. Cawkell, 1986). One reason for this is that existing processes are continually being reconsidered in the light of new technological developments, and this often leads to the redesign and redefinition of production techniques which, among other things, result in the reduction of the number of components in any given product and the sharing of some standardised parts between several products that are often only superficially made to look different as a marketing strategy.

These three stages in the development of production techniques are not synchronised with the four Kondratiev waves. The first stage, in which traditional crafts were dominant, disappears during the second Kondratiev wave; the second stage, with its emphasis on Taylorist principles, begins to make way for the third major change in the organisation of production during the third and fourth Kondratiev waves. This rather gradual process of change suggests that the organisation of production is only weakly related to changes in production technology and, this, in turn, raises questions about the intervening factors that contribute to a specific organisational structure.

A Conceptual Framework

The basic issue raised in the foregoing introductory comments is the way in which production and consumption have jointly been organised and the way in which the worker's role has changed: both relate to the production and consumption sides as well as to the interface between them (Figure 1.1a) Arguably, these three elements together determine the possibilities available to an individual by creating a set of 'binding' constraints (Hägerstrand, 1970). Thus, the focus must be on the way people can operate within the various sets of constraints surrounding any specified range of activities. To examine these relationships more closely, production has to be studied within the context of the firm, whereas consumption can be associated with the individual. The interface between consumption and production consists of three basic elements — the household, the region, and the transactions between them. The first two of these are examples of organisational frameworks where production and consumption have a specific structural form, the nature of which is determined by the individual characteristics of the different units, their own organisational structure and how these can be matched given a specific type of transaction. These transactions can be compared in some cases with the clearing mechanisms of the market, but they incorporate many different sets of constraints, including institutional, space-time and matching constraints. In this way

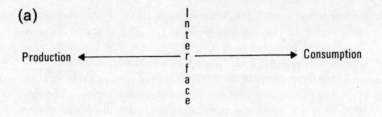

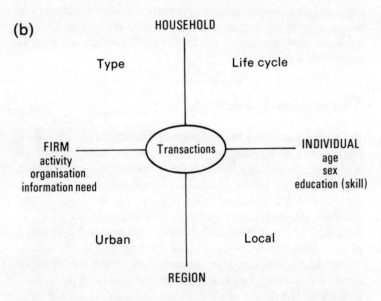

Figure 1.1: The relationships between individuals, firms and their environments: (a) aggregate relationships, (b) meso and micro relationships.

different types of transactions are shaped and possible conflicts can be resolved (Figure 1.1b).

The position of the individual in the exchange process is determined by age, sex, education and related skills. These characteristics enable people to occupy a set of positions within a household, a firm, and a region. In this way the household, as part of the interface, constitutes one of the elements that are relevant for the individual's movements in the labour market. The type of household and its life-cycle characteristics create the social environment for the interaction between an individual and a firm (Linge, 1984), which in turn is also influenced by the spatial setting of the household and the firm. At various times during the life-cycle of a household its members will re-examine such basic questions as finding a new job after becoming unemployed, or looking for a place to live after starting a family, or after retiring. In all these situations different circumstances play a role in merging the working, social and household environments into one decision process. An example of such a situation is a two-person, two-gender household, both aged between twenty-five and thirty, and having the same skills. If both have a job and one is planning to make a change the search process depends on the type of domestic arrangement within the household, the location of both jobs and the associated travel time. One may decide not to make a change because this might adversely affect the career pattern and opportunities of spouse or children. An evaluation of career patterns and an understanding of the interrelationships between various work, housing and household objectives are essential in any appreciation of the way in which labour markets operate. This, in turn, raises questions about the ways in which organisational structures of the various environmental and time-budget constraints influence choice.

Another type of environment is that of the firm which is, of course, influenced — perhaps even determined — by the type of activity in which it is engaged, its organisational structure, its production system, and the extent of its location within an urban area or region. Also important to a firm's locational decision-making process are the characteristics of the households and workers in its proposed labour market area.

Usually, the locational characteristics of a firm are studied exclusively in terms of relocation behaviour but the afore-mentioned framework is also relevant when organisational or strategic changes occur *in situ*, thus also enabling firms to readjust to alterations in their internal and external environments. In the current economic circumstances this type of locational adjustment is dominant as the birth of new firms is more characteristic of a period of rapid industrialisation.

The study of this type of locational behaviour has to take account of the complex and multi-dimensional set of interrelationships between firms, households, individuals and regions. Here the attempt is made to illustrate the type of relationships which exist between labour and the different environments of individuals, households, firms and industrial change: various aspects of these relationships are explored in more detail in subsequent chapters.

Development of Firms and Networks

The rapid economic growth during the 1960s was important for the structure and organisation of firms and, in turn, for their locational requirements. More recently, the structure and organisation of the production processes have themselves altered due to rapid technological change. The industrial firm changed from being a one-plant, one-product unit at a single location to being a multi-plant, multi-product organisation spread over several locations (Lasuén, 1971; Watts, 1981). This organisational growth had a considerable impact on the spatial structure of production. Two particular changes can be noted.

(a) The organisational structure of a firm became an important factor in its operation and created distinct spatial conditions for the multi-plant firm. This transition has been documented by Törnqvist (1970, 1978) who used a simple conceptual model to demonstrate the complex relationships resulting from the spatial flows between different units of one production organisation (internal flows) and those between units of other organisations (external flows). Törnqvist used the concept of the production-line which summarises the transformation process from primary inputs to finished consumer goods, and pointed to the spatial separation of the various stages of the production process. As a consequence of industrial change the emphasis shifts from primary production processes (dominated by physical flows) to secondary and tertiary processes with an emphasis on organisation and management (dominated, increasingly, by information flows).

(b) The external environment no longer remained homogeneous but was different for each specific part of the production organisation: locations suited to some of its activities were not suitable for others so that spatial segmentation occurred.

During the 1970s the organisational structure of the firm again changed as there was a strong tendency towards mergers which in some cases led to a diversification of output and in others to increases in the scale of production because of a growth in the market share. This process, however, seems to have ended, and firms are now again concentrating on so-called core activities which are those in which they have had long-standing expertise. A concomitant development was an increase in the independence of the various production units basically because of the change in economic conditions (such as saturated markets) and the onset of the global economic recession in the mid-1970s. As a result there was a shift in strategy with new emphasis on risk avoidance and risk-sharing behaviour (Krumme and Hayter, 1975; Fredriksson and Lindmark, 1979). The former contributed to the importance of subcontracting and encouraged a growth in the number of small firms (Keeble and Wever, 1986). The lifetime of these new small independent firms is usually rather short — in many cases even less than two years. This led to a further development of primary markets for consumer goods and secondary markets for intermediate goods. Large firms operate on the primary market, which is fairly stable, and dominate the small producers. The latter, operating on the unstable secondary market, must develop linkages with more than one large firm. This risk-sharing behaviour by both large and small producers enhances the role of physical networks for the flow of goods and non-physical networks to channel the flow of information.

Related to the changing organisational structure of the firm is the growing demand for producer services, such as consulting firms, computer software developers and engineering firms, which generates the need for non-material services and therefore fosters the growth and strengthens the development of non-material networks. For the operation of the firm both types of networks are important although their shape and function varies with the product and the structure of the organisation. The markets for primary inputs, intermediate goods and consumers' goods have international and national domains. In contrast, producer services, having a local or regional character, use more spatially confined networks. It is therefore crucial to obtain insights about the way firms create their environments and choose their locations in relation to these different networks and their respective nodes.

A related question is the difference in the spatial scales between the various networks. Firms operate simultaneously at various geographical levels so that it is important to gain a better understanding of how these networks are linked and what impacts these 'jumps' in spatial scale have for the organisational structures

7

of firms and for the locational setting of their constituent parts. The growth and spatial development of networks do not, however, necessarily lead to an increase in accessibility for all participants, which is in fact more characteristic during the early stages of network development (Taaffe et al., 1963) whereas later access becomes more selective and restricted to a subset of urban places acting as nodes. One reason for this limitation or reduced access is the increased cost of investment in high-quality networks, both in terms of capacity and in speed of communication.

There is little difference in development between material and non-material networks. Spatially, there are two opposing developments: at the local and regional levels there is an increase in the number and complexity of networks, while at a higher spatial scale there is a reduction in overall accessibility which favours certain nodes at the expense of others.

It can be argued that social, economic and spatial conditions are different in an information society and that this will give rise to changes in the spatial structure of the networks within and between the nodes, represented by firms and cities. This has implications for the location of economic activities. For the firm it means a re-evaluation of its position within the changing system. Moreover, various segments of the network develop in different ways: some retain a hierarchical structure while others develop a complementary one. It also leads to increasing differentiation between cities as nodes in different material and non-material networks which they link and create. Hence the organisational structure of a firm will vary according to its relative location in the system.

Organisation, Strategic Choices and Markets

The increased attention to cyclical patterns of growth has stimulated many authors to describe the growth path of a firm within such a context. This has led to several related paradigms including the product life-cycle theory, the innovation cycle theory (Rothwell and Zegveld, 1985) and the dynamic market theory (de Jong, 1985).

The product life-cycle theory has attracted an extensive literature, some essential features of which were reviewed thoughtfully by Krumme and Hayter in 1975. In essence, the concept postulates that a new product or process will be developed in one of the technologically sophisticated countries and, initially, the whole of the output will be made within easy reach of the innovator's research and development facilities. Growth in demand then leads to mass production and hence to a standardisation of the technology involved. This, in turn, enables manufacturing facilities to be diffused to other countries, usually beginning in a few that are already technologically advanced but spreading to others that are still acquiring technical know-how. Ultimately the stage may be reached in which the bulk of world demand is supplied by countries with relatively low-skilled labour. The feedback thus generated — for instance in the form of competition, displacement of job opportunities, and reduced profits on the one hand, and increased demand for producers' equipment and materials on the other — encourages the technologically sophisticated countries to develop new products.

Technology is the driving force in the innovation cycle theory with its role varying throughout the product life-cycle. Rothwell and Zegveld make a distinction between process and product innovations in an interrelated way. During the life-cycle the emphasis changes from key product to key process innovations. During the second stage, when the technology has been developed and mass production is being achieved, there is little room for product innovation or change.

In the dynamic market theory, the third stage of the life-cycle is the key theme. The required level of technological development is associated with the saturation of the market. During the early stage of product development infant firms, which are usually short of capital, are vulnerable to takeovers and horizontal and/or vertical mergers. When moving from the expansionary stage to maturity another cycle introducing organisational change can occur: the takeover of such a growth firm by (usually) a larger one secures growth for the latter without taking risks or losing profits. In this way it is able to continue its performance through the replacement of old activities or through diversification.

Although the product life-cycle theory can be considered as a descriptive tool, it has generated a wide range of criticisms that go beyond the concept itself and are concerned with some of the underlying principles of industrial production and its organisation.

Structure of Production

The theory is geared towards large multi-product, multi-plant firms with a sharp distinction between large and small ones. Implicitly it is assumed that small firms are always dominated by large ones (Taylor, 1987) so that the latter can determine which location is the most advantageous with respect to labour costs, tax advantages and market accessibility. In fact, however, small firms operate differently and even large ones can follow individual strategies (Harrington, 1985).

Sectoral and Technological Determinism

The only evidence for the existence of a product life-cycle is within industry rather than within other sectors, and this can be explained by the fact that innovations and technological change play such an explicit role in the process of change.

The assumption is that a given technology can be associated with a particular type of production in a specific stage in the life-cycle. Daly (1985) has pointed out, however, that in bio-technology, for example, firms in their pioneering stage and others at a more mature stage may both be using the same technology. Technological change is cutting across the traditional sectoral divisions and affects the organisation of the workplace in many ways and in many locations. At the same time, the continuous upgrading of skills of the workforce and a growing individualisation, especially in Western society, has led to a reappraisal of industrial work and jobs. The organisation of the workplace and of work itself is being evaluated together with other needs of the household (Chapter 3). The influence of social change on technological change is therefore a theme of key importance in understanding the relationships between work, the workplace and the individual both in developed and developing countries. (Some of these relationships are discussed in Chapter 8 in the context of a centrally planned economy.)

Unicausality and Timing

A basic assumption is that one technology is replaced by the next to move forward through the cycle. In some instances, such as the textile industry, there is a strong emphasis on process innovations within the same product technology to survive (Walker, 1979). Related to this is the time it takes to develop a full cycle which in high-technology industries can range from eight to thirty years (Oakey, 1984). Moreover, the need to pass through a full cycle is not apparent; small firms, for instance, may remain in the first or second stage leaving mass production to be undertaken by firms that have a better knowledge of the market.

Role of the Environment

A commonly accepted hypothesis is the comparative advantage of the metropolitan environment, but there is hardly any evidence for such a view (Davelaar and Nijkamp, 1986). On the contrary, Gudgin and Fothergill (1984) concluded that there was little difference between the urban and rural environments in the availability of skilled workers.

Organisational Dominance

The product life-cycle theory follows the scientific management (or Taylorist) principles which means that a specific approach to the organisation of production has been selected. However, other dividing principles are possible based on alternative ways of organising work (as described in Chapter 6). In this approach, the emphasis is on decentralisation of operational decision-power relating to production, marketing and sales while, at the same time, there is centralisation of strategic decision-power on investment and other management matters. This may eliminate intermediate levels of decision making which, in turn, would have severe consequences for the future distribution of skill and jobs.

These criticisms of the product life-cycle theory and its extensions have pointed to the interplay between three important intervening factors, namely the organisation of the firm, its strategy and its markets. The latter is no longer a static phenomenon but a dynamic one which can adjust to changing conditions. It can be hypothesised that the nature of the interrelationships between these factors will vary between different environments including workplace and social environments created by households (see Chapters 4 and 5). In this way the environment not only operates as a passive constraint but also possesses dynamic qualities by creating fresh conditions that may result in structural change and renewal.

Some of these relationships have been examined in a pilot study by van der Knaap and van Geenhuizen (1988) for a selection of high-technology firms. Product strategies appear to be only weakly linked with the life-cycle concept. However, several strategies were identified which differed according to variations in specialisation or diversification; increases or reductions in the scale of production; introduction of new products or the opening of new markets; orientation to particular markets; and the relative importance of innovations in the production process. The market seems to have an important role in the locational dynamics of the firm, which implies increases and reductions in production at the same site or relocation to a new site. Firms making specialised products have very different strategies for stable and unstable markets, whereas those with a diversified product range have a stronger strategic orientation to growth and non-growth markets. Another apparently important distinction is the relationship between the age of a firm, its product range and the structure of the market. A young specialised firm may experience jumps in growth while it is operating with a new product on an unstable market and may thus have a strong locational dynamic. In contrast is the behaviour of an older diversified firm which exhibits a smooth endogenous growth path with a continuous renewal of its products and a weak locational dynamic.

Thus the spatial development of the production structure cannot be fully examined by means of the product life-cycle construct. An understanding of the dynamics of growth and structural change within a firm must go beyond the neo-classical paradigm and take account of factors related to strategy, organisational structure and dynamic markets. This has consequences for classical location theory which is also based on this paradigm and assumes space to be homogeneous and production factors to be perfectly mobile. Enlarging the theory to incorporate factors related to organisational structure and management strategies has significant consequences for the role of space in industrial geography (see Chapter 2).

Concepts developed within the fields of institutional and transactional economics can contribute to the development of new paradigms. In the former emphasis is placed on the existence of segmented — and hence spatially differentiated — markets. An understanding of the relationships between these markets and their different spatial expressions is becoming a central theme in the analysis of regional social and economic change. Transaction cost economics is an essential complementary tool as it pays attention to both market and non-market orientated transactions. The latter occur within firms and also within households and, from this perspective, are considered to be governance structures and not production or utility functions. When the focus of analysis shifts to governance structures less attention is paid to regional variations in production costs and patterns of consumption.

Technology, Organisation and the Labour Market

The growth of the firm has created several important differences in the structure of production. This has given rise to a reconsideration of neo-classical location theory and a discussion of other paradigms to explain industrial behaviour. In this context a distinction has been made between large, and often capital-intensive, firms and small labour-intensive ones. The large ones (with more than 200 employees) are able to control their markets to ensure their stability; they can also afford to pay high wages and have an internal labour market with a strong division of labour (Doeringer and Piore, 1971). These are usually the dominant organisations. In contrast, the small firms (with fewer than 100 employees) are often less capital-intensive and usually operate in the traditional sector with smaller and less stable markets for their products. Moreover, they have to look to the external labour market for their personnel who may only be available in its weaker segments. The latter situation has changed to some extent by the emergence of many small firms in the high-technology sector. A third category consists of firms that rely on external markets but have a high labour turnover and a weakly developed internal labour market. Thus, not only is distinction and segmentation possible on the basis of the structure of production as it has developed during the last thirty years, but also on the basis of the variation in the demand for labour in which technological and organisational change play a key role.

The issue of technological change has been raised within the context of 'humanising' labour which had become devalued following the introduction of the Taylor scientific management system (Braverman, 1974). Some authors (including Holmes in Chapter 6) argue that the introduction of modern technology will change the organisation of production by increasing the need for flexibility and efficiency but others, such as Altmann and Böhle (1976), are not convinced that this is necessarily so. Most of the change on the production floor is created by internal training schemes for specific types of workers which create a certain, albeit limited, level of autonomous decision making. The hierarchical nature of the organisation is reinforced by the nature of the selection process, training methods and wage levels to ensure loyal attitudes that are favourable towards the management. Their conclusion is that, in terms of social organisation, there is little real change, just minor adjustments.

The arguments in favour of a change in labour organisation within a firm are based on the assumption that modern technology leaves no room for choice. Several authors have suggested that instead of a technological determinism, management is making the final choice. This is not only the case for industrial organisations (Davis and Taylor, 1976) but also for office activities (van Weenen, 1977).

The discussion so far has focused on the internal environment but the decision space of management is also constrained by the external one. The influence of the internal and external environments is difficult to disentangle because of the shadowy boundary between them. This changes over time concurrently with the expansion and retraction of a firm and is also relative to the nature and the dominance structures of the organisational linkages and networks.

It is possible to distinguish between two types of external environment, namely the social context and the market. The role of the latter has already been discussed. In relation to the social context, the view is taken that technological change has an impact on society as well as the production organisation. According to Altmann and Bechtle (1971), this impact comes to the fore in the institutional relations between management, labour unions, political parties, government, and less formalised power groups; the set of societal rules that regulates the behaviour of firms; and the relationships with organised groups, such as schools, consumer organisations and households.

Technological and organisational change along with the strong economic growth experienced during the three decades after the Second World War have altered the internal structure and external environment of the firm. This has led to a reappraisal of labour market theories to the extent that they still explain the structure and movements on the labour market (Chapter 2).

Recently several attempts have been made to compare and classify labour market theories but even these approaches by geographers vary widely. Lever (1985) concentrated on the spatial aspects, whereas van der Laan (1987) examined and compared the set of assumptions between the theories with respect to the validity of their causal relations between regions. De Smidt (1987), starting from a social science perspective, introduced two main divides (Berting, 1976), the first being along the classical dichotomy between individualism and collectivism, and the second emphasising ways in which scientific knowledge can be acquired, namely through objective and (inter)subjective approaches (Table 1.2).

The increased interest in the organisational aspects of the relationships within and between firms with regions and households shifts the focus from the individualistic to the collectivist viewpoint which is in line with tradition in human geography. It is therefore not surprising that with the inability of the standard models developed by economists to explain the changing structure of reality, an increased interest is being taken in the subjective approach in which the dual and institutional labour market theories are closely related. However, these do not express such strong neo-Marxist and anti-capitalist views as the radical approaches. The dual labour market theory is of interest as it also provides a framework for an empirical analysis of spatial labour markets. In this approach the labour market consists of different sub-markets between which there is relatively little exchange: they are permanent and not caused simply by a temporary disequilibrium of the market at large. The organisations which operate within them occupy different positions in each one. Thus, the market process is not only acting as a clearing mechanism but as a governance structure for the organisations, such as employers, unions and households operating within different sub-markets.

The definition of the dual labour market suggests a complete split into two segments. In most empirical situations, however, a complete separation does not exist as it is unlikely that there will be no interaction at all between social groups. Another and probably more important reason for the incomplete separation of the segmented labour market is that there exists a whole array of labour market segments which are related and which overlap to varying degrees. Examples are segmentations based on the size of the firm, on the type of jobs and skills offered, on the type of industrial activity, and on age or gender. The spatial implications of the dual labour market approach are evident. Instead of one homogeneous labour market there exist many regional ones which vary in character according to their specific segmentation structure. These markets are not independent but have different kinds of relationships with each other.

Table 1.2: A classification of labour market theories

	Objective	Subjective
Collectivism	Classical Marxian theory	Institutional models
	'Radical' approaches	Dual labour market theory
Individualism	Neo-classical models	Interactionist model
	Post-Keynesian theory	Arena approaches
	Human capital theory	Behavioural approaches
	Labour queue model	

Source: after Loveridge and Mok, 1979.

Organised Labour

The role played by trade unions as part of the external social environment in which firms operate has been largely neglected by geographers. The case study of worker activism in The Netherlands set out in Chapter 9 points to the significant spatial variations in strike activity even in a country so geographically compact. Much more research, however, is required to tease out some of the impacts on union activities of technological and organisational change.

For example, the Spanish Ministry of Economy has estimated that some 30 per cent of the workforce (or about three million people) have jobs in the so-called 'black' economy (i.e. that part which does not declare income for tax purposes). It can be hypothesised that unofficial employment thrives where there are rigid labour markets, small companies and widespread farming activity, all of which are features of the Spanish economy. Despite recent reforms to the labour market it is still difficult for employers to dismiss workers; 60 per cent of companies employ fewer than 20 people; and agriculture occupies one-sixth of the

Spanish workforce (twice the EEC average). Some support for such a hypothesis seems to be given by the fact that in recent years much of Spain has been relatively free of labour unrest whereas there have been major strikes in the Basque country, a region dominated by large industries (like steel making and shipbuilding) but lacking activities such as textiles, clothing and footwear which tend to employ people 'unofficially'.

In some countries the relationships between workers, households and enterprises leave none of the participants with much room for manoeuvre. Thus although there has been some relaxation recently, the People's Republic of China still has one of the world's most tightly controlled job allocation systems. Basically, China's urban workers depend on their production units for housing and, in the absence of a comprehensive social security system, for life-long employment and welfare support. On the one hand, this makes workers reluctant to change jobs and, on the other, it means that managements of enterprises cannot easily respond to the changes in organisational and skill needs that are necessary to modernise Chinese industry. Moreover, in the Chinese People's Republic, as in many developing countries that have only embryonic government-sponsored welfare networks, the role of the extended family (in which old people care for young grandchildren while they themselves are looked after by their families) adds yet another dimension to the connections between the household and the workplace.

Trade unions are wholly or partially banned in some countries. In Malaysia, for example, union activities are outlawed in industries like the manufacture of electronic components and equipment: as workers can be hired and fired on an hourly-wage basis, overseas investors have been attracted to this country (or influenced to stay there), thus affecting the nature of the international labour market available to firms. As another instance, South Korea's labour laws allow only enterprise-based rather than industry-based unions which reduces the possibility of coordinated action. Both government and management recognise that if wages rise (often from very low levels) faster than productivity, South Korea's international competitiveness will be affected; the government's aim is to hold down labour costs while that of managements, forced to give in to some blue-collar worker demands, is to reorganise their workforce so as to use their white-collar employees more efficiently.

The role and membership of trade unions in developed

countries is also changing. In some, an increasing propensity for workers in the service sectors to unionise has compensated for the decline in union membership in, particularly, heavy smoke-stack industries. In the United States, however, there has been an overall decline in membership from 25 per cent of the workforce in 1980 to about 17 per cent in 1988, and the collective bargaining power of even some of the traditionally powerful unions has been waning as evidenced by their acceptance of lower pay rises recently than they received three years ago. Job security has replaced higher wages as the negotiating priority. Yet the weakening of the unions leaves behind the problem of protecting employee rights in the workforce, a function that is now likely to be taken over by the legislatures and courts which may possibly promote regulations that are much more inflexible than those achieved under collective bargaining. This well illustrates the contention made earlier in the chapter that the various environments in which individuals, regions and firms operate are constantly changing.

Conclusions

The labour market is not only related to the firm but also to the household. It is important to recognise this connection because the members of a household actively participate in this market to try to satisfy their goals. If these are not met the market will remain incomplete.

The time-path of change is becoming increasingly important, with the several long-term processes having dynamics of their own. The rates of change in social organisations and in the organisation of labour differ and, in turn, vary with the rate of technological change. This creates adjustment problems, both in time and space, as the intervals between events differ as do the nature of the rates and the localisation of the change. An understanding of these types of variations requires longitudinal analyses that consider not only the locational behaviour of firms but also the wider social and organisational context.

It is not only the cause of change which is of interest but also the way people react to, cope with and manage its impacts. Little is known about whether people have explicit strategies and how these develop or what their spatial implications are (see Chapter 10). While some are fairly obvious, such as the adjustment of the skill levels in a household, others may exist but have not been recognised. The same kind of query relates to the strategies of firms: changing the corporate structure, subcontracting and the growth of small firms are examples of responses that have been identified but other, perhaps more subtle, coping strategies may need to be pursued. As indicated previously, a crucial role is played by such institutional agents as governments and trade unions because these create the conditions for various kinds of solutions. Managing spatial change is thus an active process.

An emerging spatial paradox should be noted. One consequence of the process of industrial change is the growing internationalisation of production but another is the increasing spatial differentiation at the regional and local levels. The links between these international and sub-national levels of spatial development are the organisational contexts in which the activities take place that are reflected in the growing complexity of their connecting networks. Because of the increased importance of non-material networks, the position of people as the main actors in the various organisational structures is again becoming a central focus in industrial geographical analysis.

2

Labour Market Models in their Spatial Expression

Sergio Conti

This chapter attempts to give a spatial role to an essential concept in industrial geographical analysis, that of the labour market, a concept which is not traditionally given a spatial function. The complexity and vagueness of the problem are such that it is not possible to reach such an objective directly. It implies, on the contrary, that a rather tortuous path will have to be followed, starting from basic labour market theories, whose essential features need to be re-examined along with their theoretical and ideological bases. By summarising the neo-classical and Marxist approaches and the theory of segmentation, the fundamental lines of the debate can be drawn but this necessitates gross simplifications in order to unravel the problem. Nevertheless this is the only way to introduce the empirical dimension discussed in the second part of the chapter. Here, these three basic theories will be tested on the basis of their explanatory ability, using as an example the industrialised economy of Italy.

Even at this level of analysis further simplifications will have to be made: each economy is in continual transformation and relationships between regions change. No change can ever be interpreted univocally but each theoretical structure provides its own explanation which sometimes contradicts others and at other times links into them. As all social scientists have their own concepts and lines of thought, each emphasises one line of interpretation rather than another. This chapter will emphasise segmentation theory more than others as the basis which allows us to formulate hypotheses for a general theory of the labour market in a geographical context. It is the only one which recognises the increasing complexity of economic and territorial relationships under advanced capitalism, and of the Italian case in general.

Basic Labour Market Theories: A Review and Commentary

Neo-Classical Theories

In the neo-classical (or marginalist) approach labour is considered as much a factor of production as land or capital. It is thus part of the process of allocation of certain 'scarce resources' and so the analytical schemes designed to determine the conditions of market equilibrium are applied to it. Once it has been established that the marginal productivity of labour is diminishing, that wages are equal to the marginal labour product, and that demand and supply of labour are a function of wages, the principal aggregate variables of the labour 'market' (employment and wage levels) are automatically determined by the conditions of equilibrium. In this framework labour theory contains the same assumptions as all of neo-classical theory, which puts at the centre of attention the pricing mechanisms, substitution as the adjustment process through which equilibrium is reached and the free entry into the market of economic subjects which tend to maximise their own utility both as suppliers and users of labour as a production factor. Even on an approximate level the neo-classical model is thus symmetrical: labour demand and supply converge towards a point of equilibrium, as 'labour is paid a wage equal to the value of its marginal product, which depends on product markets (output price), production technology and, again, the skill levels of individual workers (marginal productivity)' (Storper and Walker, 1983:8).

In contrast to the classical scheme, a continuance of a certain rate of unemployment and under-employment (voluntary or frictional) is permitted, although this is seen as a disturbing element in a long-term equilibrium model. From the time of Eckaus' (1955) explanations this aspect has been adequately covered. The existence of unemployment and under-employment are the consequences of:

(a) market imperfections in those factors which limit mobility;

(b) the existence of limited technical substitutability between factors;

(c) differences in the composition of the demand and supply of goods and services, further worsened by the problem of technological discontinuity (Cassetti, 1975:52).

21

As a consequence, the great majority of workers, in a country with a large workforce but little capital, is under-employed in backward production where marginal labour productivity, and therefore wages, are very low. The structure of production is thus dualistic (Lewis, 1954; Kindleberger, 1964) — on territorial, technological and consumer levels — which translates into a vision of the labour market characterised by the existence of two sub-markets: on the one hand, a primary market (high salaries and good employment opportunities) and, on the other, a secondary market with contrasting features (poor health conditions, low wages and poor professional openings).

The division of the labour market into two sub-sections derives, therefore, from the dualistic structure of production whose features are partially outside the labour market itself but coherent with certain structural features (the size of the firm, the productivity levels determined by international competition, and delays in the accumulation process) (Lewis, 1954; Lutz, 1962; Graziani, 1969).

On a theoretical level certain conditions (in particular the hypothesis of the homogeneity of the workforce and unlimited factor substitutability) guarantee the 'theoretical' possibility of reaching full employment. In particular, according to Lewis, the absorption of the labour force employed in the 'backward' sector at pay levels lower than those in the 'advanced' sector depends on the speed of capital accumulation and thus the expansion of the 'capitalist' sector of the economy. In this sense, therefore, the dualistic analysis leads to a *residual* interpretation of the secondary labour market, which will, sooner or later, be absorbed by the primary sub-market. The assumption is therefore that of a homogeneous labour market but which allows the existence of an occupationally differentiated labour force (Storper and Walker, 1983:9). Yet, the continuing and spreading phenomena of poverty and unemployment, in contradiction with the initial theoretical assumption, have led many economists to examine their causes. In neo-classical terms there have been three main lines: discrimination theory (Becker, 1957; Arrow, 1972), human capital theory (Blaug, 1976), job-search theory (McCall, 1970; Salop, 1973).

The hypothesis of homogeneity which characterises the neo-classical approach does not take social relations into account. This is obvious if the labour market is considered in the same way as any other product market and labour as a production factor expressed and changed by its price; if workers and employers are presumed to be rational beings aiming, respectively, to maximise wages and profits; and if individual decisions are presumed to have no influence on general wage levels and there are no obstacles to labour mobility. A series of hypotheses derives from this which justifies the macro-economic approach (Tinacci-Mossello, 1984) just as not taking social relations into consideration makes the spatial factor, *de facto*, neutral.

> Space is reduced to the presence of two or more points in an area, indistinguishable one from the other except by the distance which separates them, i.e. the costs involved in transferring goods or factors from one to another. In these conditions all spaces are — or should be — indifferent to the entrepreneur who has to choose a location (Aydalot, 1980:313).

In fact, if we hypothesise a ratio of equilibrium between wages and productivity the location problem loses much of its weight in that any decision is inevitably balanced. It is as a consequence of this spatial indifference that the concept of external economies was created, as the only one capable of explaining the ability of a space to be a point of attraction in industrial location and the posing of transport costs as a priority factor in the definition of spatial differentiation.

Neo-Marxist Theories

Two schools of thought oppose the theoretical approaches of the neo-classicists — Marxism and that of the neo-institutionalists. This is not the place to review the analysis of the labour market central to Marxist thought. Here, labour is understood to be an 'active' production factor, rooted in human existence and not simply in input; the worker has a cultural depth which depends not only on the place of production but on the wider environment. Labour is, for this reason, a pseudo-commodity which becomes a commodity through its offers to employers.

What characterises the classic Marxist analysis of the labour market is its attempt to overcome the purely economic aspects linked to the labour-capital exchange relationship by denouncing the formal nature of the parity in which it occurs. This position depends on the analytical category of surplus value, whose existence becomes an essential condition for the starting up and completion of the exchange process within the labour market (M-C-M')[1] and in the concept of labour force as a factor in the valorisation of capital itself. From this point of view valorisation can only occur through the non-attribution to the workers of that part of wealth they have helped to create or, in other terms, through the payment of the workforce in goods whose value is lower than that produced by the workforce itself. The legitimacy of this market ratio is made possible by the presence of objective conditions underlying the visible reality of economic phenomena: they can be summarised in the existence of private ownership of the means of production thus making it impossible for workers to organise production autonomously as they are forced to sell their own labour, even under the exploitative conditions depicted above. In contrast to the neo-classical model, the classic Marxist position places the concept of capital's *control* of production and progressive de-skilling at the centre of attention (Braverman, 1974; Edwards, 1979).

It is particularly important to give a spatial dimension to the theoretical framework. In sociological analysis, even in the Marxist tradition, the relationship between society and space has not been adequately conceptualised (Urry, 1982) and the very Marxist tradition of conceptualisation of social classes in terms of relationship to the means of production has for a long time kept social processes separate from spatial ones (Hamnett and Randolph, 1986). The term 'labour market' itself, in its implication of a sufficient uniformity of behaviour among certain workers, has often been seen as a *generalisation* (Kerr, 1954:92), referring to certain geographical areas, or ethnic or professional groups. As a result, as Freedman (1976) notes, preference has been given to the more abstract term 'arena', where 'the boundaries of markets depend on the writer's interest and theoretical perspective' (Althauser and Kalleberg, 1981:121).

From industrial location studies a common reference is to a corroborated theory concerning historical trends in spatial patterning that probably dates back to Aglietta's (1979) study which has given a solid historical conceptual base to the

---

1 Money plays a crucial role in the creation of surplus value, and can be explained symbolically by the cycle M-C-M', in which the capitalist advances a sum of money (M) for the commodities of materials, machines and labour power (C), and sells the final product for more money (M'): *eds.*

development of the relationship between capitalist society and labour process. The four phases indicated — manufacturing, mechanisation, scientific management (Fordism) and neo-Fordism [post-Fordism] — represent different ways of combining capital and labour in the production process, 'a different way of organising the labour force, and a different kind of stratification and differentiation within the labour force' (Massey, 1984:23). As localisation is influenced by the nature of the labour process, each successive phase implies a growing spatial and functional *division of labour* which is, in turn, a factor of production and of the maintenance of the spatial variation in class structure (Lipietz, 1977; Perrons, 1981 ; Massey, 1984).

Dealing with the spatial division of labour the hypothesis of homogeneity in the neo-classical approach has to be abandoned. Above all it has been international studies — on the theory of imperialism, product cycle theory, analysis of multinational companies (Mandel, 1975; Palloix, 1975; Vernon, 1977) — which have introduced the phenomenon conceptually into geographic literature. The emphasis placed on large industrial companies — multi-regional and multinational — has 'freed' the problem of location from the restraints of transport costs to prefer a logic in which labour exercises a crucial function in localisation. Taking the large industrial company as an economic subject capable of 'annihilating' space, to use Marxist terminology, or copying mechanically the original scheme of the product cycle into the localisation level (which has dominated the literature for years) oversimplifies the reasoning.

On the one hand, the crude reproposal of the product cycle in its distinct phases of introduction, expansion, maturity and eventual decline, or again the emphasis placed on the workers' loss of control over production and progressive de-skilling, hide a reality which is 'more complex than is often portrayed' (Storper and Walker, 1983:19). On the other, the abstract conceptualisation of the spatial division of labour which does not take real spatial differentiation of labour as a factor of production into account, ends up being unable to provide a 'complex formal model specifying relationships between the labour market, the labour process and sectoral growth' (Warde, 1985:204). It follows that 'labour markets have been largely ignored as elements of the spatial division of labour' (Warde, 1985:204).

Two lines of analysis can be summed up here briefly. The first, which emphasises the ability of the company to define space (and therefore the social division of labour), sees technology as one of its principal strategic, and spatial, arms in maintaining its dominion. A new technology is not defined simply by the machines which represent it materially or the products produced. The labour force does not adapt mechanically and passively to the new production processes, but there will always be a lag in adapting which depends on skills.

> This means that the company, when it introduces innovation, does not choose a technology-productivity relationship but one of technology-work force. The forms and results of technology will be different according to the relationship to the work force which will use it. All technologies, production processes, forms of organisation of labour, all duties and skills can be defined by the working environment, by the mass of technical and scientific knowledge, by the level of sophistication and of automation (Aydalot, 1980:316).

It follows that if a technological innovation can *also* be defined by the workforce which will be called to apply it, the technological choice is strictly connected to the spatial choice: 'a technology is chosen in function of the character of the local workforce available to apply it' (Aydalot, 1980:317). For the company, space is a place characterised by a certain labour force. In making localisation choices the company simultaneously selects technology and space through a choice of labour. This last, together with technological choices, thus becomes a structural factor in localisation (Lojkine, 1976).

The second line of analysis emphasises the problem of the organisation of labour in society, thus showing close links with postwar functionalist sociology (Giddens, 1979; 1981). In this light technology is *not* in reality the only value involved in the spatial organisation of production. Labour is, as noted earlier, a 'pseudo-commodity' and as such constitutes a 'conscious subject of production'. This implies a need for *control* and *reproduction*. The spatial differentiation of labour is therefore more complex in that the very forms of control and reproduction are differentiated. What complicates the model even further is that the vertical, or hierarchical, division of labour must be compounded by the intersection with such concepts of control and reproduction, which are in their turn spatially differentiated. The price of labour itself is therefore much more complicated than just wages (Storper and Walker, 1983).

Thus, if the economist traditionally underlines two aspects (the technical one of the degree of the workers' adaptation to a technology, and the monetary one of the relationship between wages and productivity) and the sociologist of Marxist inspiration often insists on the relationships of force and control, spatial analysis cannot avoid the specificity of the socially produced conditions of reproduction which thus generate local differentiation (Castells, 1977; Urry, 1981).

Theories of Labour Market Segmentation

The concept of labour market segmentation is also in contrast with the neo-classical scheme even though it is based on a *duality* which was already dominant in neo-classical interpretations. Moreover, it contains within it an implicit reference to the Marxist theory of social classes.

There are several schools of thought. In summary, dualism, understood as a disturbing element, frictional and temporal in neo-classical analysis, is taken here to be an element 'closely linked to the heterogeneity and instability of modern industrial economies' (Berger and Piore, 1982:45), and as a fundamental feature of advanced industrial societies which are always divided into segments. This is even more true nowadays as an array of problems (such as population growth, changes in social customs and the disordered development of metropolitan areas) means that the labour market is very diversified from both the geographical and the sectoral points of view, with the coexistence of areas which have reached a point of employment saturation and others characterised by phenomena of marginality. Thus, if 'market imperfections exist on too large a scale to be considered "frictional or temporary"' (Loveridge and Mok, 1976:3) it follows that the labour market or the labour process is structurally divided into separate sub-markets or sub-processes (segments) which 'are distinguished by their different characteristics, behavioral rules, and working conditions' (Edwards et al., 1975:xi).

The existence of a dual structure within the labour market has been noted systematically by Doeringer and Piore (1971) — developing a methodology already presented by Kerr (1954) and Dunlop (1957) — to explain both the reasons for continuing discrimination of various kinds (e.g. income, employment) and also to understand the more general bond between capitalist development and the utilisation of different labour force sectors. A dual labour market structure must necessarily show:

(a) a clear sub-division between sectors at different wage levels;
(b) limited mobility between sectors;
(c) the existence of different social status of those belonging to the two basic sectors;
(d) a different degree of job stability (Brunetta, 1981:386).

These fundamental aspects come together to determine the characteristics of the two or more markets in which the different labour forces act. The *primary market* is characterised by the presence of jobs (mainly in large-scale industry) with advantages from the point of view of wages, working conditions, career possibilities and job stability. In contrast, the main features of the *secondary market* are low-paid jobs, instability, limited protection for employed workers, little possibility of improvement and the tendency for mechanisms of discrimination to continue.

In this framework a not insignificant part of the consolidation of dualism is played by factors of an institutional nature, such as the action of trade unions and the overall effect of the legislation in the major industrialised nations (relating, for instance, to insurance, minimum wages in the primary market, and unemployment benefits) (Piore, 1968).

The problem of labour market segmentation is obviously more complicated than suggested here, starting from the labour market dualism which develops *within* single production units (primary and secondary) (Doeringer and Piore, 1971). This area has been clearly and critically analysed by Althauser and Kalleberg (1981). Faced with the sometimes very large differences in working conditions which cannot be eliminated even on a long-term basis, there has emerged a conceptualisation of the labour market divided into sections, each one delimited on the basis of employment, geographical or institutional factors, which have a *very low level of communication* between them.

This is a school of thought which is highly critical of both neo-classicists and Marxists. In both of these, despite the obvious disagreements, is the *unitary* character of industrial society that derives from the processes of integration immanent in industrialisation itself, tending to smooth the differences which society inherits from the past, so that society is developing along lines established by those groups which have a particular relationship with emergent structures in society (Berger and Piore, 1982:190).

In any case it is hard to sustain that from the whole collection of labour market segmentation theories it is possible to draw a clear line between neo-classical or Marxist analysis. On the one hand, the extension of the dualistic model to models with multiple segmentations has occurred mainly through the work of scholars with a neo-classical background (Becker, 1957; Krueger, 1963; Arrow, 1972). According to them, labour market segmentation and the obstacles in passing from one part to another depend above all on the characteristics of the workers themselves (for example, poor aptitude) rather than on structural divisions in the system. On the other, modern theory of labour market segmentation has seen its most important developments carried through by economists of the institutionalist school (Kerr, 1954; Dunlop, 1962; Piore, 1968; Reynolds, 1978) and also Marxists (Gordon, 1972; Harrison, 1972; Edwards, 1975; Reich, 1981). In the light of this, the segmentation between primary and secondary markets can be attributed mainly, if not exclusively, to employers' (and government) strategy aimed at maintaining and strengthening their economic and political predominance. It is therefore functional to the capitalist system in that it allows the owners of the means of production to control production processes as the working class is divided into various sections, making it impossible to organise effective class opposition. The basic phenomenon to note here is the presence of marginal workers (who can be considered the modern version of Marx's *Lumpenproletariat*), an inherent aspect of the capitalist system whose survival depends on the existence of 'an industrial reserve army', benefiting from the divisions in the labour force. It is now relatively easy to maintain that, despite the wide-ranging theoretical analyses, the major limit present in all models is the attempt to fix rigid divisions in the labour market. In this way the multiplicity of combinations which give rise to a vast range of differentiated situations is not noted. On the contrary, precisely because of the many different forms of segmentation a general theory is needed which can explain special cases and avoids them being taken to represent inappropriate general models.

This means that labour market phenomena cannot be considered in a vacuum, but must be placed within the framework of the problems of industrial structure, the evolution of production techniques and market forms, and the politics and structure of society.

Levels of Empirical Application

Neo-Classicism and Dualism of the Economic System, and the Question of the Economic Periphery

That social reality (and the labour market) is differentiated and that any change happens because of different rhythms is not, obviously, a new discovery, but is the obvious starting point for every commonsense discussion on the change of a 'complex object'.

Unfortunately, the multiplicity and diversity of the variables of contemporary social reality have not really been understood by economists even 100 years after the death of Marx and the birth of Keynes and Schumpeter [all 1883] (Becattini and Bianchi, 1982:22). Proof of this can be seen in the studies and debates in the postwar period which are taken up later in relation to the Italian situation.

During the 1950s and 1960s interpretations of a strict neo-classical inspiration prevailed in which the presence of a dualistic labour market was connected to a much larger model of the dualistic development of the Italian economic situation (Lewis, 1954; Lutz, 1962; Kindleberger, 1964; Graziani, 1969).

The distinctive element in such a sub-division was centred on the size of the production unit. There was, therefore, a modern sector made up of large units which used capital-intensive methods where the accumulation of capital was realised and where productivity and pay increased together with a modest rise in employment. The *traditional* sector had the function of absorbing the residual labour force. In these conditions, therefore, the dualism of the labour market was made to correspond to a sectoral dualism (Galbraith, 1967; Averitt, 1968) and to coincide with territorial dualism, where the South concentrates a great part of the backward sector and the secondary labour force to which all those who cannot enter the primary sector, despite being willing to work, have access (Del Monte, 1982). In such a way, a vast homogeneity at the centre of the system (or in the two sub-systems) comes to light, precluding a more systematic and rigorous territorial analysis.

As regards the interpretation of the development process it can be ascertained that there are two Italies — the North and the South — each with its own economic, social and demographic characteristics. The dualistic schemes (whether of neo-classical inspiration or that adopted by Marxist analysis) have been unable to forge the link between the first Italy (the North-West) and the second (the South) in order to form a 'third' Italy capable of taking off through its 'higher speed of industrialisation, increase in employment, income, exports, and ability to react to a specific economic trend' (Becattini and Bianchi, 1982:23). Quantitative data on the industrialisation process and the logic of the affirmation of the 'third Italy' have already been examined by innumerable rigorous studies (Arcangeli et al., 1980; Brusco and Sabel, 1981; Fuà, 1983; Fuà and Zacchia, 1983; Brusco, 1986), together with new conceptualisations variously rooted in the traditional background of social sciences (such as diffuse industrialisation, rural urbanisation, industrial districts and system areas) which flooded, and continue to stimulate, a whole intellectual area. The labour-capital relationship is here specific: on the one hand, the lower and middle-class entrepreneur and, on the other, a dispersed working class, weak and poorly organised in small companies and home-based work. The two classes can be placed along a continuum (Bagnasco, 1982) which presupposes considerable reciprocal mobility. This then raises the question of the social structure in these regions.

From this point of view it is thus a question of an analytically unitary area in which the small farmer is historically rooted, a population therefore dispersed across the countryside and relatively autonomous production relationships (Bagnasco and Pini, 1981). Other investigations have demonstrated the 'urban' origins of the entrepreneurs, that is to say a second, crucial endogenous variable. The urban structure is typified by a closely woven network of small and medium-size towns which have spread rich urban services (commerce, banking, craftsmen, local administration, culture) throughout the area. Therefore, while this historic network of towns 'explains', from an endogenous point of view, the entrepreneurs, the countryside explains the labour market (Paci, 1980) without negating its own agricultural traditions (faced with the crisis of traditional agriculture) but assumes the characteristics of an adaptable and cheap labour force which fits the needs of the small firm. It is thus possible to speak of diffuse industrialisation and of an urbanised countryside.

31

The industrial periphery, as a conglomerate of regions which falls between the 'centre' and the 'margins' of the system, can be considered in an analytically unitary way. This is a gross but useful simplification in that it gives an initial justification for a triadic structure of the labour market and denounces the inadequacies of the neo-classical conception of the 'secondary' market and the same theories of the 'double labour market' (Piore, 1968).

New Interpretative Schemes: Decentralisation of Production and the Labour Market

Once the full congruity of the peripheral phenomenon regarding the modality of the development of the region has been verified, the analysis of the transformation of the labour market can be taken back prior to the decentralisation of production carried out by large companies. Faced with the rigidity of the labour force in the dynamic, leading sectors of the economy and the problem of escalating salaries, the strategy of the decentralisation of production, was to (a) render the production cycle more flexible, and to (b) utilise a cheaper and more manageable workforce. This summarises many analyses (Schaefer, 1977; Massey and Meegan, 1978; Fothergill and Gudgin, 1978), according to which the production cycle would be restructured by attributing new production functions to marginal workers in small companies.

This explains, in part, Italian economic history of the 1960s and 1970s when large companies sought greater flexibility, resorting to decentralised companies or informal working practices. Such an interpretation nevertheless presents both theoretical and empirical limitations.

(a) Theoretically the discussion is in terms of interpretations which have the merit of rejecting the neo-classical thesis on the disappearance of the peripheral sector. On the contrary, the precarious (peripheral) sector is seen to be consequential rather than accidental in the selfsame accumulation mechanism. Nevertheless, the autonomy of the peripheral sector is shown to be more apparent than real and large parts of the population remain excluded from the history of the social classes.

(b) On an empirical and descriptive level, the reality of Italian peripheral industry shows that production has its own markets and only incidentally and sporadically turns to major companies for outlets; the types of products manufactured differ from those of major companies; and the siting of decentralised enterprises is directed mainly towards other areas.

In these circumstances, it is at least necessary to uphold the existence of a further differentiation of the labour market, part of which corresponds to, and follows, its own logic and cannot easily be placed within the single and dominant political and economic model of capital accumulation which, as such, justifies the macro-economic and aspatial approach, and almost totally disregards the social context.

Contemporary capitalism has great structural complexity, whose form cannot be derived from abstract features of the mode of production. Only inquiries into the nature of single social formations can uncover the variety and continuously changing nature of the social structure (Bagnasco, 1981:40).

The Italian Model: An Expression of Labour Market Segmentation

The problem must now be faced by giving a spatial dimension to the discontinuity of the economy and the labour market, namely that which constitutes one of the unsolved problems of conceptualisation. Hence, the question arises as to whether there exists a link between the labour market, class structure and regional formation. This can be considered with reference to Italian peripheral industry.

The problem of the spatial organisation of the periphery has already been canvassed: there exists here a particular city-countryside relationship, where the city, as a network of technical and personal knowledge, and as a channel into the international market, explains the rise of the entrepreneurial class. The 'urbanised countryside' would explain the availability of a cheap, flexible labour force in that it is still tied to the land which provides goods for self-consumption.

The presence of a certain type of labour market is the expression of specific social relationships. In the industrial peripheries (or those in the process of being industrialised) a 'strong' link exists between some types of agricultural production and forms of industrialisation. As has been shown, the areas of diffuse industrialisation are typified by the fragmentation of land ownership, the absence of capitalist concerns and the predominance of the share-cropping or rented land relationships (Bagnasco, 1981). The presence of such social relationships of production has driven the members of family communities to seek integrative forms of income, working from the home and moving temporarily to the nearest cities. Thus, a new phase has begun in which agricultural activity, formerly of major importance, has given way to industrial activity, without the former actually being abandoned. At the same time, the special relationship which smallholders have with the market has accustomed them, as small producers, to meeting market demand. This has created a 'positive' work culture (Michelson, 1985), based on personal initiative. In many areas the organisation of work in 'family businesses' concerning both its own reproduction and its presence in the market has contributed to the development of organised entrepreneurial abilities which, together with the technical knowledge acquired in the cities, sometimes lead the head of the family to establish a micro-unit of production, on a craft or industrial basis (Paci, 1980).

The particular family structure thus emerges as the all-important link. The crisis in traditional agriculture does not erase the 'extended family' (Bagnasco, 1982) but maintains and modifies it as the unitary centre of eco-social functions and decisions (Vinay, 1985). Even families who are no longer farmers continue to be economically and socially bound to agriculture and thus in this sense it is possible to speak of an urbanised countryside. Research on successful entrepreneurs has shown that the family organisation of craft or industrial concerns is preserved and often the family structure of capital coincides with the management group of small and medium-size concerns.

From an organisational point of view, the 'industrial district' reminiscent of Marshall (Becattini, 1986) is that which best enables an understanding of this reality, typified by the existence of systems of small, well-integrated concerns operating in similar fields of manufacturing vertically related products. Obviously the complexity of the product and the level of technological mechanisation lead to more than marginal differences, just as the historical paths taken in the structures of these areas can differ. From this at least three cases can be picked out (Michelson, 1985:88):

(a) those in which a production cycle, formerly vertically integrated within large factories, has been dispersed over a wide area;

(b) those in which the dispersal of industry has to be induced by decentralisation of production carried out by large-scale enterprises;

(c) those in which basically small and similar production units have begun to specialise in specific phases of production, diversifying and sub-dividing in ever increasingly complex cycles.

An industrial district is not to be understood as a structure in which the company appears as the decision-making and organising centre, but rather in the sense of a close link between local communities, knowledge, know-how, and institutions, held together by a tight network of business relations, technical and otherwise, thereby falling under the new heading of 'agglomerate economies' which substitute (or are another form of) the scale economies typical of large, vertically integrated industries.

In this area the social mobility of workers — vertical and horizontal — is an important mechanism regulated by the market which, in isolation, would lead to imbalance if other fundamental regulating social factors did not intervene. These include the family, the institutional arrangements, and a settlement system which entails a tight overlap between production and reproduction. Here the concept of 'fixed social capital' (Treu, 1983) comes into play; this is generally understood to include the physical-spatial organisation inherited from the past and recently set in motion (above all by local government) and strictly incorporated within a specific territorial area. This endows the local system with a reticulated urban structure (Dematteis, 1985) evolved through a self-regulating process in which endogenous factors prevail.

Searching for a Theory

Two conclusions have been reached so far in this chapter. The first is the questioning of the economic paradigm, that is an analytical scheme for which the 'subjective' aspects of the phenomena studied (in this case, labour) rarely possessed autonomy in the problems they posed. This paradigm has been challenged through two fundamental processes which Habermas (1984) clearly understood, namely (a) the emergence of the categories of social complexity, and (b) the erosion of the classic Marxist model of linear relationships between state, social classes and location in the sphere of production

It thus follows that the social structure no longer possesses a single physiognomy. Class divisions are no longer clean horizontal splits which can be explained by position within social relations of production, but by the 'horizontal' inequalities that give rise to groups which cut across and confuse traditional class lines (Sabel, 1979; Paci, 1981).

A second significant aspect, perhaps more consonant with the problem discussed here, is the relevance of the relationship between society and territory, or rather the importance of the organisation of economic-social matters at a local level. For this reason the 'relatively' separate organisation of the economy corresponds to social formations with specific functions. These social formations are organised on a territorial basis, so we can speak of 'regional formations'.

This is not to deny that the analysis of specific territorial systems must be included in complex processes which act from above. Having said this, the analysis of regional levels is necessary for the understanding of real processes, of the dialectic between the exogenous and the endogenous, between the old and the new. (The term 'region' is used here in a generic sense to identify areas of varying size, homogeneous in relation to the processes under consideration.)

A segmented society and labour market, founded on the existence of occupational groups and of differentiated strategies, is a feature peculiar to industrial society and makes any dichotomic interpretation out of date, presupposing an irremediably dated image of capitalist economy.

The problem is how to explain theoretically the discontinuity and multiplicity of social strata from the different segments of the labour market as a particular feature of industrial society and not as an anomaly (as is implicit in the competition and the traditional Marxist models).

The structure of the segmented labour market as a fruit of the intersection between political structure and socio-economic structure provides a first fundamental base of interpretation. It explains the particular forms of segmentation which emerge in different societies and countries which in turn means that the theory and logic of the international division of labour has to be taken into consideration. It also explains why in certain countries the traditional sector has diminished while in others it has survived or even grown. While this level of analysis may do for an economist, a sociologist or a political scientist, it does not explain the existence and the reproduction of specific 'regional formations', which, in turn, explain the structural features of segmentation (Figure 2.1).

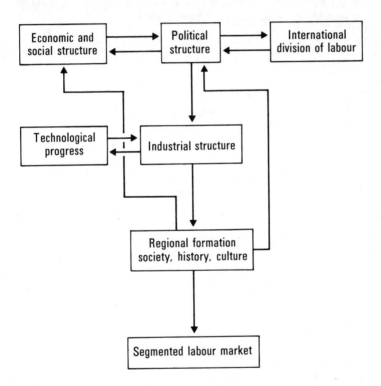

Figure 2.1: This diagram summarises the basic relationship between regional formations and the segmented labour market. The theoretical affirmation of such analytical categories is not alien to the significant and continuous changes in the industrial structure, resulting from exogenous processes (e.g. changes in the international division of labour) and endogenous ones that stem from the history, economy and culture of the various regional formations.

Society is organised on a territorial basis. Each different labour market, on different scales of analysis (from the worldwide to the regional), reacts to the transformations of the economic structure which acquires renewed mobility (including spatial mobility) so the search for the lowest labour costs possible gives new relevance to labour markets and their territorial discontinuity. At the same time the structural features of each of the spatially organised segments creates a tight-knit interdependence between supply and demand, giving a discontinuity which has its roots in its own historical social and cultural dynamics.

3

Industrial Change in Poland and the Working and Living Environment

Bronisław Kortus

The problem subsumed in the title of this chapter should be considered in a wider context of structural changes. These belong to a class of socio-economic processes, realised in time and space, which consist of economic and technological changes, demographic changes, changes in people's demands, expectations and behaviour, and spatial changes (Figure 3.1).

These structural changes are nowadays observed everywhere, but their intensity is different: in Poland they are occurring more slowly than in many other countries. The relationships between industrial change and the working and living environment, discussed in this chapter, are the essential elements of the general structural changes and belong particularly to those between economic-technological changes and those in people's demands, expectations and behaviour.

Many Polish authors have written about structural changes, but mainly in relation to their economic, demographic and spatial aspects: few have been concerned with people's demands and behaviour.

Industrial Change and Quality of Life

In the geographical and other social science literature about Polish industry little attention has been paid to the relationship between people's life and work, even though much has been written about this by historians concerned with conditions in the nineteenth century. This neglect of man in the production process results from an ideological and political doctrine. The problems of production had priority: man was only an element among the productive

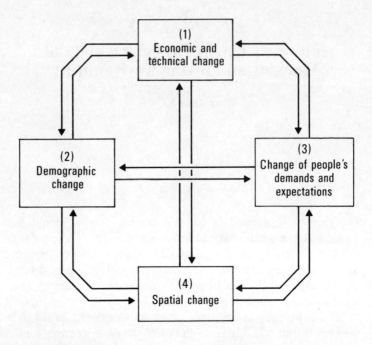

Figure 3.1: Structural change.

forces to be treated as labour-power and analysed in terms of availability, sex, age structure and skills, or in terms of spatial mobility such as migration or commuting (Kortus, 1985). A rare exception was the sociologist Szczepański (1973) who maintained that besides economic and technological factors one should recognise and appreciate the motives guiding people as individuals, social strata or social groups. He stressed also that one of the consequences of the industrialisation process is the increasing differentiation of social needs and expectations.

Changes in this attitude were, however, brought about by events during 1980 and 1981 when Polish workers demanded to be treated as the subjects rather than the objects of production. A stern slogan launched by the Gdańsk shipyard workers in August 1980, declaring that 'we are not just robots', ended such treatment of workers.

The early 1980s also revealed many other irregularities in the Polish socio-economic system, such as a strong centralisation of planning and management, and the neglect of agriculture and social infrastructure in economic and other policies. Many basic mistakes committed during the industrialisation process were brought to light, including the implementation of a high capital and resource-consuming model of industrialisation, with strong preference being given to heavy and other industry, while at the same time imposing many negative influences on people and on their life and work (Jałowiecki, 1982; Kukliński, 1986; Kortus, l986a,b).

In the meantime, Polish social scientists — including geographers — began to investigate problems relating to the quality of life and the social effects of economic growth, in which the role of industry was crucial (Rutkowski, 1984, 1986; Ciechocińska, 1985; Lodkowska, 1985; Gorzelak, 1986). There were also studies of opinions and attitudes of people, appraising the results of Polish industrialisation processes and policies (see Chapter 4).

Economic Policy and Quality of Life

A significant investigation into the relationship between economic growth and the quality of life is that of Rutkowski (1984, 1986). He studied the social efficiency of the economic growth of Poland as a resultant of

(a) the economic effects [EG] like investment outlays and the output of main industrial products; and

(b) the social effects [ES] like consumption levels of foods, durable goods and services;

and also as a resultant of

(c) the population welfare standard [D] like equipment in social infrastructure such as housing, education, health care, communication and recreation facilities; and

(d) the economic potential [ZW], i.e. existing capacities in the production, transport and service sectors (Figure 3.2).

The indicators EG, ES, D and ZW are aggregated standards obtained by a statistical procedure from twelve to fifteen analytical indices (Rutkowski, 1984, 1986). The curves illustrate the relationships between ES and EG and between D and ZW in a given time (t). Upward trending curves indicate the faster increase of the social effects compared with the economic ones (as in the

(a) $\quad es_t\,(ES, EG) = ES_t - EG_t$

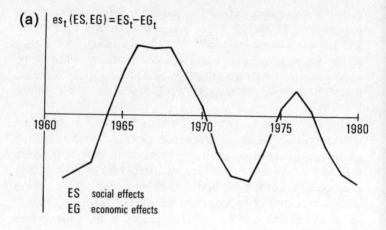

| 1960 | 1965 | 1970 | 1975 | 1980 |

ES social effects
EG economic effects

(b) $\quad es_t\,(D, ZW) = D_t - ZW_t$

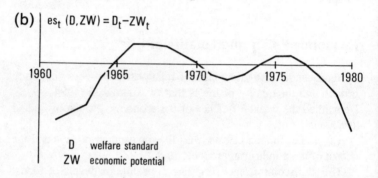

| 1960 | 1965 | 1970 | 1975 | 1980 |

D welfare standard
ZW economic potential

Figure 3.2: Social efficiency [ES] of Poland's economic development 1960 to 1980. (*Source:* Rutkowski, 1986:23-8.)

1960-67 and 1972-76 periods), while downward trending ones (as in the 1967-72 and 1976-80 periods) indicate the reverse situation. The latter case, that of 'inadequate development' caused negative reactions of the population which found expression in successive social crises — in 1956 (as a reaction to the inefficient growth in the 1950-55 period), in 1970 and again in 1980.

This cyclical character of socio-economic development in Poland has been confirmed by other authors (such as Cheliński, 1984 and Kukliński, 1987) who analysed the volume and sectoral structure of investment between 1950 and 1985 (Table 3.1). During the whole postwar period investment in industry was preferred while agriculture and infrastructure were discriminated

Table 3.1: Investment structure in Poland, 1950 to 1985 (per cent)

Branches	1950-55	1956-60	1961-65	1966-70	1971-75	1976-80	1981-85
Industry	43.5	38.8	40.2	39.3	43.8	39.3	29.0
Construction	2.3	2.3	3.1	4.0	5.1	5.0	2.3
Agriculture and forestry	10.2	12.5	14.3	16.5	14.1	16.6	18.4
Transport and communications	12.2	8.9	10.3	11.2	11.4	9.1	7.1
Social infrastructure (commerce, housing, education, science-culture, health services)	26.2	35.4	31.2	27.9	24.7	28.6	41.6
Others	5.6	2.1	0.9	1.1	0.9	1.4	1.6
Total	*100.0*	*100.0*	*100.0*	*100.0*	*100.0*	*100.0*	*100.0*
Average annual change during 1950-85 period (constant prices, per cent)							
Total investment	8.1		5.4	7.4	17.3	− 4.3	− 3.5
Gross national income	7.6		6.2	5.9	9.8	1.2	− 0.8
Net industrial output	10.2		8.9	7.7	10.8	2.6	− 1.1

Source: Kukliński, 1987, Tables 1 and 4.

against. The very great differences between investment in industry and in social infrastructure which occurred, particularly during the 1950-55 and 1971-75 periods, badly affected the quality of life. This corresponds with the cycles shown in Figure 3.2. At the same time the industrial growth contributed to low social efficiency because over 60 per cent of industrial production was of capital goods rather than of consumer goods.

The causes of the cyclical nature of socio-economic development in Poland cannot be stated unequivocally, but one explanation is that they stem from regulations and decisions (Cheliński, 1984; Rutkowski, 1986). Landau (1987) discovered a strong association between the cyclical character of economic growth in Poland and its political situation: the crisis cycle seems to be a rule of socialist development, not only in Poland (Lissowska, 1987).

One consequence of the disparity in the allocation of investment funds was that the development of service activities was disadvantaged. Broadly speaking, the proportion of employees in the service sector determines the quality of life. In 1985 the tertiary sector employed only 34.4 per cent of the total Polish workforce, although even this represents an increase from the 20.7 per cent thus employed in 1950. This sector remains underdeveloped in comparison with other countries as shown in Table 3.2 which sets out the proportions of employment in industry to all non-agricultural activities. The growth of industry, then, did not bring about much development in the service sector or much improvement to the quality of life.

The literature already cited about the quality of life in Poland is largely concerned with its variations over space. The results all confirm that the highest level of the quality of life — measured by income, consumption, education, culture and welfare services — is found in heavily industrialised and urbanised regions. This is only to be expected because during the postwar period industrial plants (which are 95 per cent state-owned in Poland) sponsored from their own budget most of the social infrastructure (such as professional schools, kindergartens, health service units, sport and recreation facilities, and those of mass culture) and, during the initial phase of industrialisation, also housing. In the Katowice voivodeship, for example, 70 per cent of such facilities belong to industry, and in the Łódź voivodeship the figures range from 30 to 70 per cent.

Thus, regions and administrative units (voivodeships, districts

Table 3.2: Employment in industry in proportion to all non-agricultural sectors (industry = 100)

POLAND								
1950	1955	1960	1965	1970	1975	1980	1984	1985
224	212	222	220	222	227	232	238	243

INTERNATIONAL COMPARISONS

France	1968: 305	Yugoslavia	1971: 267
	1984: 409		1981: 302
United Kingdom	1971: 274	Czechoslovakia	1970: 212
	1980: 337		1984: 229
FRG	1970: 232	GDR	1970: 207
	1984: 287		1984: 208
Italy	1971: 261	Hungary	1970: 205
	1984: 392		1984: 245
The Netherlands	1971: 370	Bulgaria	1970: 211
	1981: 482		1984: 212
United States	1970: 348	Rumania	1970: 220
	1984: 441		1984: 192
Canada	1971: 424	USSR	1970: 254
	1984: 513		1984: 271

Source: calculated from Poland, *Rocznik Statystyczny*, 1986: 543.

and cities) endeavoured to attract industrial plants — especially large ones — which had greater financial resources to create the local social infrastructure. One such plant is the Electro-Carbon Factory which opened in Nowy Sącz in 1965. In this way industrialisation also became a basic instrument of regional policy in Poland (and in other socialist countries), which aimed to level out the socio-economic disparities of the social structure of the country that were a legacy of the past. Thus, initially, industry was generally accepted because it provided an economic base and a catalyst for social change. However, recently some negative effects of industrial operations have been recognised which, because they were not in official statistics, could not be considered in the above-mentioned studies about the quality of life. These negative effects mainly relate to the worsening health situation of people, the increasing degradation of the natural environment, and poor working conditions. Most of these negative symptoms were revealed after 1980, such as in a five-volume study of the situation of the working class in Poland (Wójcik, 1984).

Social and Environmental Costs of Industrialisation

Forced and, in some cases, aggressive industrialisation in postwar Poland caused social, biological and environmental costs. Some demographic indices show alarming trends. For example, the death rate of working-age males in Poland, one of the highest in Europe, increased by about 30 per cent between 1965 and 1980 (Table 3.3). As a result, life expectancy of males in Poland has decreased by about two years. The causes have not been fully explained, but they are mainly associated with bad working conditions and psychological stresses brought about by the poor organisation of work.

Table 3.3: Mortality rate of working-age males in Poland, 1965 to 1985 (per thousand)

Years	Males in total	Males in working-age group (18-64)					
		20-24	25-34	35-44	45-54	55-59	60-64
1965	7.9	1.6	2.0	3.4	7.5	14.6	24.0
1970	8.8	1.6	2.0	3.7	7.6	15.6	25.5
1975	9.5	1.7	2.1	4.0	9.0	15.5	25.0
1980	10.9	1.8	2.4	5.0	10.9	18.7	26.6
1983	10.4	1.7	2.2	4.3	10.2	18.4	26.9
1985	11.1	1.5	2.1	4.4	11.2	19.9	29.1

Sources: Wójcik, 1984; Poland, *Rocznik Statystyczny*, 1966-1986.

The deterioration in living conditions and people's health was also brought about by environmental pollution. The priority given in economic policy to production and the neglect until now of the need for environmental protection have led to considerable degradation. It has been estimated that industry (including power generation) is responsible for over 70 per cent of air and water pollution in Poland. In 1983, twenty-seven 'areas of ecological danger' were identified, and these are mainly where there was heavy and 'dirty' industry. These cover some 11 per cent of Poland where 36 per cent of the population and 51 per cent of the industrial workers live. Medical and geo-medical investigations show that in some of these areas, such as Upper Silesia and Kraków, the number of people with cancer is growing due to the poor state of the natural environment (see Wójcik, 1984, vol. 5, *Ecological Danger*; and Kassenberg and Rolewicz, 1985).

The ecological impacts of industry meet with particularly vigorous protests, with people demanding the realisation of the slogan 'quality of environment is an integral element of the quality of life'. The decision of the voivodeship authorities in Kraków in December 1980 to close the aluminium smelter at Skawina (15 km southwest of Kraków) is a good illustration because it was the result of a public outcry of the people of Kraków city and region against the particularly noxious effluents being emitted. Another example was the closure of a wood pulp factory at Jelenia Góra. These decisions were made using a new environmental law which came into force on 31 January 1980.

Finally, the obsolete structure and low technological level of Polish industry make the conditions of work very hard (Wójcik, 1984: Kortus, 1986c). As many as 37 per cent of industrial jobs are not mechanised. While over 30 per cent of all workers operate in unfavourable health conditions, in some industries this proportion is much higher: for example, at the Lenin Steel Works at Kraków the figure is 37 per cent. As a result, there is a growing incidence of work-related illness (Table 3.4). The situation worsened during the late 1970s which also contributed to workers' protests in 1980. This phenomenon is differentiated both by industry branch (Table 3.4) and also spatially with the greatest intensity of work-related illness being observed in the voivodeships of Katowice, which had about 20 per cent of the work-related illness incidence in the country, Kraków, Gdańsk and Wałbrzych, showing an association with the obsolete industrial structure, low technology and the deterioration of fixed assets.

Table 3.4: Incidence of work-related illness in Poland, 1971 to 1981 (per 100,000 employees) and in selected industry branches

Years	In all professions	In industry
1971	52	-
1974	61	-
1979	64	96
1980	67	99
1981	86	150
1982	82	135

In some selected industry branches in 1981

Non-ferrous metallurgy	2,087
Coal mining	344
Transport equipment industry	289
Chemicals	172
Ferrous metallurgy	145
Ceramics	134
Engineering	121
Glass industry	117

Source: Wójcik, 1984.

Another effect of poor organisation and low technology of work is accidents on the job which have increased from 192,000 in 1970 to 237,000 in 1983; fatal accidents rose from 1,300 in 1970 to 1,500 in 1980. In 1985, 0.6 per cent (1,260) of the total accidents at work (212,500) were fatal. Industry in 1985 accounted for 51.8 per cent of total accidents in the workplace and 37.3 per cent of fatal ones (Poland, *Rocznik Statystyczny*, 1986:81). (It should be noted that all data refer to employed people in the socialist sector and thus exclude those engaged in private agriculture and other private activities.) Of all accidents at work, 39 per cent were caused by poor organisation of work, 33 per cent by technical reasons (such as problems related to design or safety standards), 26 per cent by own-fault, and 2 per cent by other, non-specified, causes (Wójcik, 1984).

The growing incidence of work-related illness as well as accidents at work caused the number of invalids to rise from 73,000 in 1970, to 124,000 in 1980 and 169,000 in 1985 (Poland, *Rocznik Statystyczny*, 1986:176): these data also refer only to people employed in the socialist sector. In 1984-85, 30 per cent of incapacitated people in Poland were under fifty years old.

Conclusions

These and other negative effects of industrial activity and, in particular, the bad and inhumane conditions of work, have made such jobs decreasingly attractive. Thus, since the 1970s there has been an outflow from the dirty and backward industries to other places of work. A case in point is the Lenin Steel Works at Kraków, where an outflow of workers has been observed since the end of the 1970s, mainly because of the hard working conditions. In 1983 the deficit of workers in this plant was estimated at over 5,000 which caused disruptions to its operations (Soja, 1986).

This is an element of a wider behavioural phenomenon, namely the negative attitudes of people to such industries (see Chapter 4). The growing contradictions between rising societal achievements, hopes and aspirations on the one hand, and the irrational organisation and management of industry, its poor effectiveness, its outdated technologies and its harmful environmental impacts on the other, are the sources of people's critical attitude towards such industries and, more generally, towards this mode of development.

While industry realised most of its quantitative productive aims and plans, the needs of workers and their families were satisfied only to the extent required for the simple reproduction of labour-power. In essence, the character and functions of Polish industry after the Second World War were not unlike those during the period of the First Industrial Revolution.

There is thus an urgent need for industrial change in Poland, not only in terms of restructuring and technological modernisation, but also for change in its aims and functions to bring fulfilment to the lives of workers, their families and Polish society.

4

Attitudes to Industrial Development and Quality of Life in Poland

Bolesław Domański

Consideration of the impacts of industrial change cannot overlook the perspective of the people. Investigation of such public perceptions contributes to a more complete understanding of these impacts and may also have practical implications for appropriate planning policies and their implementation. This chapter seeks to test some hypotheses about factors influencing urban community attitudes towards local industrial development in Poland and, in particular, tries to assess how much such attitudes depend on objective local conditions and how much on more general beliefs or values.

The Context

Space does not allow a review of the very extensive literature on 'quality of life' issues. This term is used here mainly to refer to the subjective aspect of the concept, and a narrower term — 'level of living' — is employed to cover various elements of material well-being (corresponding to the needs of 'having' in Allardt's 1976 approach). However, before reporting the results of the particular empirical work undertaken, it is appropriate to mention other similar studies and also to discuss briefly those elements of the level of living that are most affected by Polish industrial development.

There have been many geographical and sociological studies about public attitudes towards industry but the majority have focused on individual factory and other developments (Bultena, 1979; Glasson and Porter, 1980; Johnson and Zeigler, 1983; Thompson and Blevins, 1983; Smith and Irwin, 1984; van der

Pligt et al., 1986). Only a few have investigated attitudes towards local industrial development as a whole (Green and Bruce, 1976; Maurer and Napier, 1981; Krannich and Humphrey, 1983) or, explicitly, the influence of industrial development on changes in the subjective quality of life (Knox and Cottam, 1981). Studies of the latter kind have been closely related to work trying to determine attitudes towards local environmental pollution (Caris, 1978; van Liere and Dunlap, 1980; Ester, 1981). Together, these suggest that attitudes towards industry largely depend on the employment situation on the one hand and the growing environmental sensitivity on the other. When recession and deindustrialisation progressed some signs of a decrease in this sensitivity occurred, and situations in which local communities have supported local industrial development against national environmental organisations have become more common (Bultena, 1979; Glasson and Porter, 1980; Spooner, 1981). The significance of the local labour market situation for attitudes towards industrial development has increased substantially.

In many ways, however, the Polish context seems to be different. Until 1980 the environmental sensitivity of Polish society had been regarded as low (Kozłowski, 1986), and discussions of environmental problems in the mass media were almost non-existent. At the same time, industry was an important source of inter and intra-regional differences in the level of living. Throughout the postwar period only very limited resources have been allocated to social infrastructure development in contrast to those directed to industrial investment. The few studies available about Polish community attitudes towards industrial development showed that even those causing serious environmental impacts were perceived to be beneficial (Babiak, 1972; Żechowski, 1973). The situation changed rapidly in the early 1980s when the public became increasingly aware of the mounting and disastrous environmental pollution of the country.

It must be emphasised, however, that in Poland — as well as other countries in Eastern Europe — the demand for industrial labour is in many places greater than the supply. Thus people, especially in large cities, can usually choose the firm or plant in which they want to take a job so that enterprises have to compete to try to attract labour. This competition, it must be remembered, takes place in a situation in which some essential social needs remain unsatisfied. The very great shortage of dwellings is probably the most acute problem, with the others being the low standard of the old housing stock, the underdevelopment of services and the inadequate supply of consumer goods. In these circumstances industrial enterprises can attract workers by offering them better opportunities to obtain some very basic needs. Thus, they try to

(a) get control over the allocation of dwellings newly constructed by state cooperatives or to construct their own residential buildings;

(b) provide their own bus service for commuters which is especially important because of the gradual deterioration of the country's 'open' public bus service during the last decade;

(c) provide health care services, kindergartens, crèches and post-primary schools;

(d) sell goods in short supply in factory shops and canteens;

(e) offer comparatively high wages and various kinds of financial assistance, such as loans and repayment of bank credits.

All this means that industry in Poland affects the level of living not only and not mainly through the job opportunities it provides. Another implication of a situation in which workers are scarce is that the attitudes of labour and of entire communities are of much greater practical significance for industrial organisations even from a purely economic point of view.

It has been suggested that the explanation of the importance attached to various impacts of industrial development should be in terms of Maslow's widely accepted theory of a hierarchy of needs. According to Maslow (1970) needs are not additive, i.e. greater satisfaction of need A does not necessarily offset the lack of fulfilment of need B. Human needs are hierarchical and appear in some definite order: lower needs must be satisfied at least to a certain basic level before substitution of needs can occur and higher ones can come to the fore.

An Empirical Study

Hypotheses and Methods

The results reported here are part of a broader research project undertaken to test a set of hypotheses about factors influencing inter-city variations in urban community attitudes towards local industrial development in Poland. Some of these hypotheses are discussed below.

(1) There are greater inter-city than intra-city differences in attitudes towards local industrial development, i.e. the attitudes depend more on factors affecting entire urban communities than on personal characteristics of individuals.

(2) The importance attached to environmental effects of industrial development is the most differentiated one so that it is a crucial dimension of the entire attitude. It stems from the conviction that public attitudes towards industry have been positive for a long time and only the recent increase in environmental concern is likely to change it markedly.

(3) The importance of environmental effects of industrial development depends more on cultural factors, particularly environmental sensitivity, than on objective local conditions including pollution levels. This hypothesis is based on the fact that environmental hazard is not a new phenomenon in Poland whereas the greater importance being attached to it is a recent one.

(4) Environmental sensitivity, and arising from it negative attitudes towards local industrial development, spread from Kraków by the neighbourhood and hierarchical effect. It seems justified to expect that the increase in environmental sensitivity is not spatially uniform. Spatial aspects of the diffusion of ideas have been widely discussed (Hägerstrand, 1967; Brown, L., 1974; Brown, M.A., 1981) and its social and cultural characteristics have been analysed from a sociological point of view by Shils (1975) in his core-periphery concept.

(5) A high level of industrialisation in a town is a significant secondary factor that may influence negative attitudes, apart from environmental sensitivity and high pollution levels. This may be associated both with some disillusionment about actual indus-trialisation effects and with perceived prospects for further development of the town in alternative directions.

(6) Dependence of a town on one large industrial plant makes community attitudes towards industry comparatively better.

(7) The community attitude towards urban industrialisation in general is usually more negative than the attitude towards industrial development of a given town as the former is more affected by environmental sensitivity.

Twenty-five towns in southern Poland were selected for this

research so as to allow for variations in the main hypothetical factors, i.e. the hierarchical rank of the town, distance from Kraków and other major regional centres, extent of air pollution, and level of industrialisation. Some 300 people responded to a preliminary questionnaire and 3,862 to the final one which was distributed through primary schools and addressed to the children's parents. As a result the sample of respondents was biased towards younger people (5 per cent of respondents were aged fifty or more even though this age group made up 14 per cent of the region's urban labour force) but age was found to have no effect on attitudes investigated. The sample was also slightly biased in educational level (59 per cent of respondents had completed secondary education as against 40 per cent of the regional labour force as a whole) which to some extent affected the attitude of individuals but made little difference to variations in attitude to industrial development in the twenty-five towns.

Following Fishbein and Ajzen (1975), attitudes were seen to be based upon beliefs and evaluations so that the 'image' (mental scheme) of local industrialisation was considered to be part of the attitude towards it. Every attitude was measured by some complementary indicators; those relating to the attitude towards local industrial development in particular towns are set out in an Appendix to this chapter. A stepwise multiple regression analysis was used to determine which of forty-six demographic, social, economic, environmental and locational characteristics of the towns/communities affected differentiation in attitudes. The results were treated with care and their interpretation was based on detailed study and understanding of particular phenomena in the Polish city context so as to come to valid conclusions about actual relationships (impacts) underlying revealed empirical regularities. Although the possible impact of the personal characteristics of respondents was also examined, only the attitudes of urban communities are set out here.

Differentiation and Structure of the Attitude

It is worth emphasising that there is considerable agreement between the perception of the level of industrialisation of particular towns and the same level measured 'objectively'. The level of industrialisation is usually slightly understated in towns with less than about 10,000 population but otherwise town size has no effect on people's perception.

In line with hypothesis (1), attitudes towards local industrial development were found to be comparatively homogeneous within town communities. Tests of variance for the main attitude indicators show that differences are much greater between urban communities than within them so that a 'town community attitude' can be understood as meaning one that is predominant in the community. In addition, it suggests that personal characteristics of individuals have a rather modest impact compared with factors influencing entire communities and/or that there is strong interaction between the attitudes of members of the town community.

The attitude towards the industrial development of particular towns is extremely variable. On the one hand, there are communities that fully support the industrial development of their own towns while, on the other, some communities have an entirely opposite view. This divergence can be better understood by examining the five most important effects of local industrial development selected by respondents from among the nineteen listed in the questionnaire (see the Appendix). A matrix of intercorrelations between the importance attached to particular effects (i.e. between percentages of respondents mentioning these effects) was calculated and subsequently ordered so as to put strongly intercorrelated effects next to each other. The ordered matrix of intercorrelations, together with two additional criteria — a significant correlation of a given effect with the overall attitude indicator, and a sufficiently great importance attached to this effect (a limit of 15 per cent of respondents was used) — show comparatively independent principal groups of related effects that can be treated as dimensions of the attitude. Figure 4.1 demonstrates that three dimensions can be identified among effects of further potential local industrial development (the picture for effects of existing local industry is very similar):

(a) a dimension of positive effects including seven consequences commonly associated with a positive attitude towards local industrialisation;

(b) a dimension of negative environmental effects with health hazard, nature damage, bad quality of agricultural produce and dirt being the most important effects (with other environmental effects being more specific to some towns);

(c) a dimension of negative social effects which has the least significance because the importance attached to these effects is similar both in towns with positive and with negative attitudes.

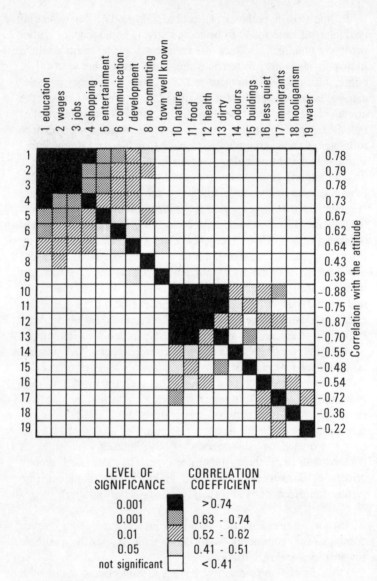

Figure 4.1: Intercorrelations between the most important effects of potential further industrial development of the towns investigated. (For description of the effects of industrialisation, see Appendix.)

This structure is related to the fact that even at the individual level there are only two principal ways of perceiving local industrial development: a negative one associated with the great importance attached to a few environmental effects, and a positive one based on the significance attached to the benefits perceived to stem from industrialisation. The dimension of environmental effects is found to be a crucial one in accordance with hypothesis (2). The variation in the importance attached to these effects in the twenty-five towns was much greater than the differentiation in the positive and social effects. Thus the importance given to environmental effects has the greatest significance for the overall community attitude.

Factors Affecting Urban Community Attitudes

Contrary to expectations expressed in hypothesis (3), the community attitude towards local industrial development of particular towns (ALI) depends more on local conditions than on general beliefs and values. Environmental sensitivity (ES) and the general attitude towards urban industrialisation in Poland (GA) have only a slight modifying impact on ALI. Although a positive attitude towards urban industrialisation in general is rare, positive ALI scores prevail (Figure 4.2). The main factors exerting very strong influences on positive attitudes are the poor social infrastructure and the lack of basic amenities (such as running water, toilet facilities and gas in many flats). In line with Maslow's theory, a higher need for a clean environment is quelled because more fundamental requirements for essential amenities and infrastructure remain unsatisfied. Local industrial development is regarded as the main, or even the only, way to change this unsatisfactory situation.

Only in communities where fundamental needs are met — in towns having comparatively good basic amenities and infrastructure — can the negative attitudes prevail. This is a necessary but not sufficient condition. Negative community attitudes towards local industrial development may result from one of two factors. The first and most obvious is the existing high level of air pollution, as in Kraków, Tarnów and Nowy Sącz. From Table 4.1 it is clear that all the most important effects perceived to arise from existing local industry are of an environmental character. The profile of the most perceived effects of further industrial development is very similar, as illustrated by the results

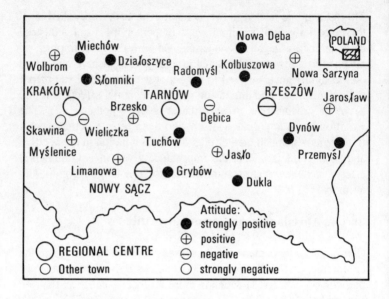

Figure 4.2: Attitude towards local industrial development of the towns investigated in southern Poland.

from Tarnów in Table 4.2. However, second, negative attitudes are also typical for industrialised towns that have no noxious activities and have not experienced negative environmental effects. In Rzeszów, for example, there is great concern about further industrialisation (compare Tables 4.1 and 4.2). Rather, prospects for development are seen to be in high-order prestigious cultural and educational services. This is in line with hypothesis (5) that a high level of industrialisation can influence negative ALI.

The predominance of negative attitudes is found in all urban communities in which health hazard is perceived to be the single most important effect. Evidently, when environmental pollution is understood to be a health hazard rather than simply as dirt the attitude becomes a negative one. In Maslow's terms it probably means that when environmental pollution is perceived as affecting health it becomes associated with the very fundamental human need.

The town of Kolbuszowa in Table 4.2 illustrates the perception of the benefits flowing from industrialisation which is typical for

Table 4.l: The most important effects of the existing industry in three selected towns in southern Poland

KRAKÓW	
1. health hazard	81.7
2. nature damage	55.4
3. bad quality of agricultural produce	50.2
4. damage of historical buildings	45.8
5. hooliganism	40.2
6. immigrants, it's more difficult to find a flat	35.4
7. water supply difficulties	31.2
8. it's dirty	29.9
9. *wide job opportunities*	*19.9*
10. *education prospects*	*17.5*
NOWY SĄCZ	
1. health hazard	46.8
2. immigrants, it's more difficult to find a flat	46.8
3. *wide job opportunities*	*35.8*
4. water supply difficulties	30.3
5. it's dirty	29.4
6. hooliganism	27.5
7. nature damage	26.6
8. bad quality of agricultural produce	23.9
9. *no need to commute*	*22.9*
10. unpleasant odours	22.0
RZESZÓW	
1. *wide job opportunities*	*55.9*
2. *education prospects*	*47.0*
3. immigrants, it's more difficult to find a flat	41.7
4. *good wage prospects*	*36.0*
5. *no need to commute*	*32.0*
6. *rapid development of the town*	*28.7*
7. *good communication*	*27.9*
8. health hazard	27.1
9. *the town is well known*	*24.7*
10. hooliganism	21.1

Notes: Percentages show the proportion of respondents mentioning particular effects among the five most important ones. Positive effects are shown in italics. Full names of the effects are listed in the Appendix.
Source: Author's fieldwork.

Table 4.2: The most important effects of the potential further industrial development in three selected towns in southern Poland

T A R N Ó W	
1. health hazard	51.0
2. nature damage	36.4
3. *wide job opportunities*	*34.0*
4. immigrants, it's more difficult to find a flat	33.0
5. *good wage prospects*	*29.6*
6. less quiet life	26.2
7. *education prospects*	*24.8*
8. *good communications*	*23.3*
9. bad quality of agricultural produce	22.8
10. unpleasant odours	21.8
K O L B U S Z O W A	
1. *rapid development of the town*	*52.9*
2. *wide job opportunities*	*41.2*
3. *good wage prospects*	*37.3*
4. *education prospects*	*33.3*
5. *good shopping prospects*	*31.4*
6. *good communications*	*31.4*
7. water supply difficulties	29.4
8. *the town is well known*	*21.6*
9. immigrants, it's more difficult to find a flat	21.6
10. health hazard	17.6
R Z E S Z Ó W	
1. *wide job opportunities*	*42.8*
2. health hazard	41.4
3. *good wage prospects*	*35.8*
4. *rapid development of the town*	*34.4*
5. immigrants, it's more difficult to find a flat	28.8
6. *education prospects*	*28.8*
7. hooliganism	26.5
8. less quiet life	23.7
9. nature damage	22.8
10. bad quality of agricultural produce	20.9

See notes to Table 4.1.

communities with a positive attitude; rapid overall development is seen to be the most important consequence while there is a very weak environmental anxiety.

A tourist function is a secondary factor conducive to negative

ALI as an alternative direction of development perceived as contradictory to local industrialisation, whereas the dominance of a single large plant makes the attitude more positive, thus confirming hypothesis (6). However, the latter mainly refers to the evaluation of existing local industry and much less to the evaluation of further such activity.

Although ALI is negatively correlated ($r = -0.504$) with the size of the town (the bigger the town the more negative the attitude), this is only a result of a correlation between this size and some other factors influencing the attitude (particularly better infrastructure and housing as well as a higher level of industrialisation). The partial correlation and multiple regression analysis prove that the size of the town has no direct impact on ALI itself.

Among variables having statistically significant relationships with ALI indicators is distance from Kraków and from other regional centres. This reflects the greater importance attached to environmental impacts of industrial development in town communities located near regional centres. Thus, hypothesis (4) about diffusion by social contacts between communities of nearby towns (the neighbourhood effect) has been confirmed. However, the influence of regional centres refers mainly to environmental sensitivity (ES) and general attitude (GA), a problem discussed in greater detail elsewhere (Domański, forthcoming).

Figure 4.3 presents a generalised schema of factors influencing the attitude towards the industrial development of particular towns. It also indicates that the general attitude towards urban industrialisation in Poland depends on the environmental sensitivity on the one hand and on the more specific attitude, ALI, on the other. Thus in the case of GA hypothesis (3) is partly supported. The environmental sensitivity depends mostly on deeper values which have not been examined. Hence the differentiation of ES is small compared to that of GA and particularly of ALI. The index of determination indicates that up to 92 per cent of the variation in ALI can be accounted for on the basis of variables representing local conditions (town/community characteristics) while these account for only 80 to 83 per cent of the variance in GA and only 70 per cent in the case of ES.

Environmental sensitivity, measured as the position that a clean environment holds among the needs that people associate with urban industrialisation, appears to be high in all the communities investigated. Despite the widespread ES and, stemming from it,

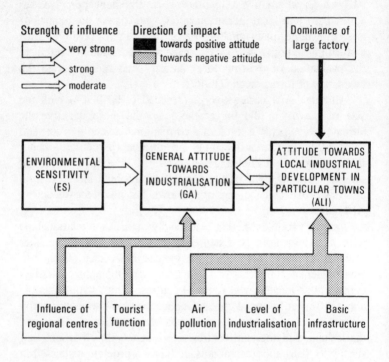

Figure 4.3: Principal factors influencing attitudes towards local industrial development.

the rather common negative or ambivalent GA, more than half the communities show a clearly favourable attitude towards the industrial development of their own towns, a confirmation of hypothesis (7). This suggests that the environmental sensitivity of the majority of the communities is a new and not very deep phenomenon. This also results from the underdevelopment of social infrastructure and unsatisfactory housing in several towns, and from the persistence of the belief that industry is the exclusive engine of development. A positive attitude can be called 'traditional' in the sense that it seems to be 'natural' for Polish urban communities unless local conditions induce a negative one.

None the less, in seven of the twenty-five communities negative attitudes predominate. In these the concern is not just about plants causing heavy pollution but also about apparently 'clean' factories making, for instance, agricultural equipment or footwear: concern about noxious industry has influenced the attitude towards manufacturing in general. Negative attitudes towards local industrial development seem to be more common, and in some cases more extreme, in Poland than in Western communities probably because of the more serious environmental problems in Poland and the different employment situation.

Local Industrial Development and Quality of Life

The attitude towards local industrial development is, in general, sharply differentiated. This reflects the various perceptions of the impact of this kind of activity on the quality of life, ranging from the 'traditional' perception of industry as a factor improving the quality of life (or at least, the level of living) to its overall condemnation for causing this quality to deteriorate. This dualism is manifested also in the analysis of the opinions about the quality of life in the twenty-five communities investigated. As in many other studies since Marans and Rodgers (1975), satisfaction has been used as an overall indicator of the perceived quality of life in a given area (Knox and Cottam, 1981; Pacione, 1982; Sofranko and Fliegel, 1984; Connerly and Marans, 1985).

In numerous studies of this kind — including this one — the usual proportion of residents declaring themselves to be satisfied to live in their town is 75 to 85 per cent. In southern Poland, however, two groups of towns showed substantially lower rates of satisfaction (Figure 4.4). In Kraków, Skawina and Tarnów these evidently arise from public awareness of the extent of industrial pollution and its health consequences. The case of the town of Skawina is extraordinary because two-thirds of its respondents said that they were dissatisfied with living there: there is no factor to compensate for the impact of its very great pollution problems whereas Kraków and Tarnów have their historical heritage and their roles as regional centres. Low satisfaction was also expressed by people in the small towns of Działoszyce, Słomniki and Radomyśl which have no industry and extremely poor basic infrastructure and housing.

Thus industry can still affect the perceived quality of life of local communities in Poland, positively or negatively in respect to local conditions. These determine which of the two, functioning at the level of individuals' general schemata of perception of industrial development, is adopted by the majority of the town

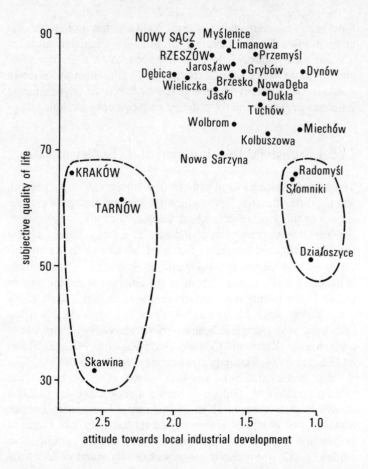

Figure 4.4: The relationship between subjective quality of life (SQL) and attitude towards local industrial development of particular towns (ALI).

community concerned. Expectation of the development of social infrastructure and better housing appear to be the principal reasons for perceiving industrial development to be beneficial. This probably contrasts with Western communities where the concern is mainly about jobs. The massive industrial pollution in Poland, which is giving rise to growing environmental sensitivity, underlies the development of negative attitudes towards further industrial activity in towns with comparatively better infrastructure and higher levels of industrialisation or great pollution.

Appendix

Indicators of ALI were based on the responses to five questions.

In Question 1 respondents were asked whether they considered their town, as compared with others of a similar size, to be (a) very strongly industrialised; (b) strongly industrialised; (c) of average level of industrialisation; (d) poorly industrialised; (e) very poorly industrialised.

In Question 2, using the same five-point scale, people were asked to say how high they thought the desirable level of industrialisation for their town should be. Comparison of the answers to Questions 1 and 2 was taken to be an indication of the respondent's preference for an increase, decrease or the maintenance of the status quo in the level of industrialisation.

A similar role was played by responses to a more direct Question 3 which asked whether you personally would be more satisfied with living in your town if it were (a) more industrialised than now; (b) at the same level of industrialisation as now; (c) less industrialised than now; or (d) whether the level of industrialisation of your town is of no significance to you.

The following three indicators of community attitude were constructed based on responses to Question 3 and a similar three on a comparison of Questions 1 and 2: (a) percentage of respondents supporting the industrial growth of the town; (b) percentage of respondents supporting a decrease in the level of industrialisation in the town; (c) mean value of answers to Question 3 (and mean value of answers to Questions 1 and 2).

In Question 4 respondents were asked to point to the five most important effects of the existing industry in their town from among the following phenomena: (a) living in the town more unhealthy; (b) the town better known, more important; (c) wider job opportunities; (d) more hooliganism and demoralisation; (e) worse quality of agricultural produce; (f) more dirty; (g) better wage prospects; (h) better communications with other localities; (i) nature more damaged in town surroundings; (j) education easier to obtain; (k) more rapid development of the town; (l) greater inflow of people from villages and other towns, more difficult to find a flat; (m) historical buildings more damaged; (n) no need to commute over a long distance; (o) easier shopping; (p) less quiet life; (q) unpleasant odours; (r) greater entertainment prospects; (s) water supply difficulties.

Using the same list of phenomena people had to choose the

five most important effects of further potential industrial development of their town (Question 5).

Responses to Questions 4 and 5 were used to examine the attitude structure. In addition, the ratio of positive and negative effects mentioned by respondents of a given town was used as an indicator of the evaluation of existing industry (Question 4) and of the further potential industrial development (Question 5).

5

Gender, Employment and Territory in Metropolitan Environments

Paul Villeneuve

This chapter is about women and men, firms and households, cities and suburbs. It seeks to understand the evolving relations between these categories, particularly their present restructuring in large metropolitan areas. Notable aspects of current metropolitan restructuring include the rapid increase of the participation of women in the wage labour force, the decline in the size of households, the intensification of subcontracting relations between firms, the social transformation of numerous inner city neighbourhoods, the decentralisation of manufacturing and polarisation between social classes. These aspects of urban restructuring are perhaps most sharply observed in rapidly growing metropolises like Los Angeles (Davis, 1987; Soja et al., 1987). What are the links between these empirically observed phenomena, and is it possible to sketch a unified conceptual framework capable of giving meaning to these diverse — and sometimes divergent — tendencies?

This framework should be able to accommodate both agency and structure (the dialectical relations between social structure and human agency have been discussed by Giddens, 1979:49-95, and critically evaluated by Storper, 1985a). It should also attempt to bridge gaps between industrial and social geography, and to amalgamate the social and the spatial into the 'territorial', an issue that is on the research agenda of several geographers such as Raffestin (1980), Pred (1985) and Scott and Storper (1986b). Furthermore, this framework should view human territories as being structured in time through myriad interactions between individuals given to intentionality and some rationality. However, it should also recognise that most of the territories so structured are themselves non-intentional: Boudon (1984) has perhaps presented the clearest exposition of the unintended social consequences of the intentional actions of individuals. In this framework, the basic units of analysis should be the relations between the individuals rather than the individuals themselves, and analytical priority should be given to relations of substance over relations of similarity and dissimilarity: individuals may interact directly or they may simply have similar characteristics, but one kind of relationship does not imply the other (see, for example, Sayer, 1984:82).

Given these principles, the canvas of our interrogations unfolds in a spiral of agency and structure. How do women and men interact to constitute organisations such as firms and households and, in turn, how do firms and households interact to constitute territorial forms such as cities and suburbs? Also, concomitantly, how do cities and suburbs 'inform' (in the sense proposed by Bateson, 1972:379-410) interactions among firms and households, and, in turn, how do firms and households inform interactions among women and men?

Tentative answers to these questions are attempted in the four sections of the chapter. First, it is argued that transaction cost economics, a perspective giving equal importance to market and non-market transactions, provides an appropriate conceptual framework to study present urban and industrial restructuring processes. Second, interactions between women and men and between firms and households are discussed from the point of view of transaction cost economics. Firms and households are seen as governance structures, rather than production or utility functions. Transactions take place within and between governance structures, and a key issue concerns the reasons for internalising or externalising given transactions. The last two sections of the chapter seek an understanding of the differences between cities and suburbs in terms of this set of ideas. Gender relations and employment relations are jointly considered. The third section argues that a crucial aspect of the evolving division of labour between households and firms is the externalisation of tasks by households. This process parallels the increasing participation of women in wage labour, and it significantly differs from city to suburbs. The fourth section considers one of the important ways by which this process feeds back on gender relations within households: occupational asymmetry between spouses, an indicator of their differential power in households' decision-making, is also shown to evolve differently from city to suburbs.

Market and Non-market Transactions

Typically, industrial geography deals with production while social geography is concerned with reproduction. This specialisation of objectives hinders an adequate understanding of present restructuring processes. A common language is needed which can handle both the institutions of production and those of reproduction. Transaction cost economics may well provide a starting point, a perspective being developed by Arrow (1974) and Williamson (1985) following earlier work by Knight (1921), Commons (1934) and Coase (1937). Clark (1981) and Scott (1986) have shown the utility of this body of thinking for the study of industrial organisation and production. It is a fully relational approach which adopts a micro-analytical perspective for studying economic organisation. In opposition to neo-classical economics, transaction cost economics recognises at the outset that governance structures other than the market are also suited for the purpose of coordinating economic activity. Indeed, a key issue is the choice of the appropriate structure for conducting certain types of transactions, whether externally between firms through the market, or internally within (hierarchically organised) firms.

In this approach, the firm is seen as a governance structure for conducting contractual relations rather than solely as a production function. This has the advantage of clearly prioritising social relations as the context in which technical relations of production take place. Labour is not considered as just another factor of production which has to be optimally combined with other factors. In the employment relations, labour and capital are in conflict but they are interdependent. Choices of location and technology are made in the context of the contractual bargaining constituting the employment relation. They are intervening decision variables.

Clark (1981) has discussed the relevance of developing an adequate view of contractual employment relationships as a key issue in the understanding of the spatial division of labour. In particular, labour and capital are in perpetual conflict over the control of the production process and the conditions of employment. Strategies of firms to centralise or decentralise certain activities may well intersect in complex ways with their strategies to either internalise or externalise the labour process. Locational considerations are also a key component of labour strategies, whether these are elaborated by individuals or by unions. They may range from 'exit' to 'voice' (Hirschman, 1970) and, like the strategies of management, they are subject to the contexts formed locally, nationally and internationally by market conditions and other institutional arrangements.

Transaction cost economics, much like Berry's (1973) 'process metageography', represents reality as flow: a firm is visualised as a network within a network. A transaction takes place when 'a good or a service is transferred across some technologically separable interface' (Williamson, 1985:1). Seen in this way, the firm — or for that matter, any other organisation, the household for instance — is not a rigid set of persons and objects easy to delineate. Rather, its boundaries are more or less permeable and ever fluctuating. They actually depend on the balance between internal and external transactions. These two broad categories of transactions are distinguished on the basis of the type of governance structure that they imply. External transactions are conducted mainly in a market environment while most internal transactions are non-market in nature. While it may not be possible to decide a priori what the balance between market and non-market transactions should be in order to minimise total social costs, it is nevertheless possible to investigate empirically what the balance actually is in real world situations such as metropolitan environments.

Gender Relations, Employment Relations, Households and Firms

Consider metropolitan environments as being formed of cities and suburbs, a binary division that provides an easy approach to the more difficult categories of centrality and peripherality. Cities can be viewed as being formed of places of residence and places of employment. For simplicity, call households the places of residence and firms the places of employment. Likewise, suburbs are formed of households and firms. Beyond built form, at the level of social space, what is it that fundamentally differentiates cities from suburbs? Neo-classical models of industrial and residential location have provided answers by conceptualising households as utility functions and firms as production functions, as indeed they are. However, households are more than consumption units and, likewise, firms are not only production units. A first difficulty in this conceptualisation arises when it is realised that households are also key elements in the production

70

process of an essential commodity, labour; and that firms are also consumers of labour and intermediate goods and services. This difficulty is one of semantics but it points to a more fundamental issue: consuming and producing may not be the most basic activities. What if transacting is more basic, in the sense that it structures both consumption and production?

Households, as well as firms, can be seen as governance structures for conducting internal and external transactions between people. The focus here is on two particularly important categories of transactions, gender relations and employment relations. These are seen as socially defined relations of substance rather than relations of form, although without deciding which are necessary and which are contingent relations. Rather, the key issue in identifying such large categories of relations is to specify what exactly makes the transactors interdependent in each category. There is no difficulty in seeing gender relations as constitutive of households and families; and, in the same way, employment relations can easily be taken as the basic components of firms, large and small. Gender relations have been neglected, however, in studies of firms, just as employment relations have been neglected in studies of households. Now that the participation of women, especially married women, in the wage labour force is no longer confined to the blue-collar working class, gender has become an issue at work and work has become an issue at home. In other words, gender relations and employment relations are increasingly interlocking, and in so doing they are restructuring households and firms as governance structures.

Governance structures can be hierarchical but they need not be, and hierarchical transactions constituting these structures can be unequal but they need not be either. The issue of the degree of equality or reciprocity in transactions is a particularly difficult one to handle empirically. In markets, the degree of equality depends on the market structure: size and spatial integration, stability of demand, degree of product differentiation and capital intensity of production. In non-market governance structures, the degree of equality depends on contractual rules that can either be specified in detail, as they are in (non-market) economic exchange, or they can be left to the 'generalised willingness to respond to the needs of others' as in interpersonal relations between kin and friends (Curtis, 1986:176).

A central place system is an example of a hierarchical market governance structure where transactions are not necessarily unequal. A corporate bureaucracy, on the other hand, constitutes a hierarchical non-market governance structure inside of which transactions tend to be unequal, although many would argue that when authority is matched with equivalent responsibility, inequality is much reduced. Authority and responsibility in organisations have been discussed by Arrow (1974:63-79): authority has to be distinguished from power and influence (Curtis, 1986), and responsibility is valued both in terms of achieving an organisation's goals and for the self-respect of the individuals concerned.

The patriarchal family is also a hierarchical non-market governance structure based on unequal gender relations. Such a family is taken here to be the traditional nuclear family with the husband as the sole participant in the wage labour force and a rigid division of labour between spouses. While these attributes do not necessarily lead to unequal gender relations, they are — as Curtis (1986) has shown — significantly related to patriarchy defined as the authority of men over women. However, the patriarchal family is only one type of household and a rapidly decreasing one in North American metropolitan environments. Other forms, including dual-earner and single-parent families, as well as non-family households, are now developing at rapid rates. Most of these are much smaller. Drops in fertility rates are well documented, although the fact that they vary greatly between ethnic groups has not been sufficiently emphasised. Metaphorically, one can almost say that a process of vertical disintegration is at work in large segments of the domestic economy. It may be, from a transactional perspective, similar to processes going on in some industries. Thus, Storper (1985b) and Scott (1986), among others, have convincingly argued in favour of an approach emphasising the study of the historical and contingent conditions giving rise to various degrees of vertical disintegration in specific industries, such as labour-intensive manufacturing and business services; with the necessary adaptations, their arguments can be extended to the domestic sphere of the economy.

Thus, transactional boundaries between households, markets and firms are continually being restructured and, in turn, this modifies the geography of cities and suburbs. A limited sketch of these modifications will now be attempted with two aspects being highlighted. First, the ways in which gender relations inform employment relations will be explored, and it will be shown that the positions of women in the wage labour force have evolved differently between city and suburbs. Second, the reverse side of the coin will be examined. One particular way in which employment relations inform gender relations will be documented: occupational asymmetry within couples will also be shown to change differently from city to suburbs.

Gender, Employment and Urban Centrality

In the 1970s many married women have entered metropolitan labour markets throughout North America. For example, the number of two-earner families in the Montreal metropolitan area increased from 135,000 in 1971 to 288,000 in 1981 (more detailed analyses of these and related data are available in Séguin and Villeneuve, 1987; Villeneuve and Viaud, 1987; Villeneuve and Rose, 1988; Rose and Villeneuve, 1988). One important geographical aspect of female employment in Canadian metropolitan areas is its greater centralisation, on the average, compared to male employment. To be sure, female employment decentralised during the 1970s, but in 1981 it was still much more centrally located than its male counterpart. Table 5.1 illustrates this situation with data from Montreal. In this Table, interactions between places of residence and places of employment are recorded in terms of binary categories: women and men, city and suburb. These data reveal a number of basic changes that have taken place during the 1970s. For example, the spatial distributions of female and male workers at place of residence have converged much more than their spatial distributions at place of employment: 51 per cent of female workers were living in the city in 1971 as compared to 42 per cent of male workers; in 1981, the figures were 35 and 31 per cent; on the other hand, 64 per cent of female workers as compared to 53 per cent of male workers were employed in the city in 1971 and 52 and 42 per cent respectively in 1981. This greater centrality of female employment in Canadian metropolitan areas differs from the situation in the United States where female employment is more decentralised than male employment (see Pratt and Hanson, 1988), a divergence which can be interpreted in the context of the specificity of Canadian cities (Goldberg and Mercer, 1986).

This observation on the centrality of female employment holds when total employment is disaggregated into economic sectors. Only sectors clearly related to labour force reproduction, such as

Table 5.1: Percentage distribution of labour force at place of employment by place of residence, metropolitan Montreal, 1971 and 1981

Category/location	Female workers						Male workers					
	1971			1981			1971			1981		
	City	Suburbs	Total	City	Suburbs	Total	City	Suburbs	Total	City	Suburbs	Total
Total labour force												
City	43	8	51	27	8	35	29	13	42	19	12	31
Suburbs	21	28	49	25	40	65	24	34	58	23	46	69
Total	64	36	100	52	48	100	53	47	100	42	58	100
Labour force in health, education and welfare												
City	42	7	49	29	7	36	39	8	47	30	9	39
Suburbs	18	33	51	24	40	64	25	28	53	25	36	61
Total	60	40	100	53	47	100	64	36	100	55	45	100

Table 5.1 (continued)

Labour force in business services

City	45	6	51	30	6	36	35	8	43	26	9	35
Suburbs	32	17	49	35	29	64	36	21	57	34	31	65
Total	77	23	100	65	35	100	71	29	100	60	40	100

Note: These are small, highly aggregated, journey to work matrices. They show: (a) the more pronounced centralisation of the total female workforce compared to the total male labour force; (b) the shorter work-trips of women compared to men; (c) the closing of the gap between the sexes on these two variables during the 1970s; and (d) the opposition between a neighbourhood-orientated economic sector such as health, education and welfare, and a downtown-orientated sector like business services. These data were derived from special tabulations made available by Statistics Canada. A much more detailed analysis can be found in Villeneuve and Rose (1988).

health, education and welfare, show a greater peripherality of female compared to male employment. Jobs in these sectors are strongly feminised and are located, generally speaking, nearer residential areas than are jobs in sectors less geared to 'reproductive activities'. The distinction between productive and reproductive activities is, of course, a difficult one because, ultimately, almost all productive activities contribute to the reproduction of labour power; it is certainly not equivalent, however, to the distinction, often used here, between domestic economy and wage labour market.

The data in Table 5.1 suggest a possible interpretation of the role of gender in the way the spatial division of labour between households and other institutions gradually evolves in metropolitan environments. Economic base theory classifies employment into basic and non-basic. In constructs such as the Lowry model the reasoning associated with this classification has been used in order to explain the location of households and jobs (Webber, 1984). The reasoning was not, however, formulated in terms of gender and employment relations. If it is reformulated in those terms, two observations readily come to mind. First, there is some overlap between such categorisation schemes as basic versus non-basic activities, and productive versus reproductive activities. Geographically, non-basic activities are also often said to be 'neighbourhood-orientated', while basic activities are said to be 'site-orientated' as they show a strong tendency to cluster either downtown or in other sub-centres within metropolitan areas. Second, tendencies originating at two opposite geographical scales influence, over time, the proportion of women in each of these two broad categories of employment. Both tendencies affect the restructuring of governance structures in metropolitan economies.

At the micro-scale, traditional 'female jobs' are, in many respects, transfers to the public sphere — the market, the state, the community — of tasks previously performed in the home. In other words, female participation in wage labour may still be partly a correlate of the 'de-domestication' of an increasing portion of the tasks associated with labour force reproduction. With time, these tasks are gradually separated from the home, but since they keep strong linkages with tasks still performed in the home they show a marked neighbourhood orientation. This process is an important component of the changing division of labour between home and the public sphere. Journey to work studies have repeatedly found that women have shorter work trips than men. The process just described may, in part, account for this.

At the world scale, one component of industrial restructuring is the concentration in downtown large metropolitan areas of an increasing variety of office jobs. These are found in headquarters of multinational corporations, in financial institutions, in state institutions and in a wide array of rapidly growing business services. Women have long been office workers. Even by 1900, they formed more than one-quarter of the clerical workforce in the United States, and by 1970, this had risen to three-quarters, the technological basis for which has been examined by Oppenheimer (1985:111-32). Whereas, in some metropolitan areas, like San Francisco (Nelson, 1986), there has been a considerable separation between 'front office' and 'back office', elsewhere this has not occurred. In Montreal, for example, an important proportion of the unmotorised female clerical force lives within subway reach of the downtown area. This indeed is an important factor underlying the centralisation of female employment.

Thus, one set of 'female jobs' seems to come from a transfer of 'reproductive' tasks from the domestic economy to the commodity circuits: the state and community organisations. Another set originates in commodity production itself, first in the division between the shop and the office and, second, in the bureaucratic hierarchies developing in office work. These two very different sources of women's labour force participation have wide implications for the social structuring of cities and suburbs.

Consider, for instance, position in the labour market. Do women occupying jobs in 'externalised' reproductive tasks have the same opportunities as women working in bureaucratic hierarchies associated more directly with commodity production? In particular, is the occupational segregation of women more pronounced in neighbourhood-orientated sectors compared to downtown sectors? In other words, how do gender and employment relations intersect in each of these two broad categories of activities?

The empirical analyses conducted in Montreal indicate that neighbourhood-orientated sectors, such as education, health and welfare, and recreational and personal services, were likely to show less occupational segregation by gender at the beginning of the 1970s than downtown-orientated ones (Table 5.2). Women in these sectors were, then, less concentrated in the low-paying, less-qualified jobs than they were in downtown sectors such as

Table 5.2: Occupational segregation between sexes in economic sectors, metropolitan Montreal, 1971 and 1981

Economic activity	Segregation index		Change in index
	1971	1981	1971 to 1981
Primary, construction, capital-intensive manufacturing	47	45	–2
Labour-intensive manufacturing	32	31	–1
Transport, utilities, trade	35	33	–2
Finance, insurance, real estate	39	32	–7
Education, health, welfare services	27	27	–
Communications, recreation, personal services	26	24	–2
Business services	46	36	–10
Public administration, defence	25	21	–5
Total	34	31	–3

Note: The segregation index is derived from the occupational structure by gender of each economic sector. The index is one half the sum over $i = 1, \ldots 7$ of the absolute values of the differences between the percentage distributions of male and female employment across the $i = 1, \ldots 7$ occupational groups in each economic sector. The seven economic groups are: managers, professionals, supervisors, upper-level white-collar, skilled blue-collar, lower-level white-collar, semi and unskilled blue-collar. The index indicates the percentage of women or men that would have to be redistributed across the occupations to arrive at no occupational segregation. Since women systematically occupy lower occupational ranks than men, changes in the index are a measure of women's occupational mobility. See Villeneuve and Rose (1988) for more details.

financial and business services. Public administration was the exception. Jobs in this sector tend to be located in the Montreal central business district but, at the beginning of the 1970s, its occupational segregation by gender was lower than in the private tertiary sectors due, probably, to equal access programmes. During the 1970s this situation greatly altered. The occupational mobility of women has been more pronounced in the faster growing downtown sectors. By the end of the decade, occupational segregation by gender was lowest in public administration, and substantially reduced in finance, insurance and real estate, and in business services, although it was still higher in these last two sectors than it was in neighbourhood-orientated sectors.

A relationship between occupational mobility and spatial mobility was also observed. Women working in downtown sectors, where occupational mobility was most pronounced during the 1970s, also saw a larger increase in work-trip length than those working in neighbourhood-orientated sectors. This greater spatial mobility was largely accounted for by access to the subway system, built at the end of the 1960s, and which is limited to the central part of the metropolitan area.

These empirical observations suggest quite different labour market trajectories for women depending on where they live. Women living in inner city neighbourhoods have easier access to jobs in both reproductive activities and downtown activities, while those living in suburban neighbourhoods are more restricted to jobs in reproductive activities. These differences would be the same for men if it were not for their much higher car ownership. More generally, women control more limited private resources then men. Collective actions and collective services may then be important for them.

Households and Urban Centrality

The question arises as to how this access to a wider range of job opportunities for women living in inner city neighbourhoods relates to their position within the household and the domestic economy. Does the transfer of reproductive tasks from the domestic economy to the public sphere take place in the same way throughout metropolitan areas? And how does the relative position of women and men in the occupational structure affect their relative position in the household?

The transfer of tasks from the domestic economy to the public sphere is clearly an externalisation of transactions from households seen as governance structures. Households may, for a number of reasons, 'subcontract' parts of the reproductive tasks to restaurants, cleaners, and other firms and institutions. In principle, it is possible to measure precisely the degree of externalisation in various settings. Although this has not been done empirically, it can be surmised from factorial ecologies and from studies of space-time budgets that home-orientated households should have a lower propensity to externalise reproductive tasks compared to smaller outwardly orientated households. It may be noted in parenthesis that such expressions as 'home-orientation' and 'outward-orientation' are not meant to be precisely defined but merely evoke the constructs of social area analysis, 'familism' and 'urbanism', distinctions that have been analysed by Langlois (1984) in the case of two-earner households. Home-orientated households are, so to speak, more vertically integrated. The degree of externalisation is also influenced by household technology, especially now with the proliferation of domestic 'high-tech' equipment and instruments. Factorial ecologies also indicate that home and family-orientated households are over-represented in suburbs while outwardly and career-orientated households tend to locate nearer to the city centre.

These general tendencies suggest an interpretation of the evolving contrasts between city and suburb in terms of the notions of hierarchies and markets as they are theorised in the analysis of transaction costs. A first step may be to distinguish various ways of organising domestic production. Accumulating evidence shows that suburbs may have comparative advantages for capital-intensive productive activities while inner-city areas would present comparative advantages for labour-intensive production. This possibility was first proposed by Scott (1981) who called it a 'peculiar form of the Heckscher-Ohlin theorem', and tested it successfully in Toronto; Norcliffe (1984) expanded and qualified Scott's proposition, while Blackley and Greytak (1986) and Villeneuve and Rose (1986) have also found some empirical support for it.

If households are considered to be productive organisations and not only consumption units, it is possible to ask whether this proposition also applies to them. Self-contained suburban 'electronic cottages' provide a more capital-intensive base for domestic production than dwellings equipped with less sophisticated appliances. The significant dimension may not, however, be capital intensity. Viewing the household in terms of a production function (instead of a utility function) merely transfers to the domestic sphere an approach criticised above for being narrowly technological. Rather, if the household is seen as a governance structure, the degree of capital intensity of domestic production can be interpreted in a wider context. Gender and employment relations form this wider context which is constituted, first, by the position of household members relative to the wage labour market and, second, by gender relations within the household.

Consider for example the way the position of household members in the labour market influences residential location decisions made by the household. Neo-classical residential location models — like that of Alonso (1964) — postulate that the main breadwinner, usually the husband, takes his job location as fixed and decides on a 'utility maximising' residential location. If his wife is working, these models would also posit that she takes as given the location of the residence as determined by the husband's decision and then decides on a utility maximising job location.

This way of theorising has been strongly criticised. First, several authors have questioned the postulate stating that the job location decision of the husband is anterior in the decision process (Simpson, 1987). Rather, at the intra-metropolitan level, job and residential location decisions may increasingly be viewed as joint decisions, even in the case of single-breadwinner households. Surely, recent increases in home-ownership rates would tend to increase the importance attributed to place of residence in the joint decision-making process. One study in Vancouver has shown how employees working at the head office of a large utility corporation have adapted to the relocation of their employment place by modifying their work-trip length rather than by moving: thus, Ley (1985:37) noted that 'while workers would prefer to live close to their place of work, a majority are prepared to tolerate a long work-trip for the benefits of good housing'. Second, the postulate of utility maximisation with regard only to distance travelled to work and to housing space consumed does not take into account either (a) other 'production factors' essential to labour power reproduction such as trips to schools and health care centres, or (b) the possible conflicts between household members, particularly if both spouses are employed (Markusen, 1981:23).

Conflict may arise over the desirability of certain neighbourhoods. Residential preferences of men and housewives tend to correlate much more strongly than those of men and employed married women. Men and housewives tend to prefer suburbs while employed women tend to prefer well-equipped urban neighbourhoods (Shlay and DiGregorio, 1985). Other studies document the gender difference in work-trip length (Madden, 1981; Howe and O'Connor, 1982; Hanson and Johnston, 1985; London et al., 1986; Singell and Lillydahl, 1986; Villeneuve and Rose, 1988). The differential tends to be larger for dual-earner families with children than for those without. The latter tend to live nearer to the city centre, a finding consistent with the high proportion of dual-earner couples observed among gentrifiers. Moreover, the contribution of each spouse in dual-earner families to the residential and job location decision has been shown to be a function of the difference in occupational rank between spouses. Thus, the weight of each spouse in the decision-making process appears to depend very much on the relative position of each in the metropolitan occupational structure.

This raises the issue of gender relations within the household. It has been suggested that the generalisation of the dual-earner family may contribute to the erosion of patriarchy as a system of gender relations (Markusen, 1981). Analyses in Montreal lend only partial support to this statement. Women's participation in wage labour may be a necessary condition for the erosion of patriarchy but it is not a sufficient one. For spouses to come to deal with each other as equal, not only do they have to be both doing paid work, but similarity of occupational rank is also an influential condition. This is not to suggest, however, that equality in couples entirely depends on the position of the spouses on the labour market; equality, as suggested earlier, has many facets.

In the Montreal metropolitan area the proportion of dual-earner families was slightly higher in inner city as against suburban neighbourhoods at the beginning of the 1970s (Table 5.3). A decade later the proportion in the suburbs was significantly higher than that in the city. Although this appears to contradict the images of cities and suburbs painted earlier, this is not so when occupational asymmetry within couples is taken into account. The notion of occupational asymmetry is simply defined as the difference in the occupational ranks of the spouses within a couple (Villeneuve and Viaud, 1987). An index of average occupational asymmetry was obtained for city and suburb. At the beginning of the 1970s, asymmetry was more pronounced in central neighbourhoods, compared to suburbs, although variations among

Table 5.3: Double-earner families in metropolitan Montreal, 1971 and 1981

	City		Suburbs	
	1971	1981	1971	1981
Percentage of double-earner families	25.6	38.3	25.2	43.5
Index of occupational asymmetry between spouses	0.44	0.41	0.39	0.48

Note: a double-earner family is one where both spouses work outside the home. The percentage of double-earner families is taken on the total number of census families. The index of occupational asymmetry is obtained by: (a) arraying husbands' occupational rank by wives' occupational rank; (b) computing the average occupational rank of husbands and that of wives; and (c) taking the difference between husbands' average rank and wives' average rank. To compute average ranks, managers were given a score of 7, professionals a score of 6 and so on (see the note to Table 5.2 for a list of the groups used). The square matrices ranking husbands' occupations by wives' occupations were special tabulations provided by Statistics Canada. See Villeneuve and Viaud (1987) for a detailed analysis.

neighbourhoods were strong. A decade later, asymmetry had markedly increased in suburban neighbourhoods while it had decreased in the city. The suburbs now had an increasing proportion of dual-earner families where the husband was either a manager, a professional or a supervisor, and his spouse had a much lower-level job status and, not infrequently, was a part-time employee.

These results seem to indicate that gender relations evolve differently in home-orientated households, often living in suburban environments, as against outwardly orientated households showing a propensity to live nearer to the city centre. In home-orientated households, two situations are the most prominent.

First, the spouses can specialise, almost totally, with one being concerned with domestic production and the other (usually the male) the paid work. This form of specialisation is, of course, anchored in traditional views of gender relations where 'the husband' is expected to bring home a 'family wage', a concept which has been discussed by Morris (1987). However, it is no longer tenable for a growing proportion of households. The spouse doing paid work may not earn enough to support the standard of living of the household, or the spouse undertaking domestic production may no longer accept this form of specialisation. A debate surrounds this question of specialisation from the point of view of economic efficiency. Some maintain that the division of labour among spouses between household and market is most efficient but that it does not have to be gender based; others argue that specialising solely in domestic tasks generates no increasing returns to time spent doing them because of the routine nature of most of these tasks. These issues have been canvassed by Owen (1987). In any case, the proportion of two-earner households is increasing even among home-orientated families.

This produces the second situation most common among these families: the husband remains the main breadwinner and his wife does some paid work and continues to perform most domestic tasks. Thus, Ross (1987) found in a large nationwide US sample that 76 per cent of wives in fulltime employment still undertake most of the housework. It is in this type of household that occupational asymmetry is likely to be high. These households are also likely to show a suburban orientation which limits women's access to as wide a variety of jobs.

Somewhat different tendencies are occurring in inner city neighbourhoods. In many of these, particularly the ones undergoing rapid overall social change, occupational asymmetry within two-earner couples is decreasing. This finding can be related to studies showing that well-educated husbands and those with more modern sex-role beliefs are more likely to participate in household tasks, and that the smaller the difference between the husband's earnings and his wife's, the greater his relative contribution (Ross, 1987:816). It can also be related to studies of gentrification. Rose (1984), for example, showed the crucial links between gentrification and gender relations, while Ley (1986) and Filion (1987) document the extent of the process in Canadian cities.

Gentrifiers are often double-earner couples. Pooling two incomes may be a necessary prerequisite to have access to certain inner city neighbourhoods undergoing gentrification, just as it is necessary also to have access to home ownership in certain suburbs as has been suggested already. The difference between two-earner households in suburbs and those in inner cities is that the latter are more and more likely to show weaker occupational asymmetry: that is, greater equality of occupational rank between husband and wife. As a corollary, two-earner households may contribute more to increased neighbourhood social class diversity in inner cities than in suburbs. This would be the case, for instance, if dual-earner households, in which each worker's occupation is middle-level, were locating in neighbourhoods where workers in single-earner households have high-level occupations, although this hypothesis — similar to the one proposed by Pratt and Hanson (1988) — has yet to be fully tested. In other words, some 'marginal gentrifiers', an expression proposed by Rose (1984), are couples without much job security, for which inner-city living means better access to a volatile labour market. Living in well-equipped inner city neighbourhoods also presents important advantages for single-parent families and other small, less mobile, households who transact heavily with their immediate environment.

Conclusion

From a transaction cost point of view, centrality and accessibility are synonyms for a large proportion of households and firms, while for others, maintaining a sufficient level of accessibility can be compatible with peripherality. This is a well-known principle in economic geography. Less well-known, however, are the ways by which external transactions of firms and households interact with their internal transactions. It has been argued here that if firms and households are considered as governance structures, encompassing their narrower representations as production and utility functions, important sociological constructs such as gender relations and employment relations can be shown to act as contexts for the transactions conducted within and among firms and households.

One important category of transactions, property relations, has not been considered here although it has been the subject of an important statement by Macpherson (1978). Various forms of property rights are crucial in the spatial organisation of urban environments. For instance, Clark (1982) has discussed these in terms of social obligations between individuals whose very individuality is constituted through social relations. Property relations interact in many ways with gender and employment relations. Explicit contractual arrangements are perhaps more current in matters of property than they are in matters of gender and employment. Private property is only one form: it is the right to exclude. Common property, the right not to be excluded, is another basic form. State property in these terms is more akin to private property than to common property. The market is usually thought to require private property as a necessary condition for its functioning. Non-market governance structures may rely more on various degrees of common property. Thus, rights to exclude or not be excluded intermingle in complex ways.

In any particular circumstance, decisions have to be made as to which transactions can be left to conveniently 'blind' and self-regulating governance structures such as various markets, and which ones have to be dealt with through other contractual arrangements. The main contention of this chapter has been that an analysis of transaction costs, as outlined here, can usefully extend the spatial interaction paradigm and deepen our understanding of the human geographies around us.

6

New Production Technologies, Labour and the North American Auto Industry

John Holmes

New technological developments embodied into new methods of manufacturing are resulting in some important and fundamental changes in the organisation and geography of production systems and labour markets. These changes in technology are themselves a response by firms attempting to adjust to new competitive conditions brought about by major structural changes in the world economy, and a recurring theme in discussions of these changes is the need for increased 'flexibility' with respect to both machinery and workers.

The adoption of these new production technologies will have far-reaching consequences for workers, in terms of the redesign of jobs, changing skill requirements, changing methods of workplace management, and changes in the form and content of collective agreements. Furthermore, the interaction between these changes and the spatially discontinuous nature of labour markets will likely lead to changes in the geography of manufacturing in particular industries.

Foremost among firms developing and adopting these new manufacturing processes have been those in the auto industry. In fact, recent changes in production technology in the North American auto industry have been of such wide scope and significance that it is possible to speak of the emergence of a new model of production in the industry (Altshuler et al., 1984; Canada, Employment and Immigration, 1986; Holmes, 1987b), a model which represents a sharp and distinct break from the Fordist model which characterised automobile production in North America from the late 1930s through to the late 1970s.

This chapter focuses explicitly on the implications of technological change in the North American auto industry for the organisation of work and workers. The first section provides a brief synopsis of the arguments presented in earlier papers (Holmes, 1987a, b; Holmes and Leys, 1987) regarding the broader context of economic change and social transformation within which contemporary technological change in North American industry is occurring, and discusses the broad implications of flexible production for labour. After briefly describing the salient features of the new developments in manufacturing technology, the second section examines the implications of the new technologies for the displacement of jobs and the design of the remaining jobs. The third section examines broader and more general shifts in patterns of labour/management relations and collective bargaining in the North American auto industry which encompass and yet go beyond the changes addressed in the previous section.

The Context of Contemporary Technological Change

Transition from Fordism to Post-Fordism

A central question when trying to analyse contemporary developments is the extent to which they are merely cyclical responses to changing economic conditions which are readily reversible, or evidence of more permanent and fundamental change. The available evidence increasingly supports the contention that these technological changes in the manufacturing and service sectors are of fundamental importance and that this period does indeed represent a *transitional* period between two separate and distinct phases of capitalist development in North America. In fact, the entire social, economic and political fabric of North America is undergoing a transformation on a scale that is probably unprecedented since the 1930s (Davis, 1986; Holmes and Leys, 1987).

This author agrees with those who see the prolonged economic downturn of the 1970s and 1980s in North America as the crisis of a specific form of capital accumulation — a model commonly referred to as Fordism — which had underlain and sustained the long postwar economic boom, and in which production was organised around a unique combination of Fordist production techniques, standardised products and mass consumption. In the early 1970s Fordism began to fall apart as a result of the breakdown in a number of key regulatory mechanisms which had underpinned it. One of the principal restructuring strategies adopted by North American manufacturers in response to the crisis of Fordism has been the development during the late 1970s and early 1980s of new manufacturing techniques which encompass changes in both 'hard' and 'soft' production technologies. Hard technology refers to the kinds of physical plant, machinery and equipment used in the production process, while soft technology refers to the way in which people and equipment are organised in relation to each other and the task at hand. These changes in production technology and organisation are designed to increase productivity; lower the costs of labour, inventory and capital goods; and enable firms to respond rapidly to changing market and competitive conditions.

Many writers refer to these new production methods as *neo-Fordist* although it seems more appropriate to call them *post-Fordist*, a point elaborated in Holmes (1987b). Whereas Fordism was characterised by homogenised consumption norms, standardised products, mass markets, dedicated specialised production equipment, an inflexible and hierarchical division of labour within the plant and highly particularised labour processes, post-Fordism *appears* to be characterised by a more differentiated range of products corresponding to increased heterogeneity in consumption and a more complex, differentiated market, flexible (reprogrammable) machines, a reconstruction of skill, and a 'flexible' workforce with reduced levels of direct supervision. No matter what precise form this post-Fordist model eventually takes it appears likely that we can expect to see continuing efforts to make production systems more flexible as well as more productive (Piore and Sabel, 1984; Cohen and Zysman, 1987).

Flexible Production and Labour

A central element of this drive to make production more productive and flexible is attempts to increase labour flexibility. The latter has been a central theme in recent business and government approaches to employment policy in Western Europe and North America, so much so that the phrase 'flexible labour market' has come to conjure up almost everything that conservative forces regard as necessary for economic and social regeneration (Atkinson and Gregory, 1986).

These authors (1986:13) identify three interwoven objectives in this push for increased labour flexibility:

(a) to improve the employer's ability to adjust quickly and cheaply to a more uncertain, volatile and competitive market and to the increased pace of technological change;

(b) to stimulate growth of productivity through the introduction of new automated equipment and the concomitant revision of work practices and organisational changes which affect both the tasks performed by the individual worker and the broader organisation of work within and between plants;

(c) to reduce labour costs either through using cheaper sources of labour or by using forms of what Christopherson (1987) refers to as 'contingent' labour (for example, temporary and contract labour) which allow rapid and inexpensive changes in the level of employment in the firm.

These objectives have been reflected in two different types of management strategy. First, and particularly during the initial phases of the crisis while firms were still struggling to maintain the Fordist mass production model, they were less concerned with increasing flexibility than with cost-cutting through decentralisation of work to low-wage areas, wage reductions and speed-ups. However, more recently as they have realised that the competitive cost differential with low-cost offshore producers was simply too enormous to be closed by straight wage-cutting and concessions alone, an increasing number of firms has moved towards a more cooperative and flexible 'high wage-high productivity' strategy in which efficiency and productivity gains have been sought through automation, increased cooperation between labour and management, and the development of a more flexible workforce.

One of the most striking and important changes in the structure of labour markets which has resulted from these developments has been the division by many firms of their internal labour market into separate components: core and peripheral workers. Employers hope to persuade the former to accept more flexible work practices by stressing a mutual long-term commitment between employer and employee, and to get flexibility from the peripheral workers 'by exposing them more and more to raw market forces' (Atkinson and Gregory, 1986:13). Thus a firm divides its workers in this way because it seeks different kinds of flexibility. Peripheral groups are mainly used to 'achieve greater flexibility in the number of workers employed (*numerical* flexibility) and their contractual status and working time patterns are drawn up to reflect these fluctuations [in level of output]' (Atkinson and Gregory, 1986:13). Numerical flexibility can be achieved either by employing workers directly on a part-time, casual or temporary contract basis, or through contracting work out or having tasks done by people brought in through agencies supplying temporary help or by specialist self-employed workers (Christopherson, 1987).

With respect to the core groups, management does not want numerical flexibility, but rather *functional* flexibility, that is, 'versatility and adaptability in what such workers do and how they do it' (Atkinson and Gregory, 1986:13). The need for this has come in response to the changing nature of production technology, competitive strategies and markets rather than fluctuation in output levels.

These two forms of labour flexibility can well become interdependent parts of a firm's overall labour strategy. For example, in the US auto industry recent collective agreements allow companies to have a permanent part-time workforce (i.e. more numerical flexibility) in return for 'life-time' guarantees of employment for the existing core group of workers from whom greater functional flexibility is being demanded in terms of revised work practices.

Transformation of Work in the Automobile Industry

This section examines some of the implications for jobs and workers in the automobile industry of new production technologies which have been introduced very recently and rapidly (Table 6.1). The focus is on their implications for job displacement and employment loss, for skill levels, and for the content of work.

The New Technologies

Any manufacturing labour process consists of three distinct functions; the transformation (conversion) of the material being worked upon, the transfer of the material/product between the stages of the manufacturing process, and the control and

Table 6.1: Adoption of new technologies in the Canadian automobile industry

Technology	Per cent of firms using the technology			
	1981*a*	1985*a*	1986*b*	Est. 1990*a*
Hard technology				
Industrial robots	4	18	40	67
Programmable controllers	18	49	55	78
Computer numerically controlled machine tools	23	36	27	68
Soft technology				
Statistical process control techniques	9	81	80	92
Just-in-time		37	50	86
Quick tool and die change			20	
Linked/integrated systems			20	

a Task Force Survey of Canadian Independent Automotive Parts Industry, reported in Canada, Employment and Immigration, 1986.

b CAW Technology Survey 1986 of unionised auto assembly and parts plants in Canada, reported in Robertson and Wareham, 1987.

integration of the first two functions. Historically, mechanisation has proceeded very unevenly along these three dimensions (Blackburn et al., 1985). While some of the present developments involve the further refinement of the mechanisation of the transformation function (e.g. transforming robots) or transfer function (e.g. automated guided vehicles: AGVs), the major development in the last decade has been *the mechanisation of control and integration* (Kaplinsky, 1984; Blackburn et al., 1985;

Forester, 1985; Robertson and Wareham, 1987). It is this that has made possible the potential tremendous increase in the flexibility and productivity of manufacturing.

Within the North American auto industry the introduction of new 'hard' process technology has seen a progressive shift towards 'programmable systemic automation' in which a series of programmable devices, such as computer numerically controlled (CNC) machine tools, robots and programmable controllers (PCs), are linked together (Aggarwal, 1985). The goal is to form 'flexible manufacturing systems' (FMS) and 'computer integrated manufacturing' (CIM) systems which will integrate and automatically monitor and control production across the entire manufacturing system. At the present time while CNC and FMS cells are growing in importance in the plants of auto component manufacturers, in the auto assembly plants the use of PCs and more general automated process control for the scheduling and coordination of production are more numerous and important (Robertson and Wareham, 1987:16).

The most important 'soft' technology developments in the North American auto industry have been the new types of work organisation and management — many pioneered in Japan — such as operating team systems for managing shop-floor labour relations, quick tool and die change (QTD), just-in-time (JIT), and total quality control (TQC) methods which include the use of statistical process control techniques (SPC) and quality circles (QCs). These involve new types of relationships among workers, between workers and management, and between firms and their buyers and suppliers.

The degree to which the potential flexibility afforded by new hard production technologies is being attained has recently been questioned (Jaikumar, 1986; Wood, 1986; Williams et al., 1987). While acknowledging that 'it is impossible to say how malleable the production set-up as a whole will eventually become', Katz and Sabel (1985:300) argue that 'there is substantial agreement that flexible deployment of labour will be a crucial element in any successful model of adjustment in the auto industry'.

It must be emphasised that these developments in both hard and soft production technology are not discrete but interlock and reinforce one another so that overall changes are of a systemic character. For example, JIT refers narrowly to a way of organising the immediate manufacturing process and buyer-supplier relationships between firms, but to operate efficiently and successfully it must be supported by, and integrated with, a wider set of practices involving a reduction of skill and task demarcations between workers, the institution of strict quality control procedures at all stages of the manufacturing process, and flexible hard technology such that the volumes and mix of products can be adjusted rapidly to changes in demand.

Job Displacement and Employment Loss Impacts of New Technology

As Robertson and Wareham (1987:17) have observed,

> Automation eliminates jobs. As a general trend, the introduction of new technology — be it computer-based machinery or new management systems — reduces the number of jobs. That is not surprising. The design of new technology and the way it is implemented are motivated by the desire to raise productivity while lowering the costs of production. In this sense technological change implies a widening gap between production and employment.

While the general trend is clear, forecasting the precise impact of the introduction of a particular piece of technology on the number of workers employed in a particular plant is very difficult because the labour displacing potential of new technologies is subject to so many offsetting conditions (Hunt and Hunt, 1985; Allen, 1987; Robertson and Wareham, 1987).

A useful distinction can be drawn between job displacement and employment loss (lay-off) caused by technological change. For individual workers this distinction is crucial since it represents the difference between job security and employment security. Recent studies reveal that workers in the Canadian auto industry see the particular jobs which they currently occupy as being vulnerable to technological change but do not necessarily view their employment in the same way (Canada, Employment and Immigration, 1986; Robertson and Wareham, 1987). With respect to much of the technological change in Canadian auto plants during the 1980-86 period, it seems that jobs but not people have been lost.

Whether or not job displacement translates into employment loss depends on various factors such as whether production volumes increase, thereby providing workers with alternative jobs, and/or whether new products are added in a way that re-absorbs displaced workers (Robertson and Wareham, 1987:18). The impact on workers currently employed also depends on whether the timing of the introduction of new technology can either be linked to the normal rate of attrition or accommodated through voluntary early retirement, which in turn depends on the age-profile of the workforce. However, in either case there is still a loss of potential employment for future generations of workers. So far the impact of technological change in many Canadian auto plants has been cushioned by some or all of these factors. Thus Robertson and Wareham note that over half the firms they surveyed reported job losses associated with technological change but relatively few reported actual lay-offs. This is in sharp contrast to the US auto industry which has experienced a significant reduction in both jobs and workers (Holmes, 1987b).

Certain types of jobs, and in particular, production jobs, have been most susceptible to displacement by technological change. In general, it is expected that the number of direct production jobs will increase (Robertson and Wareham, 1987:24). Notwithstanding the widespread concern over the potential loss of employment caused by new technology, as Sam Gindin (Special Assistant to the President of the CAW) emphasises in his preface to the recent CAW Technology Study (Robertson and Wareham, 1987:6),

> The issue of new technology goes beyond the issue of the number of jobs. . . Included in this upheaval is a dramatic reorganization of the workplace, and technology has been both a catalyst and a central part of such change. The issues involved touch every facet of workplace life: job classifications and demarcation lines; seniority rules and transfer rights; teamwork and production standards; health and safety and the work environment; new skills and the content of retraining; the erosion of bargaining units and the degree of supervision; relations amongst workers and relations between workers, their unions and management.

These aspects of technological change are now examined.

The Effects of New Technologies on Skill Levels and Job Content

Changes in the design and content of jobs, and the patterns and relations of work between employees result either directly from changes in soft technology such as the introduction of quality circles and work team concepts, or indirectly through the new skills needed to operate new types of automated hard technology or implement new soft technologies such as SPC. The present changes in skill level and job content within the auto industry are somewhat contradictory. In some instances, technological change is being accompanied by a continuation of the trend associated with Fordist technology towards increased job fragmentation, de-skilling, machine pacing and a rigid and hierarchical division of labour, whereas, in other instances — and in keeping with the push to develop more flexibility within internal labour markets — there is an increasingly strong tendency towards more broadly defined jobs, the introduction of team working concepts, and a general upward shift in the skills demanded of individual workers.

The contradictory nature of these tendencies stems in large part from the fact that working conditions and skill levels do not depend on the hard technology being used but on the social organisation of the work process for, as Streeck (1985a:18) notes, 'depending on whether new technology is used for further automation of mass production or for flexible manufacturing, it tends to be associated with highly different forms of work organisation'. Furthermore, while auto manufacturers in virtually all industrialised countries have been confronted with strikingly similar pressures for increased flexibility, the actual outcomes have varied because, despite the international spread of the mass production of consumer goods in the 1950s and 1960s, factory organisation remained substantially different from country to country (Streeck, 1985b; Tolliday and Zeitlin, 1986; Mahon, 1987). These points serve to underscore the unevenness with which technological change and the changes in work organisation associated with it are occurring. At any particular time, within one sector, sub-sector, or even firm, there is not one labour process but many, so that it is extremely difficult, particularly during periods of rapid technological change, to draw unambiguous conclusions regarding the nature of the changes underway.

Thus, while it does appear at the moment to be the dominant tendency in the North American auto industry, there is no necessary relationship between new hard process technologies, such as robots and CNC machine tools, and flexible work organisation. Such new hard technologies may be implemented within the traditional Fordist type division of labour as well as within relatively autonomous working teams (Dohse et al., 1985; Windolf, 1985). However, the concern here is with the new forms of work organisation associated with flexible manufacturing.

The exploitation of the potential flexibility of new hard process technology is enhanced by new forms of work organisation in which tool changes and equipment maintenance are to a significant extent delegated to machine operators. Lines of demarcation are being weakened and job descriptions broadened to enable production workers to set up and monitor their own machines and to perform multiple tasks within work groups/teams. Increasingly, payment systems are based on the skills and tasks commanded by the worker (so-called 'payment for knowledge') rather than on the actual tasks performed. Consequently, the traditional differentiation between production and maintenance functions and between direct and indirect work is being eroded.

Although some writers argue that these developments are leading to a 're-skilling' of the workforce, there is a danger in simply equating flexibility (the ability to change tasks frequently) with skill. Being transferred from performing one repetitive unskilled task to doing a dozen unskilled tasks does not make a skilled worker (Windolf, 1985). Robertson and Wareham (1987:30) also emphasise this point:

> Lengthening a job cycle from 16 seconds to two minutes may seem an improvement, but when it is realized that the two minute job is a package of twenty, nine-second tasks that should really take 2.5 minutes, that assessment changes. The line between broadened jobs and more work is a critical one.

Stress levels are also rising as a result of the introduction of the tighter control and pacing of work by automated control systems which reduce the ability of line workers to engage in 'banking' or 'soldiering' as ways of creating breathing space for themselves. The move towards JIT and QTD has also increased stress levels for workers who find themselves under enormous pressure to keep the production system functioning smoothly. The capital intensity of the new technology has led to the introduction or the extension of more 'intensive' forms of production, such as shift work and multi-shift operations.

With the introduction of more and more automated process control equipment, line production workers are becoming increasingly involved with the manipulation and interpretation of symbols and numerical data rather than the manipulation of things. In that sense the task content of work is becoming more abstract and conceptual skills are becoming more important than motor skills as workers are involved in monitoring and maintaining systems rather than actually operating them. For example, to be fully implemented and effective SPC requires workers to be familiar with statistical concepts, to have the ability to interpret data and graphs and to participate in group problem solving.

This shift in required skills has been reflected in recruitment and retraining programmes. Employers are demanding higher educational qualifications since the 'basic functional skills associated with academic qualifications, such as reading, mathematics and verbal ability, are to the computer-based workplace what basic motor skills and manual dexterity were to the mechanically-based workplace' (Robertson and Wareham, 1987:27). The minimum educational qualification for new production workers hired for the new Chrysler assembly facility at Brampton, Ontario, is a Grade 12 Diploma (i.e. the completion of twelve years of formal schooling). This tendency towards 'credentialism' is likely to produce a further polarisation between the internal and external labour markets.

New workers are also subjected to extensive screening and testing procedures prior to hiring. For example, at GM's newly established Job Evaluation Centre at Oshawa, job applicants are required to attend an intensive three-day assessment programme which includes aptitude tests designed not only to assess their manual skills and aptitudes but also psychological testing to measure their interpersonal communication skills and general attitudes. In fact, 'cultural training' is becoming an important aspect of training and retraining programmes and is designed to strengthen the worker's commitment to production and to the company by developing a commonality of interest between management and workers and by increasing the adaptability and flexibility of both individual workers and the labour force in general. This is important since more tightly integrated production systems such as JIT increase management's dependence on worker commitment and reliability. The importance attached to this element of training is reflected by the fact that in the six-day retraining programme for hourly employees at the newly revamped GM Truck Plant at Oshawa, Ontario, the percentage weightings were: cultural change training 70; product training 11; process training 8; specific skills training 8; specific management skills 3 (Robertson and Wareham, 1987:47).

Through such programmes a pool of generically skilled workers is being 'created' to operate as a flexible buffer for the smooth functioning of internal labour markets. A more highly qualified labour force does not necessarily indicate an increasing skill requirement within the work process; what is being sought is the ability to adapt quickly and flexibly to changing product and process conditions.

Technological Change and the Industrial Relations System

Windolf (1985:460) notes that, 'new technology is implemented within a given legal and institutional framework of industrial relations . . . as systems of industrial relations vary from country to country, so do the effects of new technology'. At the same time, large-scale technological change is likely to create considerable tension with, and pressure to transform, the existing labour relations framework. The Fordist labour relations system which characterised the North American auto industry (and other industries) throughout virtually the entire postwar period (and which was particular to North America) is currently undergoing such a transformation. While some writers have used other descriptive labels (Kochan et al., 1986, for example, refer to 'the New Deal labour relations system'), there is agreement that this distinctive and stable system of North American labour relations appeared first in the auto industry and then spread to other industries. Some contemporary observers suggest that similarly the changes that are currently taking root in the auto industry will likely spread to other industries, thus creating a new post-Fordist paradigm for North American labour relations (Davis, 1986; Kochan et al., 1986; Luria, 1986).

Perhaps the most important outcome of these modifications from a geographical point of view has been the introduction for the first time since the late 1940s of considerable variations in wage rates and working practices between companies and plants. These are particularly significant, since one of the hallmarks of the Fordist system of labour relations was precisely the uniformity that it produced with respect to both wage rates and general working arrangements.

This final section first describes the three principal elements of the Fordist labour relations system as it operated within the auto industry, and then discusses how recent changes in competitive and market conditions, and the industrial and technological changes that accompanied them, have begun to transform this traditional labour relations system.

The Fordist Labour Relations System

The pattern for the Fordist labour relations system was set by the 1948 collective agreement between General Motors and the United Automobile Workers Union (UAW) and was structured around three key issues: the determination of wages through formula-like *wage rules* in multi-year national contracts; a *connective bargaining* (not to be confused with the more general term, collective bargaining) structure defining the relationship, or connection, between national and plant level bargaining which led to a centrally imposed uniformity in wages and general contract provisions; and a so-called *job-control focus* to the contracts which linked worker rights to narrowly and strictly defined job classifications and provided for the contractual resolution of disagreements arising over matters covered by the contract. The following brief summary draws heavily on the comprehensive descriptions by Katz (1984, 1985, 1986) and King (1986).

Wage rules

Annual wage increases, which were negotiated in three-year national collective agreements with each company, consisted of two components; a cost of living escalator (COLA) designed to protect real wages against price inflation and an annual improvement factor (AIF) (which during the late 1960s and the 1970s was set at 3 per cent) linked explicitly to expected increases in productivity. With only very minor exceptions the formula was used to set wage rates among the major car makers and parts producers from 1948 to 1979 and, once set, the national contract wage could not be modified in local bargaining. This method of wage determination effectively eliminated variations in wage rates between companies and between plants within the same company — *de facto*, firms were confronted with a geographically uniform wage rate. Luria (1986) notes that between 1948 and 1979 assemblers in all GM, Ford, Chrysler and AMC plants earned within three cents an hour of each other.

Connective bargaining

Connective bargaining defined the relationship between national and local bargaining in the industry. The national union organisation outside the plant set, through collective bargaining, the general wage level and formulated the general principles and rules governing seniority, job classifications, production conditions, and the mechanisms for resolving grievances. Each local branch of the union negotiated the detailed job classifications for the plants it represented and administered the collective agreement, but even then the national office of the union played an active role by monitoring plant-level bargaining and agreements and requiring that many features of local agreements received its approval. This connected system of national and local bargaining between companies and the union effectively separated work-rule bargaining from wage determination and meant — particularly in a period of general growth and expanding markets such as existed in the 1950s and 1960s — that there was little pressure on unions at the local level to relax work-rules in order to save jobs.

Job-control focus

The term 'job-control focus' refers to the very formalised and detailed nature of the collective agreements which linked workers rights and obligations to a set of highly articulated and sharply delineated jobs and tasks. Central to this system was an elaborate job classification scheme that formed the core of each collective agreement and was built around narrowly defined jobs which, in turn, were grouped into career ladders such that the mastery of one task ideally prepared the worker for a slightly more demanding one. Workers moved up the job ladder according to seniority and, similarly, during downturns lay-offs were in reverse order of seniority. Pay was determined by attaching a wage rate to the specific job being performed rather than to the characteristics of the workers undertaking it. Thus, current and lifetime earnings, as well as employment security, depended upon the duration of a worker's employment in a contractually defined 'seniority district' of a particular firm. While the system made it easy to lay off workers, it made it extremely difficult for management to redeploy workers within a plant: in other words, it resulted in a flexible external labour market but a very rigid internal one.

Thus from the late 1940s through until the late 1970s there was a well-functioning labour relations system which was consistent with the general Fordist model of production within which it was embedded. As Katz (1986:287) aptly comments,

> given the limited import penetration of domestic sales, the national coverage of the company agreements matched the geographic extent of the relevant product and labour market throughout the 1950s and 1960s.

Towards a New Flexible Industrial Relations System

Clearly the rigid Fordist industrial relations system just outlined has presented a major barrier to management's recent efforts at production reorganisation and, particularly, to their efforts to create more fluid job roles and a more flexible deployment of labour within plants. In the last three rounds of auto industry collective bargaining (and in the 1987 round) considerable modifications have been made to all three elements of this labour relations system.

Although the full development of a coherent alternative (post-Fordist?) paradigm for labour relations is still far from assured, the basic elements of what are being perceived to be the prototype collective agreements (akin to the 1948 GM-UAW agreement) for such a 'new' system are summarised in Table 6.2. It must also be stressed that within the North American auto industry there are considerable differences between the situations in the US and Canada where the Fordist system has remained much more intact, especially in relation to the continued use of Fordist wage rules (White, 1986). In fact, this divergence between the two countries created such tension within the UAW during the 1984 contract negotiations that the Canadians split away from the international union to form the autonomous CAW (Holmes, 1987b). The following discussion focuses primarily on developments in the US.

Wage Rules

By 1985 the collective agreements for GM, Ford and Chrysler had all replaced the AIF with so-called 'contingent' profit-sharing plans in which future wage increases are tied to the economic performance of each company and are paid as lump sums rather

Table 6.2: The general features of new style collective agreements
in the US auto industry

BASIC ELEMENTS OF
NUMMI-TYPE AGREEMENTS

- **The team concept.**
  The organization of the hourly workforce into
  small teams led by an hourly team leader.
  Team members are cross-trained and multi-
  skilled in terms of the different tasks of the
  team, with some of their pay rate related to
  'pay for knowledge'. The teams are involved in
  'problem-solving' and housekeeping and the
  leaders perform some functions normally
  associated with non-hourly staff.

- **Broad operator responsibilities.**
  Few non-skilled hourly classifications. No 'job
  ownership'. Workers perform a wide range of
  functions, including housekeeping, minor
  maintenance, minor repair, inspection and
  record keeping.

- **Consolidated trade classifications.**
  Very limited number of trade classifications.
  Consolidation 'within' and 'across' basic trade
  categories. At times trade classifications
  unique to the facility, and at times new
  specialized trades.

- **Range of wages and benefits.**
  Wages that are locally set, differentials
  between existing and new-hire rates, stretched
  progression schedules and part of the wage
  package tied to performance, productivity or
  profitability.

- **Wide range of other changes.**
  Outsourcing of many activities, from
  landscaping to payroll. Varied length of
  agreements. Changed rules governing
  transfers, absenteeism, union representation,
  etc.

Note: NUMMI is the name of the GM-Toyota joint venture which
since 1984 has operated a major assembly/manufacturing facility
at Fremont, California. *Source:* Robertson and Wareham, 1987:40.

than being built automatically into base wage rates. This has led to significant variations in wages between companies and has begun to destroy the spatial uniformity in wages which had characterised the Fordist period. In the 1987 round of contract negotiations GM attempted to push this one step further by demanding that wage increases be tied to the productivity of individual plants (*Globe and Mail*, 13 August 1987). If eventually achieved this will produce significant inter-plant as well as inter-company variations in wages. Such inter-plant variations are already beginning to appear in the contracts being negotiated for new plants which lie outside the company's Master Collective Agreements with the UAW and CAW, e.g. the GM Saturn project in Tennessee and the GM-Suzuki plant in Ontario.

Two more features of the emerging new patterns of wage setting are worth noting. First, there is a tendency towards 'wage tiering' within the large automakers such that lower rates of pay exist in the captive parts plants making components for which there is intense price competition from offshore producers. Second, some recent contracts contain provisions for different rates of pay for the same job within the same plant. Formerly, new workers began at 85 per cent of the maximum pay scale for the job and moved to the maximum rate within eighteen months but now some companies are pushing for starting pay rates of 50 per cent of maximum with a ten-year progression to the highest rate (Luria, 1986:26).

Connective bargaining

There is increasing variability in work-rules between plants. The threat of further job loss, due either to the outsourcing of parts production or simply reductions in volume, unless changes in work-rules are agreed to, has led union locals to agree to the modification of local work practices to lower costs. This kind of trade-off, where in return for increased employment security and the maintenance of relatively high wages, workers are prepared to agree to concessions on work practices, is becoming increasingly prevalent. Thus, the internal labour market is becoming more flexible at the expense of a more rigid relationship between this and the external labour market. For example, at the Packard Division of GM an earlier management strategy to lower labour costs through forcing workers to accept cuts in wage-rates has been replaced by guarantees to remaining workers of employment and wage protection in return for the ability to deploy employees more flexibly and to hire new employees on a part-time basis (Kochan et al., 1986:169-71).

'Whipsawing' (the practice of making plants within a company compete with each other for work) has been a principal tactic used by management to get such concessions and has contributed significantly to the growing divergence in work-rules between plants (*Labor Notes*, 99, May 1987).

Job-control focus

The pressure to develop greater flexibility within internal labour markets has led to a revival and expansion of Quality of Work Life (QWL) programmes (see Katz, 1986; Parker, 1986; and Wells, 1986, for detailed analyses of QWL programmes), to worker involvement in shop-floor quality circles and, perhaps most significantly, to the introduction of team forms of work organisation in some plants. Each of these developments, but particularly the last, represents a significant movement away from the traditional job-control orientation of Fordist shop-floor labour relations (Thomas, 1985).

The working (or operating) team system summarised in Table 6.2 'entails a fundamental reorganization of shop-floor labour relations because it integrates changes in work organization with increases in worker decision making. . .[It] provides both a reduction in job classifications and a broadening of jobs' (Kochan et al., 1986:160). Since 1980 GM has introduced the operating team concept into all its new plants and into some older ones that have been refurbished with large investments in new technology to create new product lines. The recent renewed push to introduce team working by GM is driven much more by the need to achieve the labour flexibility which will enable the potential flexibility and advantages of new production technology to be realised than as a simple anti-union labour relations strategy.

Conclusion

This chapter has tried to identify some of the principal impacts of new production technology on labour within the North American auto industry. The following points need to be stressed.

(a) New technology is not coincident with only one form of the social organisation of production. However, to develop a fully flexible model of production there need to be both flexible forms of work organisation and flexible hard technology.

(b) The development of so-called flexible production systems in response to changed competitive conditions in the auto industry is entailing significant changes in the nature of jobs and the organisation of labour in the industry. Firms are attempting to develop a workforce that is more functionally flexible.

(c) It is important to recognise the highly specific nature of the Fordist system of labour relations that developed in postwar North America, since it is within the context of this existing system that present technological change is taking place. In the process the industrial relations system is itself being transformed.

(d) One of the most striking features of these changes is the unevenness with which they are occurring at all levels (between different work areas within the same plant, at the inter-plant and inter-company levels, and within North America between plants in the US and those in Canada). Of particular interest are the variations that are developing in both wages and work practices between plants (i.e. geographical variations).

Both the scale and scope of present technological change pose very serious dilemmas for the labour movement. If unions resist technological change they may contribute to their industry's defeat in international competition. Where they cooperate with management in facilitating change they may be the victims of the very success they encourage. For this reason, there is still considerable mistrust between labour and management about industrial and technological change. In introducing new technology and forms of work organisation, management is driven by the goal of competing for profit. The central political issue is whether the labour movement can wrest enough control from management to ensure that it is able to share in the wealth and increased leisure that new technology makes possible.

7

Conceptualising Processes of Skill Change: A Local Labour Market Approach

Jamie A. Peck and Peter E. Lloyd

This chapter opens up the debate on skill change within the field of geography which we believe is necessary for two reasons. First, the study of skill change has typically been associated with labour process theory. While this body of work has been informative, it has developed from a tradition of plant-based research which has often hampered the development of a rounded understanding of the processes of skill change. This is a field in which geographers, with their understanding of mechanisms operating at the level of the locality and of the complexity of the tangible and non-tangible linkages between firms, could make a significant contribution. The second concern is that geography itself, at least as far as the Anglo-Saxon tradition is concerned, has paid scant attention to the processes of skill change. Skill is much more than occupational competence: it reflects the distribution of social, economic and political power in society and represents one of the key ways in which the sphere of production is articulated with the sphere of reproduction. The emergent field of 'labour geography' is beginning to address these issues (Cooke, 1983; Storper and Walker, 1983: Massey, 1984; Scott and Storper, 1986a) and this chapter represents an attempt to bring an understanding of the processes of skill change to this debate.

Labour Process Theory and the Analysis of Skill Change

Braverman's *Labor and Monopoly Capital* (1974) marked a milestone in the analysis of this topic. He reasserted the Marxist position that capitalism derived its dynamism from the process of accumulation. A feature of the evolution of the capitalist system would, from this perspective, be the progressive erosion of skills as capitalists sought to extend control over the labour process. The increasing alienation of the working class, a product of the drudgery of de-skilled manual work, would set the preconditions for the eventual crisis of the capitalist mode of production. By stressing this position, Braverman provided a timely antithesis to the body of work, which has been termed the post-industrialist school, that highlighted the liberating role of new technology and the growth of workers' skills, within a social system ostensibly geared to the satisfaction of human needs (Crozier, 1971; Argyle, 1972; Bell, 1974).

In *Labor and Monopoly Capital*, the Marxian de-skilling thesis was extended and given a new periodisation. For Braverman, it was scientific management or Taylorism which was the principal weapon for the expropriation of workers' skills by capital. This differs significantly from Marx's account in Volume 1 of *Capital*, in which it was technical change that formed the leading edge of the de-skilling process. Marx saw technology as the very foundation-stone of the hierarchical division of labour which had evolved during the early phase of industrial capitalism. Thus Marx was able to argue that technical change could totally undermine the hierarchical division of labour, as work tasks were equalised and de-skilled.

While we would concur with Garnsey (1981) that Braverman's work represented a significant shift away from Marx's crude technological determinism, fundamental flaws remain. In many ways it did no more than replace one form of monocausal explanation with another: managerial strategy, rather than technical change, is portrayed as the principal cause of de-skilling. As a consequence, the capitalist class was seen as a coherent group, conscious of its interests and uniquely capable of realising its goals (Wood, 1982).

Taylor's scientific management was regarded as the essence of capitalist rationality, an attempt to 'render conscious and systematic, the formerly unconscious tendency of capitalist production' (Braverman, 1974:120-1). This represents the capitalist class as not only rational, but commits the common fallacy of assuming that, on its perceived evolutionary path, capitalist society becomes increasingly rational (Nord, 1987). From this viewpoint, the act of capital's deciding what it wants is scarcely distinguishable from its getting what it wants: the implementation of managerial strategy is seen as almost entirely unproblematic. This is perhaps the point upon which *Labor and Monopoly Capital* has been most roundly criticised. Numerous critics have argued that the opposition of the working class is a potent force in shaping the evolution of the labour process (Palmer, 1975; Lettieri, 1976; Friedman, 1977; Coombs, 1978; Edwards, 1979; Stark, 1980; Herman, 1982; Cockburn, 1983; Rose and Jones, 1985). Not only might such opposition act to reconfigure the labour process, it could be argued that it might render both de-skilling and the real subordination of labour a persistently incomplete process. This obviously raises some problems for radical analysis. As Wood (1982) has pointed out, many of the radical writers who have stressed the role of working class opposition in the labour process *still* tend to portray management as eventually able to overcome this opposition.

Thus, while the storyline of labour process analysis is becoming more sophisticated, one still feels drawn towards the same ending. The adoption of such an a priori theoretical position is disabling for empirical analysis, because it produces a tendency to measure empirical phenomena against a particular evolutionary model of skill change. It is difficult within such a framework to come to terms with the richness of concrete circumstances because those phenomena which do not comply with the evolutionary model are often treated as backward, anachronistic forms (Rubery and Wilkinson, 1981; Zeitlin, 1981). Our first major criticism of the labour process theory approach to skill change is that the a priori adoption of an evolutionary, unilinear model of skill change is profoundly restrictive.

The Nature of Skill

A second set of criticisms concerns a related issue. The nature of skill itself is often misconceived in labour process research. It has been noted that Braverman tended to idealise craft skills (Cutler, 1978), with the likely result that he over-estimated their destruction (Thompson, 1983). Such a preoccupation with craft skills remains a feature of much labour process research. While they may closely coincide with commonsense views of what constitutes 'real skill', they remain only one form among many. Furthermore, skills are practised in the household as well as in the workplace. It is necessary not only to recognise the many forms of skill which exist but, if the complexity of skill change is to be fully understood, to acknowledge the importance of the relationships between groups of workers with different ones (Peck and Haughton, 1987). 'Semi-skilled' workers, for example, are neither devoid of skill nor of bargaining strength (Rubery, 1978; Elger, 1979) and their particular relationships with craft workers can exert an important influence on the development of the labour process (Elbaum et al., 1979; Zeitlin, 1979). In the delicate relationships between different groups of workers lie important lessons about the balance of power in the labour process. Sabel (1982:167), for example, has highlighted the fickleness of the craft workers, who at one time will be found

> siding with the unskilled against management, [at others] abandoning them to advance the narrow interests of [their] immediate peers ... the craftsman can be both docile and militant — out for himself but capable of solidarity, disposed to lead broad movements against management but also to defend narrow privileges.

It would be wrong, however, to regard the destruction of workers' skills as essential for the achievement of profitable production (Elger, 1979). Skill is not necessarily under attack from management at all times and in all places. Marx, indeed, acknowledged that some skills would continue to exist in spite of de-skilling, a process which represented an attack not on all of them, but principally upon monopolisable skills (Harvey, 1982). This stance also brings with it problems because the destruction of monopolisable skills itself raises a set of contradictions. Such forms of skill may be seen as positively beneficial by those employers seeking to maintain workforce stability. A perfectly substitutable workforce would also be a highly mobile one, presenting its own set of problems.

Narrowness of Labour Process Research

Our third set of criticisms of the labour process approach to skill concerns the narrowness of its analytical focus. The explanation of the evolution of the labour process has for too long been confined within the narrow parameters of the capital-labour relationship at the level of the workplace (Littler and Salaman, 1982; Kelly, 1985; Manwaring and Wood, 1985; Nichols, 1986). Such approaches are fast becoming as unacceptable on theoretical grounds as they are on empirical ones. Transitions which are made in Braverman's work between empirical examinations of the behaviour of managers and workers within particular plants and the associated abstract tendencies of capitalist development are made in a way which often borders on the facile.

As labour process theory has evolved, the perspective in which managerial goals were unproblematically implemented has been slowly superseded by notions of a 'balance of forces' between capital and labour. Those writers who sought to illuminate the role of class struggle as a potent force in the development of the labour process were instrumental in creating a climate in which the intersection of managerial strategy and worker resistance was viewed as an intricate, almost indeterminate, affair. Attendant upon this was the need to conceive the capital-labour relationship as one not only of naked conflict but also of compromise (Palmer, 1975; Burawoy, 1979; Edwards, 1979; Elbaum et al., 1979). Worker resistance, then, did not serve merely to delay the inevitable unfolding of the capitalist labour process, but was seen as a force capable of moulding and diverting its development (Thompson, 1978; Lazonick, 1979).

As the balance of power in the labour process was now perceived as a much more delicate and fluctuating one, it became necessary to begin the search for those factors which might condition this balance. Labour process theory had to look over the factory gates. Some of the most compelling and stimulating accounts of the development of the labour process have been characterised by their efforts to set the capital-labour relationship within the context of its economic and social environment. Labour and product market conditions and national cultural systems have been shown to impinge significantly upon the evolution of the labour process, critically tipping the balance of power in the favour of one group or another at different times and in different places (Elbaum and Wilkinson, 1979; Reid,1981; Zeitlin, 1981; Lee, 1982; Lorenz, 1984; Maurice et al., 1984; Kelly, 1985; Maguire, 1988). The enduring value of this work is that it presents capital as well as labour as a reactive class. Both capital and labour inhabit an environment which at different times will not only constrain but also open up possibilities for, or even force, particular courses of action. Such a stance should not be read, however, as one in which the structural dominance of capital is denied. Capital is seen to exhibit relative, but not absolute, dominance in the labour market and in the labour process.

The Local Labour Market and the Notion of the Skill Pool

The approach to the analysis of skill change proposed here is one in which, rather than focusing on the individual firm, the analytical resolution is raised to the level of the *local* labour market or, more specifically, to focus on the 'pool' of skills which can be indentified with particular places. While there are benefits to be had from merely shifting the scale at which analysis is undertaken, the principal value of this approach lies in the emphasis which is placed on important mechanisms that have so far only played a secondary role in skills research. In particular, local labour market mechanisms are raised to the fore, as are the multiplicity of linkages which exist *between* firms and between firms and households in local areas.

This shift in the scale of analytical resolution is a necessary one in that it allows the subtlety and complexity of the processes of skill change to be captured. Increasingly, these processes are played out, not at the level of the individual firm, but actually between firms. New forms of skill utilisation are emerging, connected with developments such as temporary and part-time working, subcontracting and out-sourcing (Hakim, 1987). These work forms, which under the old Fordist regime might have been considered 'anachronistic', are taking on some ascendancy. Indeed, it is the large Fordist factory itself which is fast becoming an anachronism. Patterns of skill utilisation are, as a result, changing in ways vastly more complex than can be captured in concepts focusing upon straightforward evolution of the Fordist regime towards de-skilling. Fordist forms of working practice are beginning, in some cases, to ossify and disappear. In other cases, they are being broken down into discrete elements to be reconstituted into new, more flexible ways of working as new technology presents a widening variety of options for the application of labour to the production process (Lloyd, 1988).

In response to these evolving changes, there is a major drive to re-think the inter-relationships between the so-called 'progressive' and 'backward' sectors of the economy (Brusco and Sabel, 1981; Rubery and Wilkinson, 1981; Sabel and Zeitlin, 1985; Holmes, 1986; Shutt and Whittington, 1987). Indeed, the scale of change in the structure of capitalist production has led some theorists to go so far as to conclude that capitalist societies are entering a wholly new phase of development. This phase, characterised by the fragmentation of the old Fordist structures and the growth of small firms, flexible work patterns and subcontracting relationships, has been variously dubbed 'flexible specialisation' (Sabel, 1982; Piore and Sabel, 1984), 'neo-Fordism' (Palloix, 1976; Aglietta, 1979) or 'disorganised capitalism' (Offe, 1985; Lash and Urry, 1987).

These changes have particular importance for the analysis of skill change because they imply that it is more than usually inappropriate to judge contemporary trends in terms of past experience. The loss of craft workers from large engineering plants, for example, is now less likely to reflect an *in situ* process of de-skilling than perhaps a more complex trend towards subcontracted production. Skilled workers may, indeed, have disappeared from the large plants, but other forms of skill are emerging in the small-firm, subcontracting sector. This is a process of skill *redistribution*, not necessarily of skill destruction, though some may be lost in net terms in the process.

Given these trends, there is a critical need to re-think the issue of skill change. The remainder of this chapter is dedicated to this process of reconceptualisation. A simple heuristic — the skill pool — is used as a means of opening up the question of skill change at the level of the local labour market.

The Skill Pool

The notion of the skill pool denotes the stock of skills present within a particular local labour market. It is by definition therefore a rather heterogeneous structure. It contains not only those skills acquired through formal training, but also those obtained through experiential learning, both in the firm and in other spheres of economic and social life. A continuum of skill can be identified which ranges from spheres of considerable specialism, requiring long periods of formal training, to those more mundane bundles of competence which are required for so-called 'unskilled' activities. More than just recognising the potentially broad range of skills present in any community, it must also be acknowledged that varying proportions of this set of locally available skills will be in use (in the wage-labour market and the domestic economy) at different points in time. The residual set of 'latent' skills obviously constitutes an important, but contemporaneously unrealised, local resource.

The local pool of skills, far from being static, will be in a constant state of flux. Processes much more complex than the simple running down of average skill levels (as the de-skilling model would predict) are at work in this dynamic system. In reality, a complex web of change is evident in which patterns of skill utilisation, under-utilisation and latency are in a perpetual state of mutually independent transformation. Add to this the dynamic of the mechanisms surrounding the creation and eventual depletion of skills (effectively, those mechanisms of 'entry' to and 'exit' from the pool) and an impression can be gained of the complexity of the processes involved in skill change. The particular stock of skills which are represented in such a pool at a point in time should appropriately be regarded as a product of the balance between the processes of skill creation and depletion and the processes surrounding their duration or 'life'.

The critical point here is that it is *at the level of the local labour market* that tendencies such as de-skilling must be identified. While certain groups of workers may be experiencing this (in the sense that they are no longer practising their full complement of skills), others will be utilising theirs to the full, picking up new ones or bringing latent skills to bear. The process of skill change, then, is played out at the level (at least) of the local economic system, and this is the most appropriate scale at which the *net effects* of these diverse changes can be assessed. As a means of beginning to unpack the processes at work at this relatively unfamiliar level of resolution for the skills debate, the process of change has been broken down into its constituent components. The principal forces in the overall process of skill change can be briefly characterised as follows.

(a) The processes surrounding the creation of skill concern the mechanisms of 'entry' to the system. This is achieved by the accretion of experiential skills as well as by formal training and may take place both within firms and in the sphere of reproduction (e.g. in the household and in the school).

(b) The utilisation of skill covers, in effect, the whole sphere of current labour demand in a particular economic system. Such demand will arise from households as well as firms and will see skills taken up into assigned uses.

(c) Latent skills are those created in a previous phase but not currently being utilised. They will be largely in the possession of unemployed or inactive individuals but will also include some skills in the possession of active participants but which are currently unused.

(d) The processes surrounding the depletion of skills concern such factors as the out-migration of skilled workers, the loss of local skills through retirement, and atrophy — through prolonged latency — among such groups as the long-term unemployed.

It is perhaps easiest to think of these four components of skill change as broadly identifiable with clusters of labour market positions (including the employed and the unemployed) and of positions within the domestic economy through which individuals will pass. It is possible using this framework to explore both the ways in which individuals make their way through the skills pool and the the ways in which, in aggregate, particular components of the system evolve relative to one another.

A useful illustrative example can be derived from women's work histories. At the individual level, the four components provide a framework for interpreting the bimodal work patterns of many married women who, following an initial period of active wage labour (skill utilisation), return to the home for the purposes of child-rearing. During this period, only their workplace skills are being under-utilised in the sense that, while they are clearly required to exercise a wide range of domestic skills, many of the ones they practised in paid work will have become latent. On eventually returning to paid work, continuing constraints on their availability and the erosion of their skills see that women will commonly remain stranded in the low skill sectors of the labour market (under-utilised skills). They find themselves unable to gain entry to work at the skill level of their initial work period (Dex, 1984). There is in this sense a 'de-skilling' taking place by virtue of the particular path followed by women workers in a context conditioned by gender roles.

It is also useful as an illustrative device to think through the implications of the existence of such a pool of latent and under-utilised skills among women at the level of the local labour market. Conditions like the ones described are precisely those which might be expected to stimulate growth in the secondary sector of the economy: a sector which offers possibilities for mobilising such a pool of skill at relatively low cost (in wage terms). Massey's (1983) analysis of the growth in female employment in Cornwall and in the depressed coalfield areas of the UK provides a good empirical illustration. From this perspective, it is clearly too simple to speak of capital seeking to exploit 'green' female labour by locating in appropriate areas. The 'greenness' itself demands explanation in contexts outside the relation between capital and labour.

The process of skill change such as that just described does not occur in a vacuum. In reality, it takes place against the background of the historically established economic, social and institutional structures that evolve in particular local contexts. These serve to constrain, as well as provide opportunities for, future developments in the skill pool (Aydalot, 1980; Storper and Walker, 1983; Moulaert, 1987). In particular, previous patterns of skill creation and utilisation may become 'fossilised' under some circumstances, as cultural and institutional forms evolve around them. Patterns of skill change are consequently very much associated with particular *local histories*. These, in turn, are a partial outcome of the role played by different localities in previous geographies of production and of skill utilisation (Webber, 1986).

Skill pools, which for example provide employers with opportunities to tap reserves of latent skills in the possession of married women returning to the labour force, are likely to have particular demographic and cultural profiles. These will serve to produce the appropriate population cohorts and domestic divisions of labour (time-budgets available to women workers) and, perhaps, some history of industrial evolution which provides a 'cycling together' of these conditioning elements. In addition, historical traditions of 'nimble fingers' or particular acquired traits and abilities will serve rather to condition the possibilities offered to potential employers. From a supply-side perspective, therefore, the configuration of available groups of workers by age, sex, skill and attitude is not independently derived but is the product of complex historical-social processes operating most revealingly at the level of the local labour market.

Developing a Local Labour Market Perspective

Labour is pre-eminently moblised at the local level (Broadbent, 1977; Lloyd and Shutt, 1985). The 'local scale', however defined, would therefore seem the most appropriate one for the analysis of skill change in particular and the labour market in general. In examining the labour market, it is necessary to take account of three key influences, all of which exert an autonomous effect on the structure and dynamism of the labour market: labour demand, labour supply, and state regulation. Concrete labour market outcomes arise from the *combinatorial* effect of these three influences (Peck, 1988). If the process of skill change at the level of the local labour market is to be fully unpacked each of these influences should be considered. This is not to say that labour demand, labour supply and state regulation exert entirely autonomous influences upon labour market structures. They are, of course, interrelated. The task for local-level research is to unscramble their combinatorial effects.

Labour Demand

The first feature of the local labour market perspective which we wish to develop is that of labour demand. Across a local labour market patterns of demand are in constant flux, but the true extent of this will rarely be fully apparent within individual capital units because here the process of change is likely to be both dogged by inertia and severely inhibited in direction. While such *in situ* alterations in labour demand (e.g. workforce reorganisation) play an important part in the broader sweep of changes which are apparent across the labour market, these must be set alongside the considerable changes taking place at the 'margin' as firms close and contract or open and expand. The aggregate result is that labour markets undergo a continuous process of dynamic change characterised by industrial, occupational, organisational and geographical transformations in the composition of labour demand. Such changes are particularly apparent over the business cycle, although they also reflect longer-term structural trends.

It becomes clear, then, that at best a *partial* picture of the overall process of skill change can be derived from examining the conditions prevailing in particular plants. Plant-based studies cannot capture the dynamism of the local labour market. There is a continuous movement of workers not only between jobs but between occupations and industrial sectors — and between paid work and the domestic economy. This means that patterns of skill utilisation are in constant turmoil. During recession, for instance, redundancies and lay-offs are often the initiators of a downward spiral of job changes, as recruitment into skilled jobs freezes up and people reconcile themselves to less-skilled employment (White, 1983; Peck, 1984). Such workers have effectively been de-skilled because they have been denied the opportunity to practise the full complement of their skills. Moreover, in 'trading down' the labour market in such a way, these workers are also bringing about the de-skilling of other, less skilled, workers, who are displaced in this downward shift.

Setting the discussion of skill change in the context of labour pools raises the important distinction between de-skilled work and de-skilled workers, an issue that has proved very difficult to address within the conventional labour process framework. Against what standard is the changing skill content of jobs to be assessed? If it is in the context set by the evolution of skill in a particular plant, how can this 'trajectory' be interpreted? The skill content of jobs can be reduced, but, at least in the medium term, the workers concerned will not themselves have been de-skilled. Indeed, they may find an opportunity later to practise their skills to the full. Moreover, changes in job content in one part of the economy may create new possibilities for skill utilisation in others.

Subcontracting, local labour markets and skills

The growth of small, specialist subcontracting firms with highly skilled workforces is a good example of a niche being opened up by the changing organisation of the production process in large firms and, in the face of this, there are good reasons for being sceptical about whether a dominant direction of skill change can be sustained across a local labour market for a prolonged period. The issue of subcontracting is also useful in highlighting an important theme which pervades the examination of firms' strategies, that of the continuum which exists between the complete internalisation of the production process (and its associated skill needs) and the purchase of skill or of goods and services in the market place (Friedman, 1977). For instance, it has been argued that the tendency toward progressive internalisation of the labour market by large firms (through the development of internal labour markets with limited ports of entry) has been breaking down, as certain aspects of these firms' activities have become incompatible with this mode of organisation. The high transaction costs associated with some forms of internalised employment relationship have consequently led to a 're-externalisation' of some groups within the labour force (Williamson, 1975; Shutt and Whittington, 1984, 1987).

The neo-classical view of the firm as an independent unit which indulges in entirely independent cost-rational decision-making and competes freely on an open market is an increasingly redundant one (Holmes, 1986). Relationships between firms are not solely competitive ones: recent work on capitalist economic systems has begun to identify a complex web of cooperation, collaboration, control and inter-dependence between individual firms (Berger and Piore, 1980; Brusco and Sabel, 1981; Rubery and Wilkinson, 1981; Taylor and Thrift, 1982; Piore and Sabel, 1984; Rainnie, 1984; Brusco, 1986; Holmes, 1986; Pyke, 1987). This has formed part of a reaction against those unilinear views of capitalist development which painted a picture of a relentless drift towards factorised, mass-production techniques, large-scale mechanisation and a completely de-skilled labour force. The realisation that supposedly 'backward' sectors, such as the small firm sector, have not only survived but show signs of a revival, has led to a more sophisticated appreciation of the dynamic of the capitalist economy in which economic diversity is explained rather than 'explained away'.

Empirical work in North West England demonstrated to the authors that the level and complexity of inter-firm linkages were such that, in many cases, the employment structures and skill mixes of individual firms ceased to have any meaning in isolation. The subcontracting links that are increasingly prevalent in much of the civil engineering sector, for example, reflect the fact that many large, hierarchically organised firms are being reorganised and fragmented. Manual employment levels in these firms have fallen dramatically. Although this may be taken by some as evidence of de-skilling, these skills have not, in fact, been lost to the local labour market. They have been *relocated*. The large firms, upon securing contracts, brought in independent, often local, companies to meet virtually all their blue-collar labour requirements. Here, some form of de-skilling has taken place, but it is a far cry from that associated with the mechanisation and routinisation of tasks in large plants. In this case, while the skills which are being mobilised have changed little, the means by which they are utilised have been revolutionised. Employment opportunities for skilled workers in large plants are now not only less numerous, but they are also less secure. A process of peripheralisation has occurred in which the strategic power of skilled workers has been reduced not by robbing them of their skills, but through a reconfiguration of the structure of local labour demand.

While many similar developments within the realm of inter-firm linkages, production subcontracting and outwork have been linked to the need for increasingly flexible production systems

(Piore, 1979; Rubery and Wilkinson, 1981; Dicken, 1986; Holmes, 1986), it is of course quite possible that such activity might simply be a 'temporary' symptom of the current crisis of profitability facing many parts of the manufacturing sector. Alternatively, these relationships may be consolidated and stabilise during subsequent more buoyant periods. Perhaps such methods of organising production have always represented an historical alternative to mass production (Sabel and Zeitlin, 1985) and, after years of simmering near to the surface, are beginning to boil up.

Much is often made of the unequal power relations between contractor and subcontractor (Taylor and Thrift, 1982). In many cases, the attractiveness of the subcontracting system is that it is both expandable and expendable, but it could also be argued that this system has evolved into a more stable, symbiotic one as a technical division of labour between independent firms has become clearly established (Dicken, 1986). The civil engineering firms in the North West study illustrate the development of a system of mutual inter-dependence — a situation, however, in which many firms will be uncomfortable. It might be expected that both contractor and subcontractor would seek to minimise their dependence (often through the development of linkages with other firms), and/or attempt to gain a greater influence over the activities of the other (such as by organising subcontracting production schedules so as to maximise the degree of reliance upon the contractor). Rainnie (1984) and Shutt and Whittington (1987) found that large firms were able to manipulate these relationships to their advantage, but this need not necessarily be the case.

It is necessary, then, to break away from the stereotyped view that subcontracting relations are characterised by the exploitation of peripheral, small firms by larger ones. While the cost overheads carried by the large enterprises may militate against their viability as subcontractors, this does not preclude such activity. A major company involved in the production of oil-drilling equipment in North West England, for example, acted as a subcontractor to small local engineering firms during slack periods. Even though this company found such contracts were often unprofitable, this was nevertheless regarded as an acceptable cost of maintaining workforce stability. This is an example of the skill composition of a company apparently falling out of phase with its individual 'rationale'. The complex logic of skill utilisation extends beyond the factory gates and must be seen in the broader contexts of changing forms of corporate organisation, the current tendency towards the de-integration of production, and the ways in which these operate in particular local labour market situations.

Labour Supply

While we would concur with Craig and her colleagues (1982:77) that 'the number of good jobs in the economy is mainly determined by the development of the industrial and technical structure, largely independent of labour supply', it must be acknowledged that the notion of skill is intricately related to the characteristics of workers as well as those of jobs. Skill is a reflection of social status as well as an indicator of 'technical' ability. Popular understandings of skill are intimately, perhaps inextricably, related to workers' personal characteristics. On the one hand, there is a strong tendency for skills possessed by women to be persistently under-valued (Glenn and Feldberg, 1979; Kraft, 1979; Phillips and Taylor, 1980; Coyle, 1982; Cockburn, 1983). On the other, it has been argued that craft trade unions have been able to maintain their privileged position in the labour market — and hence their skilled status — in the face of reductions in the skill requirements of many craft jobs (Turner, 1962; Kahn, 1975; Rubery, 1978; Piore, 1979; Garnsey et al., 1985; Labour Studies Group, 1985). Skill must be seen, then, partially as a social construct. A link exists between the way in which the labour supply is structured (locally) and the distribution of skills on the labour market. This we will now explore briefly, using the case of trade union activity.

Skill supply and the trades unions

Local labour supply conditions exert an influence upon the nature, pace and direction of skill change. This can be illustrated with the example of militant trade unionism, which has been argued to possess a localised (particularly urban) character (Gordon, 1977; Lane, 1982). As mobile capital becomes increasingly sensitive to the qualitative aspects of local labour power (Walker and Storper, 1981; Bluestone and Harrison, 1982; Storper and Walker, 1983; Massey, 1984, 1986), these 'islands' of trade union militancy are experiencing rapid de-industrialisation. One of the results of these changes is that traditional trade union structures, another artefact of the Fordist regime, are themselves beginning to break down (Leadbetter, 1988). From this perspective, another shortcoming of the plant-based study is revealed. It is easy, with plant-based studies, to over-estimate the defensive capabilities of the trade union movement. As their structures are fragmented through developments, such as local pay bargaining and single union deals, the ability of the movement to combat de-skilling is significantly reduced. As contemporary events reveal, different unions or different local branches of the same union can be played off against one another (see Chapter 6). At the extreme, with the general decentralisation of employment, the trade union system can be by-passed altogether.

The fragmentation of large capital units creates serious problems for the trade union movement. The extent to which trade unions are able effectively to shape the development of labour processes in the future will increasingly depend upon their organisational strength *between* workplaces. Their strength in this is likely to be particularly compromised by the shift towards smaller plant sizes (Lash and Urry, 1987).

The implications of these trends for the analysis of skill change are far-reaching. Not least, they imply that new forms of skill may emerge. It has been observed that workers with craft skills in small firms tend to be far more flexible than is the case in the more sharply demarcated large plants (Peck et al., 1987). Where large firms have been successful in introducing such flexibility *in situ*, it has commonly been through an expansion in the employment of the technician grade rather than through the difficult process of renegotiating the conditions of craft employment. Both processes — the shift to the small firm and the rise of the technician grade — are fundamental to the context in which new flexible workforces are being created.

The process of skill change is, therefore, no less complex or dynamic from the supply perspective. Here, too, we would argue that it is necessary to look across the local labour market to capture the subtlety of these changes in terms of local labour supply structures. Only one aspect has been considered here, by focusing on the case of trade union activity. Equally important are factors such as local social mores concerning the supply of (particularly female) labour to the labour market (Pyke, 1986; Maguire, 1988) and the ways in which non-work and gender roles serve to give particular characteristics to the 'shape' of the local supply, offering local employers structured choices rather than a free hand in seeking to match workers to their production requirements.

State Regulation

The labour market cannot be seen as a 'self-regulating' structure. The wage mechanism alone is not capable of regulating the labour market. The state needs, therefore, to be accorded a central role in labour market regulation (de Brunhoff, 1978; Offe and Berger, 1985; Offe and Hinrichs, 1985). In particular, the state has an important role to play in the regulation of the skill creation process. This is because, although skills are essential for the operation of the labour market, it is often not in the interests of individual capital units to undertake training since they may find themselves the victims of 'poaching', effectively bearing the costs of training for other firms. Under these circumstances, the state has been drawn into an interventionist role to ensure an adequate supply of skills.

A contradiction arises from the state's role in the labour market, however, as its institutional presence has the effect of 'concretising' labour market structures (Peck, 1988). A clear example of this is provided by craft training, whose institutional structures have fallen out of synchronisation with the requirements of the labour market, producing what is seen to be a key *source* of Britain's labour market problems (Goldstein, 1984; Finn, 1987). Currently, institutional structures are themselves coming under pressure as labour market structures have been increasingly broken down and reconfigured. Although in Britain such institutional structures are now undergoing change, this process of modification is not occurring evenly across space. In some areas, for example, the traditional regulatory system has remained largely intact, while in others it has collapsed. This creates a spatially differentiated set of prior possibilities for institutional change. To exemplify this argument, the impact of recent changes in the training system on two local labour markets in North West England is now briefly examined.

State regulation, training infrastructures and local skill configuration

The two localities chosen to provide a basis for this discussion are labelled Abbotsthorpe and Stoneby, these being pseudonyms since some sensitive local labour market issues exist in the real areas from which confidential data were acquired. Both have long histories of engineering employment. Traditionally, this sector in both areas was structured in very similar ways. Both towns were dominated by a handful of large enterprises in the electrical engineering, vehicle making and ordnance sectors but also had many small machine shops and specialist engineering firms. Historically, the reliance on craft skills was great but, although this was the case in both large and small firms, the former bore most of the training costs associated with the creation of craft skills.

In both cases, the training system was very traditional, with the 'time-served' apprenticeship as virtually the only route into craft employment. Until the mid-1970s, the level of apprentice training by the large firms meant that most of the small firms in the area could rely on being able to buy skills on the labour market (by 'poaching'). In effect, by their training input, the large firms met virtually all the engineering skill needs in the two local labour markets. In interviews, both employers and workers expressed similar views about what constituted 'real skills'. At the heart of it was apprenticeship training conducted according to the guidelines of the Engineering Industry Training Board created to ensure common standards throughout Britain.

From this perspective, the two localities exhibited a very similar 'heritage' on entering the recession of the late 1970s. Their experiences during the dramatic economic and institutional changes of the 1980s have, however, been very different. The engineering sectors of both relied greatly on government expenditure, and the reshuffling of priorities which took place following the election of a Conservative government in 1979 impinged significantly upon the fortunes of each. For Stoneby the effects were disastrous and 1981-82 saw a debilitating wave of redundancies sweep across the entire area as major employers could no longer fill their order books. In Abbotsthorpe, although there was also a downturn, the engineering sector has remained relatively stable throughout what has been a difficult period for the industry nationally.

The importance of these events for present purposes lies in their impacts on patterns of skill creation and utilisation. In Abbotsthorpe, conditions of reasonable security/stability spawned little change. While training levels fell to some extent, they continued to follow the traditional pattern. Events in Stoneby, however, were very different. Considerable restructuring followed the crisis of 1981-82, which was perhaps most significant in that it brought about a transformation in the institutional character of the training system. In contrast to national trends, the government-funded Youth Training Scheme gained a strong foothold immediately it was introduced in 1983, drawing the state strongly into the training process. Although, in many cases, this provided little more than a financial buttress for the traditional apprenticeship system, it was also the initiator of important changes in the structure of the training delivery system. In particular, it saw the establishment of a large private training agency in Stoneby, geared specifically towards the needs of *small* firms in the area. This delivered both traditional apprentice training and also shorter courses at the 'sub-apprentice' level. The basis was, therefore, established in Stoneby for a new, more flexible training system, capable of satisfying skill needs across a different group of client companies (see, for instance, Peck and Haughton, 1987).

The key point to be made from this particular example is that the institutional forms which evolve alongside unfolding labour process and labour market structures should be seen as exerting a long-term and pervasive influence, significantly moulding the potential futures of different localities (Jackson, 1984; Clark, 1986b). The structures of the creation and utilisation of skill, though intricately related, are partially autonomous. Conditions in one sphere will constrain and stimulate developments in the other while each has a dynamic of its own. Economic difficulties in Stoneby set the preconditions for a transformation in the institutional structure of the skill creation process, while the more stable economic climate in Abbotsthorpe militated against such a profound and rapid restructuring. These institutional structures, so altered, may then go on to exert a pervasive influence on the process of skill change in each area, effectively 'concretising' certain forms of skills while leaving others unaffected. Such changes in labour market institutions may consequently exert a far-reaching impact upon the skill pool, as new possibilities for skill change are opened up and as others are closed off. Moreover, there would seem to be evidence that institutional structures, although often having their origin in central government policies, evolve a locally specific character. Thus, it is possible to talk of distinctive local training infrastructures, which develop their own dynamics and which condition the evolution of specifically *local* labour market structures.

Conclusions

The approach sketched above remains a tentative one. In unpacking the processes of skill change, we have sought to shift the parameters of the debate and highlight some of the ways in which geographers can — and should — contribute to this important area of research. A central feature of this approach has been to shift the scale of analytical resolution away from the level of the individual plant to the level of the local labour market. This we have found to be a prerequisite for understanding fully the complexities of skill change, which are not only played out within firms but also between firms and between the spheres of paid and unpaid labour.

The notion of the skill pool has been deployed as a means of coming to terms with the processes of skill change operating at the level of the local labour market. This has been illuminating in three ways. First, it throws into high relief the structures of the labour market. In this terrain of compromise, neither employers nor organised labour can exert anything approaching absolute control. Such necessary accommodation and mutual inter-dependence underpins the dynamic of skill change, as changes in skill in one part of the economy will at the same time both inhibit and provide opportunities for changes elsewhere. The process of skill change, then, is perceived as one which conforms to a most complex dynamic, rather than one which follows a predetermined, unilinear evolutionary path. Second, with regard to the formation of firms' strategies within the skill pool, we argue against the view that individual firms act as independent decision-making units. Rather, it is necessary to focus on the many tangible and non-tangible linkages which exist between firms. The rationale for patterns of skill utilisation is quite often not revealed until these 'families' of inter-dependent firms can be identified. Third, we argue that the most appropriate scale of analysis is the local one, for it is at this level that labour is mobilised and that the dynamic between different sources of skill utilisation is played out. It is at this level of resolution that the key regulating forces of demand, supply and the state can be seen each to have a crucial role in conditioning the creation and utilisation of skill. While each is, to a degree, autonomous, there are subtle and locally sensitive interaction effects between each element. 'Reading-off' from macro-structures in the relations between capital and labour and the state is unlikely to indicate all we need to know about the ways in which de-skilling takes place, skill shortages arise or training structures evolve. The local contingent circumstances surrounding the interaction of the key elements have a critical explanatory role.

As the 'big structures' of Fordism have begun to break down, patterns of skill creation and utilisation have been transformed. An increasingly complex technical division of labour has emerged between plants, as inter-firm relationships have become both more prevalent and more sophisticated. The plea for additional research at the level of the local labour market should not be taken as an alternative to plant-based studies. Research at the plant level continues to have an important role in the explanation of skill change, but our key point is that there must be heightened appreciation of the locally inter-dependent nature of these individual plants. More emphasis should be placed upon the 'location' of individual plants within their local labour market context. We can only claim to have taken the first steps along this path here.

8

The Changing Organisation of Labour and its Impacts on Daily Activities

Roman Matykowski and Tadeusz Stryjakiewicz

In Polish geographical literature the labour factor has not generated much interest (Stryjakiewicz, 1987). This claim is borne out by noting that among the 220-odd volumes published by the Committee for Space Economy and Regional Planning of the Polish Academy of Sciences since the beginning of the 1960s, none (excluding two small fragments, two studies of the journey to work and an analysis by Ciechocińska, 1973, on the employment problems of deglomerated plants in Warsaw) has been devoted to the problems of the labour market. This is despite numerous calls for research of this kind, especially by Kukliński (1976). This lacuna considerably reduces the possibility of comparative analysis; moreover, theoretical concepts developed in capitalist economies are of minor importance as a source of research hypotheses under Polish conditions.

The starting point for the analysis is the statement that in Poland, like other countries with centrally planned economies, a real labour market does not exist, although this notion is used. In this chapter an attempt is made to show the constraints and incentives shaping the organisation of labour in Polish industry. The labour 'market' in Poland is characterised by:

(a) a surplus of demand for industrial workers over their supply;

(b) little spatial mobility of labour, mostly because of the shortage of residential accommodation;

(c) the small influence of technological change on employment movement;

(d) a warped structure of wages, usually fixed centrally without any relationship to qualifications or the economic effects obtained.

Our basic research hypothesis assumes that the labour shortage notified by many establishments in Poland can be explained by managerial inertia which leads to a lack of job restructuring and to labour wastage. It can be said that the 'model' of employment movement in Poland is a reverse of the scheme:

innovation———>employment movement———>change of wages.
　　　　　　　　(including change
　　　　　　　　of qualifications)

Wages, rather than technical, technological and organisational innovations, seem to be the primary and most common factor of employment movement. Less important are others, such as the possibility of obtaining a flat or a contract for work abroad. Innovations are often forced on industrial plants by the outflow of labour, and this usually occurs after unsuccessfully trying other ways to adapt to the changed conditions. These include:

(a)　pressing 'the centre' to raise wages (this leads to a levelling out of wages between establishments, which secures relative stability of employment at the urban and regional scales but reduces the motivating force of wages and wage competition in socialised industry);

(b) attracting workers by means of various social benefits (such as loans, allotment gardens, helping with the building of single-family houses or the construction of the plant's own blocks of apartments and workers' hostels, assisting with the purchase of goods in short supply, securing places in nurseries and arranging holidays abroad);

(c) extending the range of journeys to work.

This process can be presented schematically.

```
                              ——> pressuring centre to raise wages

                              ——> increased social benefits

relative
drop in  ——> outflow of ——> extending  range of  journeys to
wages          workers         work

                              ——> innovation  and  technological
                                   changes

                              ——> technological changes.
```

It should be noted that the relative drop in wages is effectively an external factor that is little dependent on the decisions of any particular plant but, rather, is largely determined by central decisions (see Jewtuchowicz, 1981:161).

Apart from these constraints and incentives that can be called institutional (following from the principles of the socio-economic system), there are also various space-time constraints in industrial activity. Hägerstrand (1970, 1973) has distinguished three basic categories of constraints.

(a) Capability constraints: these limit the activities of individuals both through their own biological make-up and also through the capacity of the tools they can command.

(b) Coupling constraints: factors defining the time that the individual spends with other people, tools and materials, in order to produce, consume and do business.

(c) Authority (or steering) constraints: these stem from the occurrence in space of 'domains' (spatio-temporal cells) that are under permanent or temporary control of groups or individuals.

These constraints are interrelated and together determine the size of a 'prism' embracing all paths available to an individual, as well as suggesting a sequence of activities (given the limited resources of time and space that everyone possesses). Under Polish conditions these constraints appear primarily at the local level. Hence the problems of the organisation of labour and the changes during the 1975-84 period are discussed in detail in relation to one selected industrial centre, namely Gniezno.

Gniezno is located in the Wielkopolska region about 50 km northeast of Poznań; in 1984 it had a population of 67,400 which puts it in the category of a middle-size urban centre (i.e. one with between 20,000 and 100,000 inhabitants). In his functional classification of Polish towns, Jerczyński (1977) included Gniezno among industrial-service centres, with its workplace function strongly dominating its residential one. In a more recent classification, based on exogenous functions only, Maik (1986) categorised Gniezno as an industrial type of town. In 1984, 42 per cent of the local workforce was employed in socialised industry. In terms of industrial employment Gniezno ranks seventy-seventh among Polish industrial centres, while in population terms it ranks fifty-ninth. (In the voivodeship it ranks second after Poznań on both counts.)

Gniezno can be regarded as a 'typical' industrial centre, representative at least of western Poland, for the following reasons.

(a) It is located in the middle of an agricultural area at a communication 'node' (such a location limits alternative employment opportunities and favours commuting).

(b) It has a multi-branch industrial structure, with the leading sectors making footwear, clothing, electro-mechanical equipment and foodstuffs.

(c) Women make up a considerable share of the industrial workforce.

(d) The characteristic industrial zones in the town's spatial structure, associated with the various stages in its industrial development, continue to influence the relationships between place of work and place of residence.

(e)   There has been a 'natural' evolution of changes in industrial activity recently that have not been stimulated by externally imposed, centrally planned investments.

The analysis presented here is based on data obtained by Zacholska (1986), Matykowski (1987) and Stryjakiewicz (1988) and from the industrial plants in Gniezno and the Voivodeship Statistical Office in Poznań, and by students during fieldwork exercises in 1983. The detailed analysis of structural changes in labour covered the sixteen largest industrial plants which, during the survey period, employed between 88.5 and 94.5 per cent of the town's industrial workforce. The examination of employment was based on two indices that were the most readily available and differentiated the plants most clearly: the share of women in the workforce and the share of people with higher educational qualifications i.e. university degrees. The investigation of the structural features of the labour force was combined with an analysis of wages, innovativeness (defined by the number of innovative projects proposed by employees) and labour productivity. The latter was measured in terms of gross annual sales per worker, although because of the 'twisted' price structure in Poland this does not fully reflect the actual efficiency of labour. Comparisons with national trends were made by using the conclusions from research carried out by Zienkowski (1987) and Baczyński (1987).

Structural Change in Employment and the Role of Technological Change

In Gniezno, its region, and Poland as a whole, there has been a steady fall in industrial employment per thousand population (Table 8.l) and in the share of industry in the total workforce of the socialised economy. Another tendency has been the development of non-socialised industry, including foreign firms (see Manikowska et al., 1985), which often resembles handicraft activities; this explains why the share of socialised industry in total industry declined from 96 per cent in 1975 to 91 per cent a decade later. A systematic drop in employment in Polish socialised industry started in 1978 and has accelerated since 1981. Apart from the state of martial law, another reason was the government resolutions of 21 July 1978 and 17 July 1981 offering workers a one-off opportunity to retire early. This applied to men of 60 with at least twenty-five years' of service and to women of 55 after twenty years' service, with smaller pensions being offered for shorter periods (the regular retirement age is 65 for men and 60 for women). The legislation was intended to make jobs available for the baby-boom cohorts just reaching working age, but many more people resigned than had been expected. Indeed, in some industrial establishments in Gniezno from 72 to 100 per cent of those eligible, especially the men, took advantage of the 1981 resolution which was amended the following year (Table 8.2). It can thus be concluded that higher earnings and job satisfaction do not outweigh the benefits of leisure time due to retirement. (At the same time, however, many retired people eke out their pensions outside industry.) The baby-boom cohorts did not fill the vacancies in industry, especially as new competing sources of income appeared — including foreign firms, of which three, employing over 200 people, were established in Gniezno. In addition, increased profitability in various agricultural sectors made some of the peasants give up their factory jobs. For these reasons eleven of the sixteen plants now claim to be short of labour, even though most employ some of their pensioners on a half-time basis (although no more than 7 or 8 per cent of these pensioners go back to work in industrial plants).

Events in the sugar refining industry of the region confirm the thesis that this shortage results from extensive management of labour and the 'upside down' relation between technological and employment changes, with innovations being forced by the

Table 8.1: Selected characteristics of employment in socialised industry in Gniezno, the Poznań region and Poland

Area	Year	Number of industrial plants	Number of employees in industry (000)	Industrial employees per 1,000 people	Average number of employees per plant	Per cent of women in industrial employment	Per cent of workers with higher education	Average annual wage in industry zloty (000)
Gniezno	1975	107	12.1	220	113	50.4	2.4	42.2
	1978	114	12.5	211	110	50.9	2.4	50.0
	1981	115	12.7	200	110	53.2	2.4	81.0
	1984	115	12.3	183	107	50.4	3.0	185.0
Poznań voivode-ship	1975	1,976	147.1	126	74	38.9	4.3	43.6
	1978	2,175	144.8	120	67	39.0	5.2	54.8
	1981	2,198	138.2	111	63	37.6	5.8	84.7
	1984	2,130	141.7	110	67	38.0	6.4	201.6
Poland	1975	54,160	4,999.7	145	92	39.4	2.9	50.1
	1978	57,306	5,098.7	143	89	39.2	3.4	62.8
	1981	59,152	5,045.4	137	85	37.4	3.9	99.9
	1984	54,386	4,693.1	124	86	36.8	4.4	225.8

Sources: Materials of the Voivodeship Statistical Office, Poznań; *Statistical Yearbooks*, 1976, 1979, 1982, 1985.

outflow of labour. The first to install modern unloading equipment were not the largest producers with the greatest throughput, but the Gniezno refinery — the one having the most serious problems in getting labour, especially seasonal workers. Earlier this refinery had built a workers' hostel and organised its own transport for commuters, but it started to press for the equipment when it lost some of its commuters to the developing Konin Industrial District and the neighbouring town of Słupca with its new, large industrial plant. In the event, the Gniezno sugar refinery did not reduce employment to the extent expected by the design of the equipment but appears to have kept on its books some of the labour freed from unloading work just in case they might be needed. More generally, the problem of labour management and the poor ability of industry to design and introduce innovations have become key issues of the economic reforms that have been attempted in recent years.

Other problems are connected with the composition of labour and its relation to wages, productivity and innovativeness. The industrial structure of Gniezno differs from that of the region and of Poland as a whole because there women made up more than half the labour force whereas, nationally, less than 40 per cent were women and even this proportion has been steadily declining (Table 8.1) although the share of women in the total Polish labour force has been increasing. The large share of women in the Gniezno labour market means that the wage level there is lower than the regional and national averages, and also that the proportion of workers who have higher educational qualifications is smaller. (In 1985, 5.2 per cent of males and 3.1 per cent of females employed in Polish industry had university or technical qualifications.) This situation is typical not only of centres dominated by food and other light industries but also of those within the hinterlands of large urban agglomerations. In Gniezno these two factors coincide, with Poznań having a draining effect. Despite a general tendency for the share of workers with higher educational attainments to increase, in some Gniezno establishments (such as the sugar refinery, dairy factory and tannery) the share of this group of workers has declined in recent years. This is because, for financial reasons, people move to other, sometimes non-industrial, economic units, such as foreign firms, private handicraft-making and combines of state-owned farms. This draining away of better qualified workers from some kinds of industrial production has alarming long-term implications.

Table 8.2:   Retired employees of sixteen industrial plants in
Gniezno

Year	Number of retired persons	Per cent women	Per cent retiring before regular pension age[a]
1980	78	46.2	32.1
1981	176	40.3	68.2
1982	413	36.1	86.7
1983	76	44.7	48.7
1984	60	51.7	30.0
1985	58	56.9	19.0

[a] Regular pension age is 65 for men and 60 for women.
Source: fieldwork.

It also confirms the hypothesis that wages have a decisive
influence on employment movement, irrespective of education.
This is a point on which both the managers of the Polish economy
(see Baczyński, 1987) and workers agree. Of the 600 employees of
Gniezno industrial plants interviewed (a 5 per cent sample), 78 per
cent said that the level of wages was the main incentive to work in
a particular establishment. The level of wages also significantly
determines people's standard of living. The substantial role
played by wages seems obvious but, none the less, it deserves
special consideration under Polish conditions, as their structure
and the mechanism of fixing them (or, rather, its absence) are one
of the principal sources of the pathology of the labour market and
the difficulty it poses for industrial plants. They also contribute to
the formation of such negative social attitudes as disrespect for
work, seeking illegal sources of income and the atrophy of
competitive behaviour. They are best expressed in such popular
sayings as 'the state pretends to pay and the worker pretends to
work' or 'work or loiter, lie or stand, then go and get your X
grand' (with X changing as inflation rises).

Baczyński (1987) distinguishes several factors shaping the level
of wages in Polish industry.

(a) The branch structure: in heavy industries (such as power
generation and metallurgy) the average pay in 1983 was nearly
double that of the food, wood and paper industries.

(b) The organisation and the related degrees of monopolisation:

higher wages in establishments belonging to the so-called obligatory associations which form powerful pressure groups in the economic apparatus, as has been confirmed by Stryjakiewicz (1988) for light industry in the Poznań region.

(c) The share of women: a 1 per cent increase in the share of women in employment brings about a drop in average monthly pay of 53 zlotys.

(d) The size of the plant as well as the size of the place where it is located: both these factors have a positive relationship with wages.

Baczyński also found that while there is a positive relationship between the level of wages and even such things as the level of membership of the Party and trade unions, there is no connection between wages and the productivity of labour (correlation coefficient $r = 0.04$) and between wages and the level of accumulation. He notes, too, that the more rapid increase in wages in the industrial branches and individual establishments having the highest earnings is increasing wage discrepancies. In turn, Zienkowski (1987) points to the rapid reduction in the differences between the salaries of engineers and technicians and the wages of manual workers: whereas the former received pay that was 50 per cent higher in 1970, this had declined to 26 per cent by 1980 and 21 per cent by 1985. This has damaged the prestige of several professions requiring high qualifications and a declining interest among clever, enterprising young people in pursuing higher studies. This may be one of the reasons for low innovativeness of Polish industry which seems likely to become even more backward.

This present research has attempted to verify some of these statements at a local scale, extending the analysis to cover relations between the structure of employment on the one hand and the productivity of labour and innovativeness on the other. Bearing in mind the relatively small size of the sample (sixteen plants) and recognising the need for a cautious interpretation of the results in their verification against other data, the following conclusions seem to be justified.

(a) The relationships between the variables analysed are generally weak, even in those cases where stronger links might be expected from an economic point of view (for instance, a low correlation between wages and the productivity of labour, bearing out a national tendency).

(b) The only structural feature of employment that influences other variables significantly is the percentage of women. Plants with a large share of female labour have lower wages, a lower percentage of employees with higher educational qualifications, and lower figures for workers' innovation projects.

(c) As in the whole of the country, during the 1981-84 period there was a rapid drop in the degree of dependence between the level of education and earnings.

(d) The negative relationship between the number of workers' innovations and the productivity of labour that occurred during the whole study period corroborates the earlier claims about the poor ability of industry to adopt innovations and the negligible impact of innovations on economic results.

Space-Time Budgets and Constraints

The organisation of people's lives in the town's space-time environment is crucially influenced by the constraints mentioned at the beginning. Of particular importance in shaping a worker's daily path are coupling constraints as these determine the time an individual spends with other people at such locations as the place of work and places where goods and services are consumed. Authority (steering) constraints, in turn, determine privileged areas for the workers of some plants (such as shops on the plant's premises, allotments and factory health centres). Moreover, the organisation of workers' activities and time-budgets is determined by their working hours. Industrial plants usually operate for two (sometimes three) shifts running from 06.00 to 14.00, 14.00 to 22.00 (and sometimes from 22.00 to 06.00), although there are some factories that divide the hours differently. Employees starting work at 06.00 have no opportunity to buy everyday foodstuffs before work, and after 14.00 these are in short supply. To ease this situation the largest industrial plants have opened grocery shops on their premises. The workers use them during working hours, which reduces their effective worktime, especially in the case of supplies of attractive goods for which they have to queue.

Nearly 55 per cent of workers travel to work by bus and more than one-third walk. The average journey time for workers from Gniezno is twenty-six minutes. Nearly 30 per cent shop for groceries on their way, and most buy items like cigarettes and newspapers at 'Ruch' kiosks, some of which open very early in the morning. The municipal transport network also operates eight special bus lines to serve workers at the industrial plants but these only run early morning and afternoon services.

Some constraints and incentives are connected with the employment structure. The two largest industrial plants in Gniezno have tried to maintain their appeal (especially to their predominantly young female workforce) by setting up shops to sell their own products (shoes and clothes) as well as facilities like libraries and discotheques on their premises. However, a major obstacle to the participation of women in the workforce is the serious shortage of day nurseries and nursery schools (which have places for only about two-fifths of the eligible children). This explains why in the larger industrial plants — with a high proportion of female workers — 10 per cent or more of the women avail themselves of three-year (partly paid or unpaid) child-care leave: for Poland this index was 8.6 per cent, or 3.2 per cent of the total employment in socialised industry in 1985.

Spatial Patterns of Workplace and Journey to Work

The spatial structure of workplaces in Gniezno, as in most Polish industrial centres, takes the form of a concentric-axial pattern. The location of workplaces in particular concentric zones of Gniezno (Figure 8.1) is connected with the successive stages in the town's territorial development, while their distribution in the three sectors is associated with the location of plants along main communication routes. The eight old factories in the central part of Gniezno, which employ from 20 to 300 workers, together provide work for 1,000 people, 55 per cent of whom are women. In this easily accessible area are located the department for 'protected' labour (pregnant women and workers with occupational diseases) of the Wielkopolska Footwear Plant 'Polania' and the production department of the Cooperative of the Disabled 'Piast' which provides jobs for the disabled people of the town and its vicinity. Together these employ nearly 500, or about half of all the industrial employees in the central area of Gniezno. In the intermediate zone there are two concentrations of industry: in the eastern one 2,100 people (about 70 per cent being women) are employed, while that in the south has some 2,450 workers (80

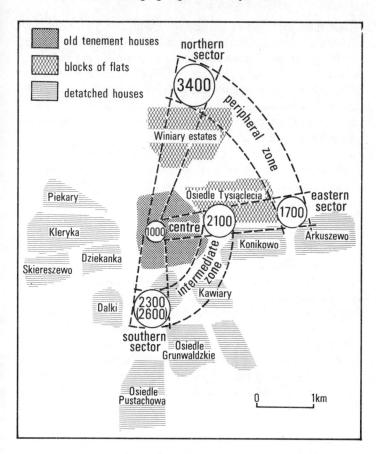

Figure 8.1: The spatial structure of industrial workplaces in Gniezno.

per cent of them being men). In the peripheral zone (with the newest industrial plants) — at least 2 km from the centre — two concentrations can be distinguished. In the northern sector industry provides jobs for 3,400 employees (of whom two-thirds are female), while in the eastern sector it provides work for 1,700 employees (three-quarters being male). In the immediate vicinity of the major workplace concentrations in the peripheral zone the largest estates of blocks of flats are being built. Hence residential construction and industry can be considered to have a kind of 'symbiosis'. In the case of the peripheral zone of the northern sector, the area of industrial workplace concentration developed earlier than the modern residential estate that has been built between this area and the centre since 1978. Thus, industry can be considered to be a factor facilitating and stimulating residential construction in the northern sector of Gniezno. The western part of the town with its single-family houses is mostly inhabited by craftsmen, professional people and owners of horticultural farms, and is devoid of industrial workplace concentrations. This spatial separation of industry and new single-family building becomes an ever more widespread feature of many Polish towns (the protection of this 'privileged' rich zone against the negative impact of industry).

Journeys to work within Gniezno were analysed on the basis of the residential addresses of the workers at the sixteen large industrial plants located in various parts of the town. The main residential areas were in the centre of the city and in the two complexes of blocks of flats built after 1960 (Winiary in the north and Osiedle Tysiąclecia in the east). The distribution of workers by residence-workplace distance varies with the zone of plant location (see Figure 8.2). Thus, in the case of plants located in the central zone (such as the Printing Works), over 90 per cent of the residential addresses are located up to 2 km from the plant, with the maximum distance not exceeding 3.5 km, whereas in the case of plants located in the peripheral zone (e.g. the Wielkopolska Footwear Plant 'Polania') the majority of the workers live from 1.5 to 3 km from work with the maximum distance of intra-urban travel being 7.5 km.

Commuting from outside Gniezno is declining in significance because of the diminishing attractiveness of industrial workplaces, and the difficulty experienced by non-resident workers in getting cooperative flats in the town. Several regularities can be noted about these journeys to work.

(a) The share of commuters in the total workforce of a plant is highly correlated ($r = 0.64$) with the level of wages.

(b) Poznań exerts a limiting influence on the intensity of this commuting which is reflected in the distinct asymmetry of its spatial structure (Figure 8.3). In addition, the old administrative-political boundaries dating back to the former Russian partition (from 1815 to the First World War) also continue to have an effect because there was a deliberate policy not to locate industry in the border zones. (Gniezno belonged to the Prussian part where locational policies were quite different.)

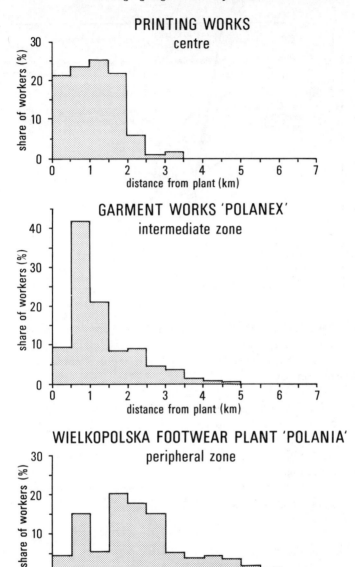

Figure 8.2: Distance travelled to work by the employees of three plants in different zones. In 1984 the printing works employed 383 (53 per cent female), the garment works 1,379 (88 per cent female), and the footwear plant 3,325 (72 per cent female).

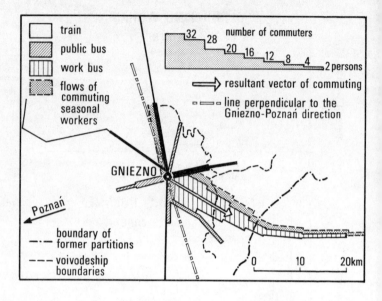

Figure 8.3: The influence of nearby Poznań and of former political boundaries on the spatial pattern of commuting to the sugar refinery in Gniezno. The plant had 286 employees in 1984 (18 per cent female).

(c) The average distance travelled by non-resident workers continues to decline (from 17.8 km in 1979 to 16.3 km in 1984).

(d) An increasingly important role is being played by the population of small towns while that of peasant workers is decreasing.

(e) The volume of commuting is determined by the frequency of the transport service (r = 0.58) rather than distance (r = 0.02).

Conclusions

These findings point to the declining role of industry in the labour market in towns and regions devoid of sectors and establishments at the upper end of the wage hierarchy, and having well-developed handicraft and agricultural activities. This conclusion also seems to have taken root in social awareness, as evidenced by the results of surveys conducted in Gniezno in 1983 among 600 industrial workers. These surveys aimed to elicit subjective estimates of

particular aspects of the national economy using three criteria —
the attractiveness of work in terms of professional performance,
earnings, and the amount of leisure time available. Of the nine
major economic activities distinguished, industry ranked last but
one in men's answers relating to earnings, and leisure time. This
negative evaluation of industrial work on the time-budget is
caused, among other things, by the discrepancy between
workplaces, places of residence and service facilities (which for
the most part are located in the centre of the town).

In the light of these opinions and findings, a thorough
economic reform that would include labour market mechanisms is
obviously and urgently necessary to overcome the economic crisis.
What is needed, in fact, is the creation of a dynamic — *sensu
stricto* — labour market, requiring the restoration of the self-
dependence of enterprises, the motivational function of wages, and
proper economic relations. Moreover, in a reformed system
industrial plants should be freed from the numerous social
functions, such as supplying workers with goods and services,
which should in fact be taken care of by other sectors of the
economy.

9

Spatial Implications of Unionisation, Employment and Labour Activism

G.A. van der Knaap and L. van der Laan

The labour market by necessity binds people. Within this market it is possible to improve one's circumstances on the basis of the processes of 'exit' and 'voice' (Hirschman, 1970; Lulofs, 1987). 'Exit' is an economic reaction of disappointed partners in the exchange process of labour and work; the exchange relation is broken off and one tries to find a transaction on better terms. 'Voice' is a political reaction: although there is some disappointment, the relationship is continued but protests are made. Because the exchange relation is maintained some 'actions of revenge' are not excluded against individuals (Birch, 1975). If the possibility of the exit alternative is small, which also means that the effectiveness of the voice is lowered, the possibility of retaliation increases. Under these circumstances the 'institutionalised protest' by means, for instance, of labour unions is an adequate solution to the threat. In addition, the collective action by unions has a regulatory function on the labour market: regulation substitutes for competition. Changes in supply and demand create uncertainty for both employers and employees, but collective negotiations try to lower this uncertainty by laying down the conditions of exchange for a longer period.

Labour unionism *as such* can have ambiguous effects on the locational behaviour of industry. In Western Europe close cooperation of institutional representatives of employers as well as employees may, within the framework of a neo-corporative society (see later), have a soothing effect on potential labour conflicts. Labour unionism then can be an attractive locational aspect, as was illustrated during the postwar period of economic recovery in the Federal Republic of Germany, sometimes referred to as the 'economic miracle' or the '*Wirtschaftswunder*'. Labour unionism, therefore, should also be analysed using another measure, the degree of activism. Both the extent of unionism and of labour activism greatly influence the locational behaviour of industry (van Kooten and van der Laan, 1987). In several European countries, such as Italy and France, the degree of activism has been an important influence on the process of industrial relocation (Dunford, 1979; Fuà and Zacchia, 1983; Tuppen, 1983; Cooke and da Rosa Pires, 1985).

An important factor for the functioning of trade unions is their socio-cultural position. In this respect the role of the unions in The Netherlands is based on three interdependent pillars. The first of these is the function of the unions within the postwar corporative social system. Capital and labour were supposed to have a shared responsibility for the development of the economy. Various legal institutions were erected on this starting point, such as the influential social-economic advisory board (SER). This harmony at the national level was copied at the level of the industrial sectors (Mok, 1985). The second is the principle of compartmentalisation: in different fields of Dutch society, social groups and institutions are organised according to their political and/or religious basis, where these are usually interrelated (see Goudsblom, 1968: 104-20). Therefore different labour unions came into existence: the most important being the protestant, catholic and social-democratic labour unions. In turn these are represented in the corporative structure mentioned above.

The third is the degree of participation in the unions by the labour force. The level of unionism as reflected in the relative membership differs between regions (discussed later) and also by economic sector. In l985, with a national average of 29 per cent, high levels of unionism were to be found in civil services (43 per cent), the building industry (42 per cent), transport (41 per cent) and particularly education (56 per cent). Farming and manufacturing had an intermediate degree of unionism with 32 and 31 per cent respectively. Low levels of unionism existed in trade (7 per cent) and banking (8 per cent) (The Netherlands, Centraal Bureau voor de Statistiek, 1985).

One of the most important functions of the unions is the representation of the labour force in collective bargaining. This results in a collective labour agreement (CAO). Most of the labour force is tied to one of the 700 agreements (see Reijnaerts, 1983). The agreement not only embraces the union members but, by means of the possibility of 'general alignment' by the Minister of Social Affairs, also the workers who are not organised. This possibility is used quite frequently. Another important feature of the Dutch situation is also the absence of the 'closed shop system' so well known in the United Kingdom and the establishment in the labour laws of the 'right to work'.

Some Determining Aspects of Labour Unionism

Before analysing the empirical spatial pattern of unionism, it is appropriate to comment on the causal aspects of this variation in space (van der Laan, 1987). The participation of the working population in labour unions depends on several interrelated circumstances. These include concentration of the employment (large-scale versus small-scale industries), their recognition by employers and government, and some specific spatial aspects such as the degree of urbanisation and the character of the region (Moore and Newman, 1975; Clegg, 1976; Visser, 1985; van der Laan, 1987). Besides these three factors, unionism is influenced by the level of employment in relation to the business cycle and the gender and sectoral composition of the workforce. However, the causes themselves are often simultaneously affected by the level of unionism. The business cycle, for instance, influences the growth of union membership but is itself affected by this growth (Booth, 1983). These two-sided effects can also be noticed in relation to the factor 'composition of the labour force' (Bain and Elsheikh, 1979, 1982).

These main causes can be summarised briefly. The first, the concentration of employment, concerns the size of firms, establishments and divisions. The greater the production, the higher the degree of organisation required but this is not a linear relationship (Elsheikh and Bain, 1980). The second, recognition, concerns the interest attached by employers to trade unionism. Government activities may strongly influence this recognition. The compulsory introduction of work councils or the existence of anti-union legislation (such as the 'right to work' laws in the US) are examples. The aspect of recognition is often placed within the framework of the 'neo-corporative society' in which there is close cooperation between institutions representing different interest groups. The direction in which industrial relations will move and, in the shorter term, the conditions of employment, depend on the bargaining process. For example, to obtain long periods of stable wages and employment all the interest groups concerned are supposed to have a true representative role. A high level of unionism will enhance such representation in the interest of all parties. The spatial differentiation in the degree of neo-corporatism will largely influence the regional pattern of labour and social conflicts (Buck, 1979).

The third main cause relates to two explicit regional aspects: the degree of urbanisation and specific territorial characteristics. The level of unionism is expected to correspond positively with urbanised areas as 'small firms and small towns are more difficult and costly to organize . . .' (Moore and Newman, 1975:437). The influence of the territorial characteristics cannot be pointed out unambiguously as the cultural standards in specific regions may positively or negatively influence the degree of unionism.

The level of employment, or more comprehensively the business cycle, also has some specific effects on unionism. Generally, labour unions have a pro-cyclic growth pattern (Arts, 1985; Visser, 1985). Bain and Elsheikh (1976, 1982) tested an econometric model of union growth in Great Britain, Australia, Sweden and the US. Within the framework of the business cycle, three variables — some with a time-lag — were particularly important in explaining the changes in unionism.

(a) The rise of consumer prices had a positive effect on the level of participation. In this process the labour union is seen as a means to withstand the threat of growing costs of living. In a recession period, with prices going down, this function is supposed to be less important.

(b) The rise of wages has the same effect as the price fluctuations. Unions get a 'reward' for their efforts.

(c) The level of unemployment has a somewhat ambiguous effect. It depends on the specific function of the union in an unemployment phase. If labour unions have a broad array of services in this phase (also in a formal judicial sense, as in Belgium and Denmark: Martens, 1985), it will act as a premium to be a member. Commonly, however, a rising level of unemployment is associated with a lower union membership.

The last main cause for the variation in unionism, composition of the labour force, also has some sub-variables like the sectoral composition and gender balance. The changing structure of the economy leads to a rise of white-collar workers and jobs in the service industries, and the participation of females in the labour force is rising (van der Knaap, 1987). However, the causal effect of the composition of the labour force is ambiguous. In Table 9.1 the effects of the shift to white-collar jobs and the willingness of people in six European countries to join labour unions are made clear. Not surprisingly, the absolute growth was mainly caused by white-collar workers and thus mirrors the sectoral shift in these economies. The last column shows the extent to which the willingness to unionise was important for growth because increases in a specific recruitment pool, such as the service sector, can be 'compensated for' by a greater reluctance to unionise. Also situations of increasing willingness to unionise can be imagined. The growth of unions in Great Britain, Denmark and Sweden, in particular, was fostered by the greater propensity of white-collar workers to unionise. Since 1960, however, the willingness to unionise in The Netherlands and Austria has declined, the shift towards more white-collar jobs having meant a less than proportional growth.

This leads to the conclusion that changes in the labour force as such are not responsible for all the changes in unionism in the various countries; rather, much depends on the capacity of unions to attract white-collar workers. Indeed, empirical evidence suggests that union membership in various industries does not depend to any great extent on the relative proportion of blue-collar and white-collar employees (Elsheikh and Bain, 1980; Visser, 1985). The relationship between unionism and the composition of the workforce should, therefore, be analysed within the limits of circumscribed spatial domains.

This reservation also applies to the relationship between unionism and gender (Visser, 1985). The proportion of women in the workforce does not explain differences in the level of total unionism between countries, industrial sectors, and companies. None the less, in those countries with a high share of female labour (e.g. Sweden), the level of unionism of women is also high. The same pattern is true for The Netherlands although there a low female workforce participation rate is accompanied by a low level of female unionism.

Labour Activism: Strikes and Factory Occupations

Strikes are often taken to be an indicator of the level and

Table 9.1: The effects on union growth of the shift to white-collar jobs in six European countries, 1960 to 1980

Country	Per cent growth			Growth explained by shift in labour force (per cent)			Shift in willingness to organise (ratio)		
	T	B	W	T	B	W	T	B	W
Austria	11	–0.1	32	23	–7	83	0.90	1.08	0.72
Denmark*a*	82	23	198	37	2	122	1.33	1.30	1.35
FRG*b*	23	5	61	12	–7	61	1.08	1.14	1.00
The Netherlands	32	18	59	29	–1	80	1.02	1.18	0.88
Sweden	78	42	160	41	21	90	1.26	1.18	1.37
Great Britain	33	9	101	–0.4	–14	37	1.38	1.27	1.47

a 1960 to 1979
b 1961 to 1981

T = Total all unionists
B = Total blue-collar workers
W = Total white-collar workers

Source: Visser, 1985:23.

149

quality of industrial relations. This can be seen from two theoretical perspectives: the institutional and the neo-Marxist view (de Nijs, 1983). The former view, as supported by Ross and Hartman (1960), stresses the role of institutions in regulating conflicts which might lead to strikes. Unions have an important function in controlling these conflicts. Within the evolving society self-regulating initiatives will lead to formalised negotiating structures in which disputes are solved on a 'rational' basis. Differences between countries in strike activity are a result of differences in:

(a) the stability of the organisations: stable and older unions are better equipped to regulate potential conflicts;

(b) conflicts of leadership: several competitive unions will lead to more strikes;

(c) the relation between management and unions: recognition by employers and consolidation of the structure of negotiations lead to fewer strikes;

(d) the political activity of the employees: 'labour-party' influence, particularly in government, will press less hard for strikes (although this depends upon the particular political structure of the country involved).

On the basis of these factors countries can be classified according to the existence of a comprehensive institutional framework.

The neo-Marxist view, in contrast, stresses the basic causal function of the production relations. These differ between countries and regions, as does the derived strategy of the elements (classes) involved. There is no evolution to a specific stable situation as was supposed by the institutionalists. The level of strike activity is based on the industrial infrastructure within which three dimensions are important, the first two being the degree of industrial and organisational complexity. These should, in turn, be placed within the third dimension: the framework of the development of (industrial) society (Ingham, 1974). Less concentration, highly specialised product making and complex production processes will hinder the development of large, central interest groups. Therefore the regulating power of unions in society will be small. This results, in the neo-Marxist opinion, in a high volume of strikes.

Some Marxist writers, like Hibbs (1978), do not stress the institutional framework, but much more the political dimension, with the level of strike activity depending on the influence of labour parties. This particularly leads to an extension of the public sector which, in turn, will reduce the number of strikes. Korpi and Shalev (1979) have an analogous view with the possibility of exchange of union and political power: the greater the opportunity for political exchange, the lower will be the frequency of strikes. Table 9.2 summarises the main theoretical findings in explaining the (in this case, low) level of strike activity, as in The Netherlands.

Strikes and factory occupations (sit-ins, work-ins) can be seen as two forms of labour activism. Both attempt to harm the employer in such a way that he is forced to meet the demands of the employees. In the 1970s, however, a change in the attitudes towards strikes occurred. Because of the deteriorating economic situation and structural economic changes, employment had to be terminated in many establishments and hence a strike would have had no detrimental effect on the employer. Indeed, factories could be closed even faster and at less cost. Then factory occupation methods were used, and these had some important advantages (Smit and Visser, 1986):

(a) control of the machinery and stock is improved;
(b) 'black-legs' can be kept out more easily;
(c) the chance of violent escalations is lessened;
(d) solidarity among the employees is often improved;
(e) political sympathy is more easily gained.

During the 1970s factory occupations became a common phenomenon in Western Europe, even in countries like The Netherlands and the Federal Republic of Germany where they were previously unknown. They were often aimed against collective dismissals resulting from closures and reorganisations of industries. Thus, there is a correlation between the business cycle and the frequency of factory occupations which increases during recessions (Visser, 1986). Other factors apart from the business cycle that have proved to be important are listed in Table 9.3.

The form of labour activism chosen depends on several considerations. Generally, however, a shift in labour activism has occurred during the last decade as a result of interrelated developments in the economic system of Western countries which are changing the power structure: these include the introduction of new techniques, the emergence of flexible labour relations and the

151

Table 9.2: Theoretical views on (a low) strike activity

INSTITUTIONAL APPROACH

Ross and Hartman (1960)

* strongly centralised bargaining structures
* stable labour unions
* centralised labour unions
* little communist influence on labour unions
* mutual recognition of unions and employers as being equal partners
* institutionalised participation in national socio-economic policy making
* participation of labour-orientated party in government
* extensive commitment of government with industrial relations

---

NEO-MARXIST APPROACH

Economic

Ingham (1974)

* relatively late in the process of industrialisation
* no complex and highly differentiated industrial structure
* centralised organisation structure of labour and employers
* centralised bargaining structure and institutionalised participation

Political

Hibbs (1978)

* participation of left-wing political parties in government
* growth of the public sector at the expense of the private sector
* shift of 'distributive struggle' to the political arena

Korpi and Shalev (1979)

* strong position of labour on the basis of:
  - high degree of unionism
  - sectoral unions united in federation
  - close cooperation of labour union and political labour parties
  - exchange of strike power with political power

Source: de Nijs, 1983.

Table 9.3: Some important factors at the emergence and at the extension of factory occupations

---

A. **Factors important at the *emergence* of the phenomenon**

    (1) company internal aspects   - the economic position of the company
                                    - the availability of action leaders
                                    - the degree of unionism
                                    - the attachment of workers to the company

    (2) company external aspects   - the economic position of the sector
                                    - the regional employment situation
                                    - the support of the labour unions and the government

B. **Factors important at the *extension* of the phenomenon**

    (1) the business cycle
    (2) the development of the industrial relations
    (3) the results of preceding occupations (including behavioural contagion)

Source: based on Visser, 1986.

internationalisation process (Delsen et al., 1986). Technological developments lead to a more heterogeneous structure of labour and hence to a differentiation of industrial relations and a greater orientation of unions to particular interests. Flexibility in labour relations is also emerging (van Voorden, 1985; Bos and Vaas, 1986). This arises because of the introduction of less rigid production methods which necessitate, for example, greater workforce versatility or the recruitment of temporary (often female) workers. This can greatly hinder collective labour actions. The internationalisation of production means that regional and national developments are increasingly being determined by circumstances on which labour unions have no influence, but proposals for the formation of a powerful international union have not yet led to any action.

On the whole these processes have resulted, in The Netherlands at least, in a shift from the traditional powerful organisation of a more or less homogeneous industrial labour force towards a defensive and relatively declining organisation with less power. This has led to a decentralisation of the collective bargaining process (Reijnaerts, 1985). In relation to the heterogenisation of the labour force, a more 'custom-orientated' policy of the trade unions has emerged, which 'means that from the perspective of the labour union, one cannot suffice in making collective agreements, but that also, and following naturally from this line of argument, activities at a local level have to be undertaken' (van Hoof, 1987:273). This also implies a regional differentiation of such activities. The tendencies towards decentralisation and regional differentiation mean that unions run the risk of losing their influence on the protection of workers' interests. Particularly in those activities and regions where union participation is low, strikes or sit-ins have a different character. Because of the differentiated and decentralised bargaining process, activism tends to be more spontaneous. Big, planned strikes organised by nationwide unions may give way to activism directed at specific group interests. During the past decade, for instance, most of the strikes in The Netherlands were unofficial in that labour unions did not at first organise them (Albeda, 1972; de Nijs, 1983).

Spatial Patterns of Unionism

Unionism shows distinct spatial variations at different scales. Because this chapter focuses on regional variations within The Netherlands, the sub-national level is accentuated. However, it is useful first to indicate the country's international position. Table 9.4 shows that the Scandinavian countries have the highest level of unionism whereas the level is much lower in France. In six of these ten European countries unionism generally rose between 1950 and 1980 but in Austria, The Netherlands, Italy and France it declined relative to the growth of the workforce. As a whole, however, the ranking of the countries showed no major shifts.

The Netherlands is among those having a moderate level of unionism and a moderate rate of growth. Figure 9.1 shows this growth and also the increasing divergence in union participation rates between the core region (Randstad) located in the west of the

Table 9.4: The degree of unionism in ten European countries, 1950 to 1980 (order by rank position in 1980)

Country	1950	1960	1970	1980
Sweden	67.7	73.0	73.6	87.7
Denmark	51.9	59.6	64.0	75.2
Norway	-	61.5	61.8	63.8
Austria	62.7	63.5	62.1	58.4
Great Britain	44.1	44.2	48.5	53.2
Italy	44.1	26.5	33.1	43.3
Federal Republic of Germany	33.1	37.1	36.3	38.7
The Netherlands	39.0	38.7	37.5	37.1
Switzerland	-	30.3	29.2	33.5
France	-	20.5	23.1	19.2

Source: Visser, 1985:20.

country, the adjacent intermediate zone to the east, and the peripheral zone in the north and south. After 1960 the level of unionism in the Randstad region stabilised while in the peripheral region it continued to rise.

This has had two effects on the regional pattern of unionism. The first is the growing deviation of provinces from the national mean: from a standard deviation of 2.8 in 1950 (the mean being 27.5) to 9.4 in 1981 (the mean being 43.3). The second effect is a shift from the areas with the highest level of unionism — Utrecht and Zeeland — in 1951 towards the provinces of Friesland and Gelderland, although the level remains still high in Zeeland. The area with the lowest level shifted from Drente towards Overijssel and South-Holland. Figure 9.2 shows the level of unionism in 1951 and 1981.

The Business Cycle and Labour Activism

Dutch postwar economic developments are fairly well documented (for instance, van Duijn, 1979; Bartels, 1980; Griffiths, 1981; Wever, 1985) so that only a brief summary of some major trends is needed here. Van Duijn (1977), for example, was able to describe the postwar period using long-wave models of the Kondratiev type. He argued that the fourth Kondratiev wave started about

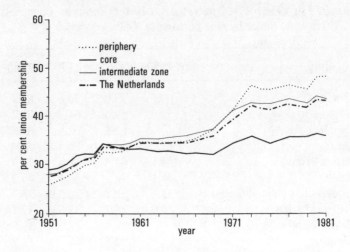

Figure 9.1: The degree of union membership as a percentage of the workforce in The Netherlands and in three sub-regions, 1951 to 1981. *Sources:* The Netherlands, Centraal Bureau voor de Statistiek, *Statistiek van de Vakbeweging* [*Statistics of the Labour Unions*], various volumes; *Statistiek van de Arbeidsvolume and Arbeidsreserve* [*Statistics of Labour Volumes and Surplus Labour*], various volumes; *Statistiek Werkzame Personen* [*Statistics of Employed Persons*], various volumes (The Hague: CBS).

1949-50 with economic growth being reinforced by the demand suppressed during the previous period and by the creation of the European Economic Community.

The first phase of economic growth started in 1950 and lasted until 1958, at the end of which was a small international economic recession in 1957-58. Immediately thereafter economic growth continued until the 1967 recession. Although growth rates continued to be rather high during the 1968-70 period, there were overtones of change. The growth then declined and had disappeared by 1978. Thus, in terms of the long-wave model, the 1967-75 period can be depicted as recessionary.

Income Development

Income per capita grew continuously after 1955 but the rate of growth was not constant, there being a noticeable change after

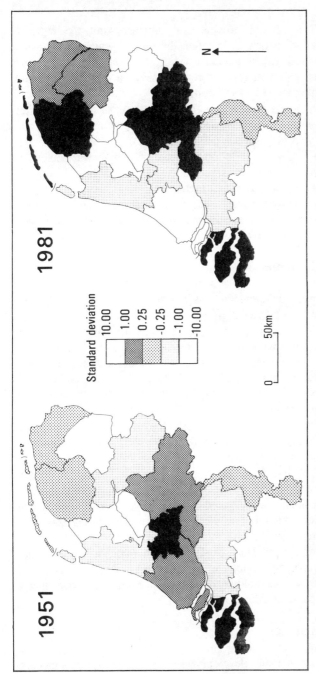

Figure 9.2: The level of labour organisation by provinces in The Netherlands (deviations from the national average) in 1951 and 1981. *Source:* The Netherlands, Centraal Bureau voor de Statistiek, *Statistiek van de Vakbeweging*, various volumes (The Hague: CBS).

1969. The rate of growth then increased but the regional differences in income distribution diminished which is indicated by the smaller values for the coefficient of variation. If annual rather than cumulative rates are considered, a more detailed and different picture emerges (Figure 9.3).

Income levels rose at irregular intervals, most noticeably after 1963 for a brief period and from 1969 to 1975 at a rather high rate. They showed very similar patterns for the core, intermediate and peripheral regions even though the rate of growth was somewhat less in the core where the level was higher (as described in van der Knaap and Erkens, 1982). In terms of income development, the 1967-75 'recession period' was very significant, but in general there is only a weak relationship between economic cycles and cycles of income growth per capita.

Job Opportunities

Such a weak relationship was not the case, however, for the pattern of unemployment growth nationally and regionally (Figure 9.4). The level of unemployment seems to have had a close correspondence with the minor recessions in 1957-58 and 1967-68. Yet the dramatic increase in unemployment occurred only after 1980 and not directly after 1975, even though the 1975-80 period experienced unemployment levels above those of the preceding twenty-five years. There was little difference in unemployment levels in the core, intermediate and peripheral zones although those in the core region were consistently lower throughout the whole period. The minor recessions of 1957-58 and 1967-68 had different regional impacts. During the former there appears to have been a strong regional concentration of unemployment, as is indicated by the large value of the coefficient of variation, but this was clearly not the case during the latter period when structural changes also occurred in the textile and mining industries. The post-1980 unemployment situation has been affecting all regions in a similar way. An analysis of the time-series of unemployment growth and change shows that a rather stable regional pattern emerged.

Labour Activism

Patterns of income development and unemployment can be

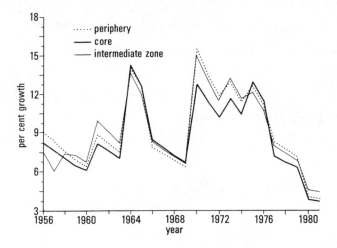

Figure 9.3: Annual growth of income per capita in three sub-regions in The Netherlands, 1951 to 1981. *Source:* The Netherlands, Centraal Bureau voor de Statistiek, *Statistiek Personale Inkomensverdeling Regionale Gegevens [Statistics of Personal Income Distribution]*, various volumes (The Hague: CBS).

compared with the two forms of labour activism, namely strike behaviour and factory occupations. Any collective action of workers which negatively affects production and does not have the approval of the employers is considered a strike (Flier and van Kooten, 1981:39; de Nijs, 1983:227). Strikes can be characterised in three ways: the intensity of a strike measured by the total number of workers on strike; the duration measured by the number of working days lost; and the localisation of a strike measured by the number of regions being affected. The latter aspect can reveal a degree of acuteness as an indication of severe social tension being suddenly released. Usually these will peak very high. The spatial pattern of strikes has varied both in intensity and duration. The strikes of 1960, 1973 and 1977 were rather general ones affecting the country as a whole, as evident from the small values of the coefficient of variation (see Figure 9.5) and the intensity of the strike. In contrast, the strikes of 1956 and 1970 had a more localised impact. Generally the strike pattern in The Netherlands has been a cyclic one with short periods of strike activity being

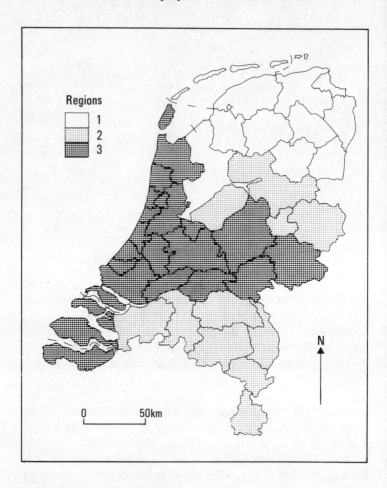

Figure 9.4: Three regions of stable unemployment in The Netherlands, 1951 to 1983. *Sources:* The Netherlands, Centraal Bureau voor de Statistiek, *Statistiek van de Arbeidsvolume and Arbeidsreserve*, various volumes; *Regionaal Statistich Zakboek* [*Regional Statistical Handbook*], various volumes (The Hague: CBS).

followed by longer periods of industrial peace. Large strikes characterise periods of labour unrest: from 1970 to 1979, for instance, the five longest strikes accounted for 75 per cent of all working days lost (Flier and van Kooten, 1981). In general the majority of strikes in The Netherlands have had a strongly

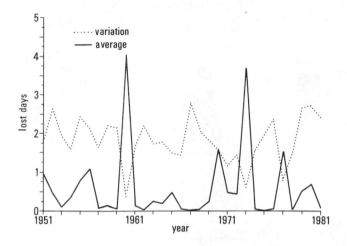

Figure 9.5: The average and variation of the length of strikes in The Netherlands in terms of the number of lost days, 1951 to 1981. [The average represents the percentage of the population, and the variation is the standard deviation divided by the average.] *Source:* The Netherlands, Centraal Bureau voor de Statistiek, *Stakingsstatistiek* [*Statistics of Strikes*], various volumes (The Hague: CBS).

localised pattern, with most occurring in the urbanised western part of the country (van Kooten and van der Laan, 1987).

A comparison of the temporal cycles of strikes and unemployment rates with their spatial patterns reveals an inverse relationship between the level of unemployment and the strike sensitivity of an area (Figure 9.6.) Thus, most of the strikes occurred in the urbanised core region which has consistently had a relatively low level of unemployment. One explanation may be that strikes occur where they are likely to be successful and hence economically powerful areas are more vulnerable to such action than economically weak ones, although as strikes have a national impact the latter will be affected too.

Earlier it was noted that growth in labour unions was procyclic, but judging from the cyclical pattern of strikes (as is shown in Figure 9.5) it might be hypothesised that these generally have an anti-cyclic character. This view is supported by the 1960 strike (post 1957-58 recession), the 1970 strike (post 1967-68 recession)

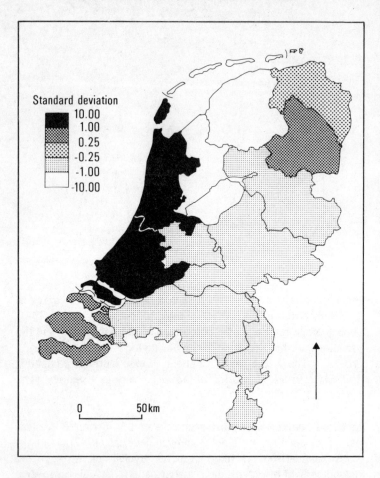

Figure 9.6: The relative number of strikes by provinces in The Netherlands, 1951 to 1981 (normalised data). *Source:* The Netherlands, Centraal Bureau voor de Statistiek, *Stakings-statistiek,* various volumes (The Hague: CBS).

and the 1977 strike (after the onset of the 1975 depression). When these strikes are put in a longer-term perspective of the Kondratiev cycles there is no support for Screpanti's (1987) finding that major upheavals tend to explode around the upper turning points of the long cycles. On the contrary, most of the strikes, measured by the number of lost working days, occurred in the post-1970 downswing.

The regional pattern of factory occupations in the 1965-82

period set out in Table 9.5 shows that these also tended to be concentrated in the western provinces of North-Holland, South-Holland and North-Brabant whereas Drente, Zeeland and Utrecht hardly had any. After correcting for the size of the working population it emerges that (apart from Drente) the more peripheral regions — especially Groningen but also North-Brabant — had unduly large scores for this type of activity. An important explanatory factor is the goal at which these occupations were directed. In more than two-thirds of the cases they were aimed at the preservation of jobs. Companies in declining sectors, like textiles and shipbuilding, were particularly vulnerable. However, Smit and Visser (1986) concluded that factory occupations in declining sectors did *not* concentrate in regions with the heaviest job losses but rather in those with only a moderate presence of such sectors. An explanation may be that the chance of success is a particularly important consideration (Shorter and Tilly, 1974). In other words, workers in stronger sectors or regions with some prospects of success are more willing to occupy their factories than those with gloomy prospects. In general, strike activity in declining sectors (apart from the textile industry) also shows this pattern (Smit and Visser, 1986).

Regional Patterns of Urban-Industrial Change

Current economic circumstances in The Netherlands, as in many other countries in the industrialised part of Europe, have been greatly influenced by three important developments at different spatial scales during the last thirty years. These are:

(a) strong industrial growth and deconcentration at a national level between 1950 and 1970 (cf. Keeble et al., 1981);

(b) the suburbanisation of a wide range of activities between 1960 and 1980 at a more local and regional level and also at the level of the firm (cf. Burtenshaw et al., 1981);

(c) a changing structure of production processes since 1970 which overlap and interact in time and space, and create new quantitative and qualitative demands for labour (cf. van der Knaap, 1987).

The period of strong economic growth and deconcentration was characterised by a change from labour-intensive to capital-

Table 9.5: Factory occupations by province, 1965 to 1982

Province	Per cent share of factory occupations	Per cent share of working population	Relative representation
	(a)	(b)	(a – b)
Groningen	8.3	3.8	4.5
Friesland	4.5	3.4	1.1
Drente	-	2.4	– 2.4
Overijssel	9.8	9.3	0.5
Gelderland	5.3	8.6	– 3.3
Utrecht	2.3	6.6	– 6.3
North-Holland	17.3	18.9	– 1.6
South-Holland	22.6	24.1	– 1.5
Zeeland	1.5	2.2	– 0.7
North-Brabant	21.6	13.7	7.9
Limburg	7.5	7.0	0.5
Total	100.0 (N=126)	100.0	-

Source: based on Visser, 1986:233; and on data from the Centraal Bureau voor de Statistiek.

intensive industries, an increasing scale of production and larger firm size, and a growth in the number of basic industries (Jansen et al., 1979). The consequence was a selective spread of mainly labour-intensive industries employing unskilled and semi-skilled labour from the core towards the more peripheral regions in the north and south. Although this did not always involve the physical relocation of plants, it reflected the relative shifts in the industrial composition of the national economy. Within the core region this has meant the expansion of capital-intensive industries using people with specialised skills and the eventual replacement of such activities by market-orientated services.

It has been shown elsewhere (Lloyd and Dicken, 1977) that the extent of labour organisation varies by industry class, with the least organised groups being those in commercial services. Hence change in the spatial structure of employment also influences the degree of organisation by particular sections of the labour force. Thus, it is important to recognise that this change occurs at a low spatial level of the firm and the city, and also that this is part of a spatially selective process. It is not sufficient to make a distinction simply between large and medium-size cities but it is also necessary to know the location of these cities and the industrial dynamics which govern changes in urban labour markets (van der Knaap and Louter, 1986).

The emerging pattern of spatial specialisation thus has considerable implications for the geographical organisation of labour. First, there is a strong growth in the weakly organised segments of the Dutch labour market. Second, existing geographical patterns are fragmenting and this may lead to spatial changes in labour activism. Strikes have previously been concentrated in the core region but there may be a shift of such activism towards the southern part of the country where industry will continue to be dominant and where the organisation of labour on traditional lines will remain relatively powerful. This trend is likely to be reinforced by the declining influence of organised labour on the economic activities in the core region and especially in its northern part, which experienced a strong growth in commercial services. Such changes may have an impact on the location and investment decisions of firms and operate in favour of the northern part of the core region where unions are likely to have a limited influence.

Conclusion

It appears that the level of strikes is positively associated with the degree of industrial concentration and negatively with the technical and organisational complexity of the firm and the degree of product specialisation. From this it can be argued that there is a change in the character of labour activism from strikes to factory occupations. The highest strike incidence can be observed in areas with relatively low levels of unemployment, particularly in the core region. Income effects are only weakly associated with strike activities and have, if at all, an anti-cyclic character.

Finally, the changing pattern of urban-industrial employment has an impact on the location of jobs and their future growth pattern. This in turn has consequences for the organisation of labour and the institutional reactions of these organisations in labour disputes. This will influence the spatial pattern of labour activism considerably.

In The Netherlands there is distinct evidence that new areas of specialisation will emerge which have concentrations of modern types of industry as compared with areas of producer-orientated services. These will have a different spatial pattern within the core region (Randstad) caused by the deglomeration forces; in addition new zones will emerge in the immediately adjacent areas creating a spatial separation of industrial and service activities. It has been argued that this will lead to a spatial specialisation within the core. In the southern part modern industry will be dominant, whereas the northern part will predominantly offer a range of high-order quaternary services. Thus, together with a marginalisation of industry in terms of employment there will also be a marginalisation of labour both economically and spatially. Together these may lead to a spatial marginalisation of labour activism and to a less concentrated and more diffuse pattern of industry.

10

Strategies in Local Communities to Cope with Industrial Restructuring

John Bradbury

Coping strategies are invoked by individuals, communities, municipalities, companies and the state during periods of rapid economic change, restructuring or recession. In effect, coping strategies become the mechanisms which articulate between the event of disruption and the resolution of subsequent events. Adjustments of responses and behaviour can take the form of individual action or, as the case may be, inaction; procedural action often takes the form of collective behaviour instituted either through formal or informal networks and institutional structures. These behaviour patterns can be in the form of protests, such as demonstrations or passive resistance; or they can be directed through existing social or economic conduits such as the union (if one exists), through local councils or through parliamentary networks. These can be regarded as protest actions which may be preceded or followed by self-help organisations or the restructuring of existing informal economic activities, such as cottage industries.

Strategies may be developed by organisations during periods of upswing and downswing — one purpose here is to analyse the various mechanics of these events in order to identify ordinary and extraordinary patterns of coping strategies. Furthermore, the attempt is made to tease out these events and establish some of the causal or trigger mechanisms which invoke or induce coping strategies *per se* and which result in some kind of resolution of conflict between parties.

The primary focus in this chapter is on the strategies of individuals and families in specific labour markets attached to manufacturing and processing industries. Where the strategies of individuals and families interact with those of companies and various levels of government there are differences in the level and intensity of the resolutions made. However, while the focus is on household and individual strategies these cannot be taken out of the context of corporate and government responses and behaviour. Each set of actors has different perspectives on its behaviour: individuals and households attempt to retain their capacity to reproduce themselves and to retain a surplus (Massey and Meegan, 1982; Gordon, 1984; Massey, 1984; Handy, 1985; Ford et al., 1986; Robinson, 1987). Companies attempt to restructure to retain their production facilities, to modify their labour costs and inputs or to find alternative sources of surplus value (Aydalot, 1979, 1983; Bluestone and Harrison, 1982; Gibson and Horvath, 1983; Newby et al., 1985; Scott and Storper, 1986b; Holmes, 1987a). The local state attempts to retain the equanimity of the living and work space under its jurisdiction and to expand or retain its local tax base — this may vary from place to place depending upon the viability of the municipal actors and the class position and perspective of the local state (Bradbury, 1984, 1985; Murgatroyd and Urry, 1984; Sawers and Tabb, 1984; Markusen, 1985; Clark, 1986a).

The major variation in this literature, starting with Massey and Meegan in 1982, is the concern first with the restructuring of capital and of specific firms: the recession of the 1980s then deepened, and in many localities whole sectors, communities and long-established industries declined or even disappeared in what is now often euphemistically called 'de-industrialisation'. This process left behind an abandoned social and economic landscape which is documented more clearly in some of the later studies referred to here. Much of the recent literature concentrates on the local and household scales, thus reflecting the depth and uniqueness of restructuring in many different localities.

All these actors may be in concert or in opposition because all have a perspective based on their own awareness of potential alternatives. Similarly, each has a different time horizon, according to the individual awareness of the problem and the possible action space available. The avenues open to each are unevenly distributed largely because of their position in the economic hierarchy of companies, the comparative power and status of individuals and the class basis of the state represented at the local level of the town and the community.

This chapter presents the results of a survey conducted in the labour-market zones of three non-metropolitan areas in southern

Quebec, Canada, in 1986 and 1987. The survey was conducted in Windsor, a pulp-mill town (population 5,200); Bromont, a high-technology town recently converted from a sunset textile industrial base (population 2,700); and Valleyfield, a mixed industry satellite town undergoing job losses and employment change from several declining textile and chemical industries (population 29,600). These settlements were chosen on the basis of their individual employment base, their distance from other settlements, and the potential access by the workforce to jobs outside the immediate area. Ninety respondents in each settlement were given three-hour interview schedules and questionnaires on the methods of coping deployed by individuals and households during periods of economic restructuring.[1]

What became clear in the preliminary assessment of patterns of coping in these settlements is that, overall, individual and household strategies apparently vary only a little during boom or bust periods. The major variation between groups such as white-collar and blue-collar workers lies in their potential to obtain access to different jobs if they are displaced, or to obtain retraining or relocation if they have access to facilities to assist them. In the case studies it was evident that human and corporate ingenuity has not been extended to devise wholly separate mechanisms for periods of expansion and growth and phases of downswing. In many ways people often deploy minor modifications of behaviour patterns in boom and bust periods and only the intensity and variety of operations vary. Indeed most personal or family strategies, as well as those of companies and the state, are largely concerned with expansionary strategies at almost all scales of operations from individuals to corporate institutions.

Corporate Coping Strategies

Within the international division of labour it is now clear that capital seeks new places for investment in both new and old industries by insertion into new communities or into older social

---

1   The total sample of 270 respondent households (N = 90 × 3) provides a valuable in-depth view of the population of the areas surveyed. The sample was not intended to be a classical statistical grouping. Instead, the author's preference was to seek qualitative data and to deploy these alongside secondary information and with both structured and unstructured interviews.

and economic fabrics within the existing urban milieu of small manufacturing communities. Or conversely, the sudden arrival of a new industry may create demands on a wider labour market thus drawing women or marginal workers into a new network. However, every industry appears to have individual restructuring behaviour despite the recognisable and generalised responses within the new international division of labour. Thus different communities may in turn be required to develop specific coping mechanisms and social responses to economic restructuring. It is therefore important to set a comparative research profile to shed light on the variants (Handy, 1985).

Comparative studies offer an opportunity to distinguish between coping behaviour in different sectors, regions and national spaces. The assumption here is that such studies will lead to a greater understanding of the mechanics of economic and social restructuring and to a better understanding of the new industrial geography and of the planning strategies needed to cope with regional and industrial change.

In downswings the tendency is for companies to withdraw from a range of operations and to concentrate on a system which will maintain essential services or ensure the survival of the individual or the institution. In some cases firms can manage to deploy capital in a counter-cyclical investment strategy but this requires forethought, planning and awareness, which are capacities not always available at appropriate times for corporations or individuals. This investigation has shown that, overall, capital has more strategies available to it than labour.

During downswings in resource-based regions or in single industry towns, such as those in these case study areas, various strategies may be deployed by companies to increase production, employment and exports. The overall strategy is to increase, or maintain, the flow of money into the local economy, and to increase the rate at which money can be retained there. The net flow of cash generally occurs through the external sales of locally produced goods; the accumulation of capital in fixed assets of machinery and buildings and production systems; and spending by governments, either through local investments or transfer payments to subsidies or direct production and employment networks.

Any increases in exports from a local area during a recession require an evaluation of the potential and competitive nature of the commodities produced. In manufacturing-dependent settlements competition may come from other export-orientated systems often with linkages to Export Processing Zones or lower-cost labour areas (Currie, 1984); competition between export-orientated systems can thus influence the viability of manufacturing sites or regions which do not have access to subsidies or cheap labour. To overcome these disadvantages, municipalities as well as higher levels of government may attempt to promote industrial expansion through trade delegations, or subsidies to encourage exports or the location of additional industries. Government subsidies form an important strategy in the Canadian context: under a number of projects and schemes the federal Canadian government has endeavoured to entice or encourage industries to locate, relocate and decentralise to areas which are 'underdeveloped'.

In smaller-scale economies, such as single-industry operations or small settlements, attempts to increase the inflow of capital may be directed towards the increase in production, and hopefully of sales, of the local commodity such as agricultural produce, or from mining, fishing or forestry (including logs and pulp and paper). When such an expansionary strategy has been deployed it is often accompanied by a tightening of local employment through residual rationalisation (resulting in lay-offs). Increases in exports are thus accompanied by structural problems related to the lowering of local employment and an intensification of local plant activity, which is quite the reverse of what may be desired. Furthermore, an expansion of exports may have other deleterious effects such as an increase in the drain-off of cash, or the flooding of an already sensitive primary materials market in which increasing numbers of commodities from similar areas are competing for a shrinking income.

A further method of increasing capital inflow into a local area, or at least to increase the amounts generated locally, is derived from the local state. Common strategies embrace subsidies, advertising, industrial park development and municipal employment. The industrial landscape of most small towns, at least in areas adjacent to major centres in Canada, and in other countries too, is never complete without an array of industrial parks and advertising claims as to the advantages offered by the local area. Municipalities invest in railways, roads, infrastructure and sign posts and expensive fences to enclose their enticing wares. All too often these areas end up as empty spaces or, at best, a half-filled and lonely collection of unlinked industries. During downswings this particular strategy is still invoked as a desperate measure to inveigle wary industry into the fold. On some rare occasions this is successful but usually such tactics merely increase the municipal debt load in a period of crisis because there is little to entice extra employment into local areas during a recession and few mechanisms within the law to force or help retain and capture earnings for spin-off development.

Local Initiatives During Recessions

There are some unique local initiatives that came to light during a recession which also enter the overall profile of coping strategies. Here can be noted the tendency for workers to become involved in small business in the *petite bourgeoisie* alternative; this of course is limited by available capital, credit and customers. Starting a small business is apparently easy, but keeping it operating may be difficult, depending on the will or mood of bankers and the availability of credit. Evidence suggests that small businesses started before a recession last longer than those started during it; this is largely due to the stress of the downswing and the tightening of credit. Despite these obvious limitations people swell the numbers of those trying out the restaurant business, moving into gardening and landscaping, or contracting on home building or small construction. The efforts required are huge, the hours long and the survival rate low. Nevertheless these areas of change and investment are an integral part of the survival landscape during a recession.

In some circumstances the moves towards alternative employment have a cyclical quality about them for there is an implicit recognition in many communities, especially those in mining or forestry, that boom and bust are as natural to life as bread and butter. Thus people recognise the patterns and the signs in the long-run and they seek either to sit-it-out, migrate for several years, or move into the small business sector. Alternatively in the short-run, and this is especially noticeable in industries which have both a cyclical as well as a seasonal character, people move to off-season jobs. In some regions a few alternatives are available for resource-based industrial workers, but they are few and far between and by no means universal. In Newfoundland and other parts of Atlantic Canada, for instance, such job interchanges have been a requisite part of living and rather than being a luxury these job mobility and flexibility arrangements are forced on the population (Staveley, 1987). Fishermen become part-time farmers, loggers become miners or farmers go to town or send their spouses out to work. Thus there is an apparent 'natural' recognition and reshaping of the family division of labour which matches the boom and bust as well as the cyclical side of economic and social life (Bradbury, 1984).

In certain areas where no expansion of the formal economy is possible people have turned to alternative activities and to the informal economy. Local exchange systems operate on the basis of the exchange of services for equivalents in 'local exchange currencies', variously named 'green dollars' or 'blackies'; or labour for labour equivalents. In the informal economy, in contrast, a new range of survival strategies has emerged in peripheral areas in Canada: women often take up the challenge to become primary earners and increase household production and to sell surpluses; cottage industries are developed to use household-based skills, such as knitting, child-care, or woodwork or sewing incorporating local produce; and communities dig deep into their roots to establish new networks of production involving trade and exchange and the sale of labour on a network of kith and kin (Mackenzie, 1987).

In the case study towns all facets of community activity have exhibited several additional elements of the coping strategies noted here, which in the wider framework are evidenced in the attempts to ameliorate the material conditions of life, to improve opportunities for employment, to provide jobs, to give succour during periods of economic downswing and unemployment and to facilitate opportunities for migration or moves to alternative jobs through retraining and education.

Case Studies: Social and Economic Coping Strategies

The very presence of a coping strategy whether it be at the level of the individual, the community, the corporation or the state, begs the question of what it is being deployed for. During periods of change, adjustment must be made by most levels of societal organisation, but this does not reveal the structural mechanisms which bring about modifications of behaviour. Nor does adjustment necessarily mean a positive or negative behaviour response. Rather what is sought here is the pattern of change which goes beyond simple adjustment to the reflection of underlying structural changes in the economy such as would arise during periods of rapid restructuring.

Some would argue that the differences in velocity of change are simply a reflection of a continual adjustment mechanism which is part and parcel of the human response to fluctuations in the patterns of capital accumulation. Without such adjustments capital cannot be continually invested, recycled and profits drawn from it. In essence this is a continually adjusting system in the labour market structures of most employment areas. Others would argue that the adjustment behaviour is simply a normative response for a return to a form of equilibrium in which regular adjustments will be made in order for progress to occur in a linear fashion. Fieldwork evidence suggests that the former explanation and behaviour response are more likely — given that deeper structural change will rarely return to any form of equilibrium and indeed that disequilibrium is more the norm. Table 10.1 shows the extent to which structural changes have occurred in the study area: job losses and gains are represented for each major employer and the structural changes are indicated in the extent and timing of lay-offs. The differences in this Table lie largely between those 'sunset' industries undergoing destabilisation involving closures and job loss, and those of a 'sunrise' nature which are fragile but more stable than those older industries such as textiles and chemicals.

In phases of recession and economic downswing the pace and intensity of coping measures must be increased because unemployment rates are higher, de-skilling and re-skilling are likely to occur, alterations in the gender division of labour are intensified and are likely to lead to social and family/household stresses. Changes in the locational patterns of employment can bring about reformulations of the family commitment of labour and dislocation can lead to regional reorientation of the labour-shed structures. Furthermore, the moves towards high technology in some regions have inspired changes in the social class structures of traditional white-collar and blue-collar areas. Rapid changes may also lead to new job searches for individuals in sunset industries displaced by sunrise industries. These searches often have a gender and age-specific profile in which the skills that are required may be selective in terms of the characteristics of the individual workers required; furthermore, cheaper labour often implies a female or youthful workforce.

In other circumstances the industry located in an area may 'demand' certain 'concessions' from labour to the extent that wages may be drastically cut, working hours changed, individuals 'laid off' and new and multiple skills required: a whole new social contract can be demanded by capital. This is capital's coping strategy in the face of more general economic restructuring, competition and recession, but it places considerable stress on the existing social fabric of the working-class members of a community and requires adaptation, change and coping strategies on the part of the workforce. Such drastic changes also produce a ripple effect in the employed, the sometimes-employed and the unemployed members of a community. Unfortunately, while new job profiles may be opened up for some individuals, they become cut off and erased for others.

Bromont: A High-Technology Centre

Adjustment *per se* means that labour must be continuously available and at hand. Both new and old workers must be increasingly flexible during periods of economic downswing and recession. Where new labour requirements become apparent in the employment profile of a firm or a region, labour must be sufficiently fluid to fit the needs of industry. The requirements vary from place to place and from time to time. New skills must be developed by the existing workforce or workers imported into the area. Such moves during rapid periods of restructuring result in spatially and sectorally defined class conflict. Where displacement occurs, regional resentments may result in social ruptures and in new social fractions on the social landscape. In other instances social insertions can occur side by side with replacements. This particular mix, noted in Bromont, results in new zones of older blue-collar workers torn from their previous place of residence and put together with new white-collar high-tech workers. The older workers in this situation are required to pick up new skills, re-educate themselves by attending night school, move their place of residence or commute considerable distances.

This constellation of social forces has resulted in Bromont's becoming fractured spatially and socially by the insertion of three non-union high-technology firms into a small town which had previously been a quiet country village and where the major blue-collar work was in the region's textile and woodworking

Table 10.1: Job loss and gain among major employers in Bromont, Valleyfield and Windsor, Quebec Province

Employers	Plant employees			Net change	Rank by total employees (Quebec)		Rank by revenue[a] 1986
	1985	1986	1987		1985	1986	1986
BROMONT							
Canadian General Electric (jet fans)	405	473	504	+ 99	28	29	32
IBM (hybrid chips)[b]	1,350	1,500	1,500	+ 150	33	38	19
Mitel (chips)	510	214	238	– 272	n.d.	n.d.	n.d.
VALLEYFIELD							
Expro (explosives)[c]	720	600	430	– 290	92	98	214
Zinc Electrolytique Canada (NORANDA GROUP) (zinc, cadmium)	605	600	560	– 45	14	14	18
Dominion Textile (textiles)							
Beauharnois plant	460	350	350	– 110	15	19	48
Salaberry plant	[d]	212	261	[e]	-	-	-
WINDSOR							
DOMTAR (pulp and paper)[f]	786	720	600	– 186	17	17	26
Jack Spratt (garments)[g]	158	164	150	– 8	140	152	306

footnotes to Table 10.1

a   Ranked according to corporate revenue in Quebec in 1986.

b   IBM has a policy of no lay-offs of full-time workers (75 per cent of those employed in the plant); part-time workers and subcontractors are deployed extensively.

c   Plant closed for a six-week period in 1987; complete lay-off of the workforce.

d   Plant closed.

e   No real change: all workers were recalled.

f   DOMTAR will lay off another 200 workers by 1988 as plant modernisation is completed.

g   Figures do not indicate temporary lay-offs.

Sources: Scott's Directories of Quebec Manufacturers; Ministère de l'Industrie, Commerce et Tourisme: Inventaires Industrielles; personal communications with plant personnel officers; *Les Affaires*, Cahier Spécial, 13 June 1987.

industries. These new plants thus resulted in a particular coping strategy on the part of the local workforce. In the face of the possibility of their being completely replaced by imported workers they have adjusted by re-skilling. Nevertheless there are workers who do not come from the local area: these are the technical and engineering workers with Business Management and Technical University degrees who form in effect a cultural and class enclave. Interestingly, they adjust to the 'quieter' country life by internal social mixing, by occasional (sometimes regular) sojourns in the city of Montreal or by participation in local recreational activities.

Windsor: A Pulp-Mill Town

The channels in which strategies are available are circumscribed by the apparent isolation of the workplace and the community. In Windsor, distance from available opportunities is a real barrier which people attempt to overcome. However, distance from other employment opportunities has both a spatial and a cultural or a class meaning. In this particular settlement the main industry is a major pulp mill which employs more than half the local workforce and on which a large proportion of household incomes depends. The skill needs are very specific and there is little chance of alternative skills and jobs being developed. The town is essentially a blue-collar settlement with some technical and white-collar staff attached to the mill and to ancillary employment. Thus the job chances of local people are circumscribed by the upswings and downswings in the mill.

Furthermore, there are few opportunities for women of all ages in the pulp and paper industry. The very presence of the dominant industry for more than eighty years has created a patriarchal and paternalistic social climate. The social threads of the community and the job opportunities are dominated by the corporate hierarchy and by the social and technical division of labour derived from the pulp mill located adjacent to the centre of the town. Indeed the physical presence of the plant creates an air of domination by a patriarchal system. Job prospects for women married or related to white-collar mill workers or to management are probably higher than for others, but few if any female process-workers are employed. This situation has spawned a range of coping strategies for some women, and placed severe limitations on the opportunities and the range of strategies of others. In the first instance some women, generally the spouses of mill workers, have moved into commercial opportunities and run restaurants, corner stores, grocery stores and small retail outlets — presumably with some financial connections through family networks to spouses. There is some evidence to suggest that this may be a more general trend in smaller settlements and in cities as well.

Women have tried to move away from the town but find that the distance of space and culture sometimes blurs their vision of job opportunities elsewhere. As a result some attempt to improve their skills and employment status by attending night school. In other instances low educational levels provide a barrier which both designates the type of work they can get and the location of the jobs in town or elsewhere. The only other 'major' employer in the town is a clothing factory which largely employs women; this is the only kind of job opportunity for young women and many, whilst finding it as the only place of work, are also trapped by it. The chances of mobility are low and the opportunities to acquire new skills and hence, external jobs, are limited.

In a sense the jobs both men and women do are a form of capture of the local pool of labour and, as such, particular and unique coping strategies are required. Many individuals rarely break out of this captive status and single-enterprise settlements of this nature become stagnant in terms of the types of opportunities available: the major incentive is to migrate but this is limited during periods of more general recession. Single-industry communities continue to exist in Canada but they are especially vulnerable during a recession. Such communities are politically and economically isolated, constituting reserve labour pools that are 'integrated' only within the specialised logic of an individual, corporate plan whose directives may be derived externally and whose imperative is based on multinational operations (Clark-Jones, 1987: 83).

At the same time, the stress of possible closure of the pulp mill generated an internal dynamic in the community in the late 1970s to overcome the dependence on this operation and to diversify the local economic base. Mill workers and other members of the community formed a limited liability company in 1978 to promote the town's image, to invite extra industry to the town, to boost tourism and to diversify the local industrial base (Dussault, 1985). Spurred on by the pulp mill company's comments that 'closure was imminent' workers paid $Can2 per week into the community chest which by 1987 had risen to over $Can250,000. The committee of this organisation consists of skilled mill workers, municipal councillors and a representative of the local industrial commissioner's office. Clearly the size of the committee's operations does not represent a viable alternative source of investment for industrial expansion or diversification, nor is there a clear plan in the community about what path development could or should take; the organisation has thus become a form of booster for the local townsite which promotes linkages, cultural events and awareness in the community.

Valleyfield: A Mixed Industry Settlement

At the other end of the scale from the single-industry towns there are communities which are multiple-enterprise and whose economic base is dominated by heavy industry, processing and sunset industries. Such is the case of the third settlement, Valleyfield, which is near Montreal and is an outer industrial satellite with more than 100 years as a heavy and medium-manufacturing area (Table 10.2). Recently these sunset industries came under increasing pressure; some strategic closures occurred, job displacements took place, and outright lay-offs and long-term unemployment ensued. A wide range of coping strategies has been deployed by both the companies and the workforce, many being defined by immediate needs of unemployment for families and rapid and traumatic restructuring for employers. Short and long-term closures in the textile mills located at Valleyfield were a response to rationalisation at the continental level by the parent firm. In the case of metal-processing industries closures took place because of a downswing in the international usage of their output. In the case of a rubber products and tyre making firm, slowdowns in production and short-term closures took place as a result of a rationalisation programme by a parent American firm.

The companies cope in such circumstances by traditional methods of rationalisation involving a wide range of cost-cutting, labour-reducing and saving techniques. Some actions are at the behest of foreign owners who make decisions which may be rational for their multinational activities but apparently irrational for a local firm operating at an apparently profitable and efficient level. One firm closed several of its factories and gentrified some of its premises and converted them into warehouses. Other firms simply close, sell up and move out.

The firms also call upon the local, regional and national levels of the state for assistance or for legitimation of their rationalisation

Table 10.2: Principal activities of the production workforce in Bromont, Valleyfield and Windsor, 1981 (per cent)

Activities	Total	Males	Females
BROMONT			
Office machinery, supplies	50.0	59.1	31.4
Telecommunication equipment	10.0	7.2	17.4
Clothing	6.1	-	17.4
Agriculture, fishing, lumbering	4.6	5.6	-
Construction and public works	4.2	5.6	-
Other	25.1	22.5	33.8
	100.0	100.0	100.0
VALLEYFIELD			
Rubber and plastics	8.9	14.0	0.5
Textiles	7.8	8.6	6.5
Metal processing	6.0	1.0	0.8
Food and beverages	3.6	4.2	2.5
Chemicals excluding pharmaceuticals	5.2	5.2	1.0
Construction and public works	5.2	7.9	0.8
Other	63.3	59.1	87.9
	100.0	100.0	100.0
WINDSOR			
Pulp and paper	43.4	52.2	14.5
Clothing	12.6	2.4	32.8
Agriculture, fishing, lumbering	4.5	5.7	-
Metal processing	1.4	1.9	-
Construction and public works	2.7	3.2	-
Other	35.4	34.6	52.7
	100.0	100.0	100.0

Source: Statistics Canada, 1981: special tabulations.

programmes. Both the provincial and federal governments in this present case undertook an assessment of impending closure programmes to try to control them and to find employment in alternative locations. Such measures have limited success, especially during periods of a more general recession. The provincial government set up a review board to examine the procedures in the lay-offs or the closure and consider the work and skill profile of each individual; the purpose is to find individuals or families who are willing to move, to find government programmes which smooth the transition in terms of skills or costs of relocation and provide bridging funds or social welfare.

The unions in this settlement fight to keep what they have and for what they have fought since the end of the Second World War. Older union zones such as this are increasingly coming under pressure to restructure, which in local terms often results in numerous social casualties. The unions are as militant as they can afford to be given the stringent measures the companies take during periods of recession and traumatic industrial change. The degree of militancy and class power exercised by unions varies from place to place depending on the history of class struggle and on the role played by the state. Canadian unions for the most part appear to have been able to hold on to more of their industries and community structures than have union members in the US where the more conservative political milieu, at least during the last five years, has undermined local and union solidarity by creating greenfield industrial sites and deliberately relocating in areas with fewer unions or where the population has little or no record of union activity.

During the mid-1980s several strategic strikes occurred in this particular community. Conflicts lasting six months or more took place as the unions struggled to prevent loss of jobs, de-skilling, displacement and differential lay-offs. Several companies used long lay-offs ostensibly to retool, keeping the union members at arm's length in a strategic move to control the work process and the workplace before a scheduled period of wage negotiations. In these cases unionised workers wait out the period of lay-off, hoping and trusting that their jobs will once more become available when the plant reopens. In such circumstances workers rely upon union solidarity, social cohesion and blue-collar loyalty. In dire circumstances people sell off their property, including cars and furniture, and take advantage of government programmes for the unemployed. Some sell their houses and, through remortgaging and refinancing arrangements, purchase cheaper homes to avoid any losses of equity resulting from further financial collapse and the taking over of property by the banks (or other lending institutions). In other circumstances people deploy a 'wait-it-out' strategy in which they cut all their spending on extras and unnecessary items or luxuries and wait for the 'good times' to return. Such an optimistic sense, in fact, has a basis of pessimism to it for often the circumstances which generate 'temporary' lay-offs or unemployment are extended for unusual periods so that they become incorporated as a point of reference in working-class culture. It is here that the very basis of a flexible work pool waiting as a reserve army of labour is evident. Often lacking wider skills or without the capacity and opportunity to migrate or change their skills, this particular stratum of the working class becomes demoralised and ineffective as a political power. People may resort to the informal sector in which moonlighting is rampant and 'tax-less' transactions are common. Such activities are difficult to trace, except through participant observation techniques.

Conclusion

Coping strategies during a period of recession vary in accordance with the changes that are imposed on the workplace and on the workforce in any particular community. Obviously in a recession there is a greater need to develop alternative job strategies on the one hand and to maintain jobs and create additional or new ones on the other. What is apparent from this study, and absent in most government policy, or indeed in the academic literature, is an adequate understanding of the distinctive differences between industries, sectors, places and gender. The case studies presented in this chapter are an exploratory view but, none the less, point to some differences in the restructuring behaviour and strategies adopted by various communities and industries. While much more research is needed, such differences appear to be greatly influenced by class, gender and industrial sector.

The recession of the 1980s struck each of the communities in a different way largely based upon its location, its industrial base and its class background and experiences. Underlying this constellation of social forces, the restructuring imperative varies with the deeper structural components of the industry and its external linkages. The external pressures on a firm, whether they be generated in the branch plant, in the head office or derived from government pressure or business competition, exacerbate any difficulties which may be experienced at the local level. Local industries are thus transformed by a backlash (some call it a whiplash effect) syndrome which defines the context and the condition of industrial and other employment. At the same time, local labour must find new ways of coping with change whether it be in the plant, the office, the community or at home, and these changes are strongly felt during a recession.

The study has shown that people embrace strategies which will preserve what they have whenever they can. Innovative behaviour is limited to a few cases where people are sufficiently inspired or pressured to devote time and energy to working as individuals or within a community to help find new jobs or to manage without them — or at best cope with a smaller household cash flow. Community organisations such as the 'green dollar system' and the 'community booster chest' are the exception. Class differences in access to capital, credit and retooling strategies are the major variables in routes towards individual and coping strategies. The vast majority of individuals and families, at least in the working class, have little option but to wait out the bad times and hope for better ones. In some circumstances, especially in small towns and rural areas, community members, especially women, may resort to modified forms of occupations in the informal sector and to cottage industries. Further research is needed on this topic, largely to establish the extent of such activities and whether they are specially adapted for periods of recession or present at all times and only more obvious because of the declining rate of employment in the formal and wage-labour sectors. White-collar workers, however, have higher rates of mobility and a higher level of education which, on the surface at least, makes them more adaptable and employable in a wider range of jobs and locations. The state in some circumstances, mainly in strategic voting areas or ridings, constructs methods of welfare, retraining and relocation, but only if sufficient class and community pressure is placed on it. These strategies, too, appear to have a class bias depending upon the area in which they are invoked and the particular part of the community and labour force which is given assistance.

References

Aggarwal, S.C., 1985, 'MRP, JIT, OPT, FMS? Making sense of production operations systems', *Harvard Business Review*, **63**(5), 8-16.

Aglietta, M., 1979, *A Theory of Capitalist Regulation. The US Experience* (London: New Left Books).

Albeda, W., 1972, *Arbeidsverhoudingen in Nederland* [*Labour Relations in the Netherlands*] (Alphen a.d. Rijn: Samson).

Allardt, E., 1976, 'Dimensions of welfare in a comparative Scandinavian study', *Acta Sociologica*, **19**, 227-39.

Allen B.T., 1987, 'Microelectronics, employment and labour in the United States automobile industry', in S. Watanabe (ed.), *Microelectronics, Automation and Employment in the Automobile Industry* (Chichester: Wiley), 79-106.

Alonso, W., 1964, *Location and Land Use: Toward a General Theory of Land Rent* (Cambridge, Mass.: Harvard University Press).

Althauser, R.P. and Kalleberg, A.L., 1981, 'Firms, occupations, and the structure of labor markets: a conceptual analysis', in I.Berg (ed.), *Sociological Perspectives on Labor Markets* (New York: Academic Press), 119-49.

Altmann, N. and Bechtle, G., 1971, *Betriebliche Herrschaftstrukturen und Industrielle Gesellschaft* [*Business Dominance Structures and Industrial Society*] (Munich:Carl Hanser Verlag).

Altmann, N. and Böhle, F., 1976, 'Betriebsspezifische Qualifizierung und Humanisierung der Arbeit [Firm specific job qualifications and the humanisation of labour]' in H.G. Mendius et al., *Betrieb-Arbeitsmarkt-Qualification I* [*Firm-Labour Market-Qualification*] (Frankfurt: Aspekte Verlag),

185

153-206.

Altshuler, A., Anderson, M., Jones, D., Roos, D. and Womack, J., 1984, *The Future of the Automobile: The Report of MIT's International Automobile Program* (Cambridge, Mass.: MIT Press)

Arcangeli, F., Borzaga, C. and Goglio, S., 1980, 'Patterns of peripheral development in Italian regions, 1964-77', *Papers of the Regional Science Association*, **44**, 19-34.

Argyle, M., 1972, *The Social Psychology of Work* (London: Penguin).

Arrow, K.J., 1972, 'Models of job discrimination', in A.H. Pascal (ed.), *Racial Discrimination in Economic Life* (Lexington, Mass.: Lexington Books), 82-102.

Arrow, K.J., 1974, *The Limits of Organization* (New York: Norton).

Arts, W., 1985, 'Vakbeweging, conjunctur en ledenbinding [Unions, the business cycle and union membership]', *Economisch Statistiche Berichten*, 23 August 1985, 857-9.

Atkinson, J. and Gregory, K., 1986, 'A flexible future: Britain's dual labour force', *Marxism Today*, **30**(4), 12-17.

Averitt, R.T., 1968, *The Dual Economy: The Dynamics of American Industry Structure* (New York: Norton).

Aydalot, P., 1979, 'Le rôle du travail dans les nouvelles stratégies de localisation [The role of work in new location strategies]', *Revue d'Economie Régionale et Urbaine*, **2**, 174-89.

Aydalot, P., 1980, *Dynamique Spatiale et Développement Inégal [Spatial Dynamics and Unequal Development]* (Paris: Economica).

Aydalot, P., 1983, 'Villes en crise, marches du travail et regulations locales [Towns in crisis, labour markets and local regulations]', *Revue d'Economie Régionale et Urbaine*, **1**, 43-68.

Babiak, J., 1972, 'Opinia ludności wiejskiej na temat uprzemysłowienia powiatu konińskiego [Rural population opinion about industrialisation of the Konin region]', *Zesyzty Badań Rejonów Uprzemysławianych*, **52**, 112-25.

Baczyński, J., 1987, 'Jaka pozycja, taki zarobek [Like position, like earnings]', *Polityka*, **5**, 3-4.

Bagnasco, A., 1981, 'Labour market, class structure and regional formations in Italy', *International Journal of Urban and Regional Research*, **5**, 40-4.

Bagnasco, A., 1982, 'Economia e società della piccola impresa

[The economy and society of the small firm]', in S. Goglio (ed.), *Italia: Centri e Periferie: Analisi Regionale, Prospettive e Politiche d'Intervento* [*Italy: Centre and Peripheries: Regional Analysis, Prospects and Intervention Policies*] (Milan: Angeli), 84-98.

Bagnasco, A. and Pini, R., 1981, 'Economia e struttura sociale [The economy and social structure]', in Quaderni della Fondazione G. Feltrinelli, *Sviluppo Economico e Trasformazioni Socio-Politiche dei Sistemi Territoriali ad Economia Diffusa* [Books of the Feltrinelli Foundation, *Economic Development and Socio-Political Changes in Territorial Systems with a Diffused Economy*] (Milan: Feltrinelli), **14**, 3-125.

Bain, G.S. and Elsheikh F., 1976, *Union Growth and the Business Cycle: An Econometric Analysis* (Oxford: Basil Blackwell).

Bain, G.S. and Elsheikh, F., 1979, 'An inter-industry analysis of unionisation in Britain', *British Journal of Industrial Relations*, **17**, 137-57.

Bain, G.S. and Elsheikh, F., 1982, 'Union growth and the business cycle: a disaggregated study', *British Journal of Industrial Relations*, **20**, 34-43.

Bartels, C.P.A., 1980, *Regio's aan het Werk: Ontwikkelingen in de Ruimtelijke Spreiding van Economische Activiteiten in Nederland* [*Regions at Work: Developments in the Spatial Distribution of Economic Activities in The Netherlands*] (The Hague: Staatsuitgeverij).

Bateson, G., 1972, *Steps to an Ecology of Mind* (New York: Ballantine Books).

Becattini, G. (ed.), 1986, *Mercato e Forze Locali: Il Distretto Industriale* [*Market and the Local Forces: The Industrial District*] (Bologna: Il Mulino).

Becattini, G. and Bianchi, G., 1982, 'Sulla multiregionalità dello sviluppo economico italiano [Italian economic development in its multiregional perspective]', *Note Economiche*, **5/6**, 19-39.

Becker, G.S., 1957, *The Economics of Discrimination* (Chicago: University of Chicago Press).

Bell, D., 1974, *The Coming of Post-Industrial Society* (London: Heinemann).

Berger, S. and Piore, M.J., 1980, *Dualism and Discontinuity in Industrial Societies* (Cambridge: Cambridge University Press).

Berger, S. and Piore, M.J., 1982, *Dualismo Economico e Politica nelle Società Industriali* [*Dualism and Discontinuity in*

Industrial Societies] (Bologna: Il Mulino).

Berry, B.J.L., 1973, 'A paradigm for modern geography', in R.J. Chorley (ed.), *Directions in Geography* (London: Methuen), 3-21.

Berting, J., 1976, *Paradigmata, Sociaal Wetenschappelijk Onderzoek en Engagement van de Onderzoeker [Paradigms, Social Science Research and the Engagement of the Researcher]* (Rotterdam: Erasmus University).

Birch, A.H., 1975, 'Economic models in political science: the case of "Exit, voice, and loyalty"', *British Journal of Political Science*, **5**, 69-82.

Blackburn, P., Coombs, R. and Green, K., 1985, *Technology, Economic Growth and the Labour Process* (London: Macmillan).

Blackley, P.R. and Greytak, D., 1986, 'Comparative advantage and industrial location: an intrametropolitan evaluation', *Urban Studies*, **23**, 221-30.

Blaug, M., 1976, 'The empirical status of human capital theory: a slightly jaundiced survey', *The Journal of Economic Literature*, **14**, 827-55.

Blauner, R., 1964, *Alienation and Freedom* (Chicago: University of Chicago Press).

Bluestone, B. and Harrison, B., 1982, *The Deindustrialization of America: Plant Closings, Community Abandonment, and the Dismantling of Basic Industry* (New York: Basic Books).

Booth, A., 1983, 'A reconsideration of trade union growth in the United Kingdom', *British Journal of Industrial Relations*, **21**, 377-91.

Bos, T. and Vaas, F., 1986, *Flexibilisering & Segmentering [Flexibilisation and Segmentation]* (Utrecht: Jan van Arkel).

Boudon, R., 1984, *La Place du Désordre [The Place of Disorder]* (Paris: Presses Universitaires de France).

Bradbury, J.H., 1984, 'The impact of industrial cycles in the mining sector: the case of the Quebec-Labrador region in Canada', *The International Journal of Urban and Regional Research*, **8**, 311-31.

Bradbury, J.H., 1985, 'Regional and industrial restructuring processes in the new international division of labour', *Progress in Human Geography*, **9**, 38-63.

Braverman, H., 1974, *Labor and Monopoly Capital: The Degradation of Work in the Twentieth Century* (New York: Monthly Review Press).

References

Broadbent, T.A., 1977, *Planning and Profit in the Urban Economy* (London: Methuen).

Brown, L. (ed.), 1974, 'Issues in spatial diffusion processes', *Economic Geography*, **50**, 285-374.

Brown, M.A., 1981, 'Behavioural approaches to the geographical study of innovation diffusion: problems and prospects', in K.R. Cox and R.G. Golledge (eds), *Behavioural Problems in Geography Revisited* (London: Methuen), 123-44.

Brunetta, R., 1981, *Economia del Lavoro. Teorie e Politiche* [*Labour Economics, Theories and Politics*] (Padua: Marsilio).

Brusco, S., 1986, 'Small firms and industrial districts: the experience of Italy', in D. Keeble and E. Wever (eds), *New Firms and Regional Development in Europe* (London: Croom Helm), 184-202.

Brusco, S. and Sabel, C., 1981, 'Artisan production and economic growth', in F.Wilkinson (ed.), *The Dynamics of Labour Market Segmentation* (London: Academic Press), 99-114.

Buck, T.W., 1979, 'Regional class differences: an international study of capitalism', *International Journal of Urban and Regional Research*, **3**, 516-26.

Bultena, G.L., 1979, 'Public attitudes towards coal strip mining in Iowa', *Journal of Soil and Water Conservation*, **34**, 135-8.

Burawoy, M., 1979, *Manufacturing Consent: Changes in the Labor Process Under Monopoly Capitalism* (Chicago: University of Chicago Press).

Burtenshaw, D., Bateman, M. and Ashworth, G.J., 1981, *The City in West Europe* (Chichester: Wiley).

Canada, Employment and Immigration, 1986, *Automotive: Why People Count (Report of the Automotive Industry Human Resources Task Force)*, (Ottawa: Ministry of Supply and Services).

Caris, S., 1978, *Community Attitudes Toward Pollution* (Chicago: University of Chicago, Department of Geography, Research paper No. 188).

Cassetti, M., 1975, 'Le richerche sulla disoccupazione strutturale in Italia: sviluppi teorici e indagini empiriche [Researches on structural unemployment in Italy: theory and empirical studies]', in M. Cassetti, L. Frey and R. Livraghi (eds), *Le Richerche sul Mercato del Lavoro in Italia* [*Researches on the Italian Labour Market*] (Milan: Angeli), 51-66.

Castells, M., 1977, *The Urban Question: A Marxist Approach* (London: Edward Arnold).

Cawkell, A.E., 1986, 'The real information society: present situation and some forecasts', *Journal of Information Science*, 12, 87-95.

Cheliński, R., 1984, 'Etapowy charakter rozwoju gospodarczego w Polsce Ludowej [Staging character of economic development in People's Poland]', *Ekonomista*, 5, 25-42.

Christopherson, S., 1987, 'Production organization and work time: the emergence of a contingent labor market' (paper presented to the Association of American Geographers' Annual Meeting, Portland, Oregon, April).

Ciechocińska, M., 1973, 'Deglomeracja Warszawy 1965-1970. Wybrane problemy zatrudnienia pracowników zakładów deglomerowanych [Deglomeration of Warsaw 1965-1970. Selected problems of the employment of workers of deglomerated plants]', *Biuletyn Komitet Przestrzennego Zagospodarowania Kraju, Polska Akademia Nauk*, 80, 1-143.

Ciechocińska, M., 1985, 'Tendencje zmian standardów życia w Polsce w latach 1960-1981. Próba określenia rozpietości regionalny [Trends in changes of living standards in Poland 1960-1981. An attempt to define regional disparities]', *Przegląd Geograficzny*, 57(1-2), 15-34.

Clark, G.L., 1981, 'The employment relation and spatial division of labor: a hypothesis', *Annals of the Association of American Geographers*, 71, 412-24.

Clark, G.L., 1982, 'Rights, property, and community', *Economic Geography*, 58, 120-38.

Clark, G.L., 1986a, 'Restructuring the U.S. economy: The NLRB, the Saturn project and economic justice', *Economic Geography*, 62, 289-306.

Clark, G.L., 1986b, 'The crisis of the midwest auto industry', in A.J. Scott and M. Storper (eds), *Production, Work, Territory: the Geographical Anatomy of Industrial Capitalism* (Boston: Allen and Unwin), 127-48.

Clark-Jones, M., 1987, *A Staple State: Canadian Industrial Resources in Cold War* (Toronto: University of Toronto Press).

Clegg, H., 1976, *Trade Unionism Under Collective Bargaining: A Theory Based on Comparisons of Six Countries* (Oxford: Basil Blackwell).

Coase, R.H., 1937, 'The nature of the firm', *Economica*, 4, 386-405.

Cockburn, C., 1983, *Brothers: Male Dominance and Tech-*

nological Change (London: Pluto Press).

Cohen, S.S. and Zysman, J., 1987, *Manufacturing Matters: The Myths of the Post-Industrial Economy* (New York: Basic Books).

Commons, J.R., 1934, *Institutional Economics: Its Place in Political Economy* (New York: Macmillan).

Connerly, C.E. and Marans, R.W., 1985, 'Comparing two global measures of perceived neighborhood quality', *Social Indicators Research*, **17**, 29-47.

Cooke, P., 1983, 'Labour market discontinuity and spatial development', *Progress in Human Geography*, **7**, 543-65.

Cooke, P. and Rosa Pires, A. da, 1985, 'Productive decentralisation in three European regions', *Environment and Planning A*, **17**, 527-54.

Coombs, R., 1978, 'Labour and monopoly capital', *New Left Review*, **107**, 79-96.

Coyle, A., 1982, 'Sex and skill in the organisation of the clothing industry', in J. West (ed.), *Work, Women and the Labour Market* (London: Routledge and Kegan Paul), 10-26.

Craig, C., Rubery, J., Tarling, R. and Wilkinson, F., 1982, *Labour Market Structure, Industrial Organisation and Low Pay* (Cambridge: University of Cambridge, Department of Applied Economics, Occasional Paper 54).

Crozier, M., 1971, *The World of the Office Worker* (Chicago: University of Chicago Press).

Currie, J., 1984, *Export Processing Zones in the 1980s* (London: The Economist Intelligence Unit Ltd, Special Report No. 190).

Curtis, R.F., 1986, 'Household and family in theory on inequality', *American Sociological Review*, **51**, 168-83.

Cutler, T., 1978, 'The romance of "labour"', *Economy and Society*, **7**, 74-95.

Daly, P., 1985, *The Biotechnology Business: A Strategic Analysis* (London: Frances Pinter).

Davelaar, E.J. and Nijkamp, P., 1986, 'De stad als broedplaats van nieuwe activiteiten [The city as incubator for new activities]', *Stedebouw en Volkshuigvesting*, **2**, 61-6.

Davis, L.E. and Taylor, J.C., 1976, 'Technology, organisation and job structure', in R. Dubin (ed.), *Handbook of Work, Organisation and Society* (Chicago: Rand McNally College), 379-420.

Davis, M., 1986, *Prisoners of the American Dream: Politics and Economy in the History of the U.S. Working Class* (London:

Verso Editions).

Davis, M., 1987, 'Chinatown, Part Two? The internationalization of downtown Los Angeles', *New Left Review*, **164**, 65-86.

de Brunhoff, S., 1978, *The State, Capital and Economic Policy* (London: Pluto Press).

de Jong, H.W., 1985, *Dynamische Markttheorie [Dynamic Market Theory]* (Leiden: Stenfert Kroese).

Del Monte, A., 1982, 'Dualismo e sviluppo Economico in una economia periferica: il caso Italiano [Dualism and economic development in a peripheral economy: the Italian case]', in S.Goglio (ed.), *Italia: Centri e Periferie: Analisi Regionale, Prospettive e Politiche d'Intervento [Italy: Centre and Peripheries: Regional Analaysis, Prospects and Intervention Policies]* (Milan: Angeli), 44-83.

Delsen, L., Dercksen, W. and van Veen, A.P., 1986, 'De rol van vakbeweging in de komende jaren [The role of the trade unions in coming years]', *Tijdschrift voor Arbeidsvraagstukken*, **2**(1), 87-90.

Dematteis, G., 1985, 'Contro-urbanizzazione e strutture urbane reticolari [Counter-urbanisation and reticular urban structures]', in G. Bianchi and I. Magnani (eds), *Sviluppo Multiregionale: Teorie, Metodi, Problemi [Multiregional Development: Theories, Methods, Problems]* (Milan: Angeli), 121-32.

de Nijs, F.W., 1983, 'Arbeidsconflicten [Labour Conflicts]', in W.H.J. Reijnaerts (ed.), *Arbeidsverhoudingen, Theorie en Praktijk [Labour Relations, Theory and Practice]* (Leiden: Stenfert Kroese), 222-71.

de Smidt, M., 1987, 'A taxonomy of labour market theories — geographical perspectives' (paper presented to the IGU Commission on Industrial Change meeting, Rabka, Poland, September).

Dex, S., 1984, *Women's Work Histories: An Analysis of the Women and Unemployment Survey* (London: Department of Employment, Research Paper 46).

Dicken, P.E., 1986, *Global Shift: Industrial Change in a Turbulent World* (London: Harper & Row).

Doeringer, P.B. and Piore, M.J., 1971, *Internal Labor Markets and Manpower Analysis* (Lexington, Mass.: D.C. Heath).

Dohse, K., Jürgens, U. and Malsch, T., 1985, 'From "Fordism" to "Toyotism"? The social organization of the labor process in the Japanese Automobile Industry', *Politics and Society*, **14**,

115-46.

Domański, B., forthcoming, 'Public attitudes towards industry in Cracow and its region', *Bochumer Geographische Arbeiten*.

Dunford, M.F., 1979, 'Capital accumulation and regional development in France', *Geoforum*, **10**, 81-108.

Dunlop, J.T., 1957, 'The task of contemporary wage theory', in G.W. Taylor and F.C. Pierson (eds), *New Concepts in Wage Determination* (New York: McGraw-Hill), 117-39.

Dunlop, J.T., 1962, *Automation and Technological Change* (Englewood Cliffs: Prentice-Hall).

Dussault, G., 1985, *Quand le Milieu s'Implique* [*When the Community is Involved*] (Montreal: Les éditions de L'alternative).

Eckaus, R.S., 1955, 'The factor proportions problem in underdeveloped areas', *The American Economic Review*, **45**(2), 539-65.

Edwards, R.C., 1975, 'The social relations of production in the firm and labor market structure', in R.C. Edwards, M. Reich and D.M. Gordon (eds), *Labor Market Segmentation* (Lexington, Mass.: D.C. Heath), 3-26.

Edwards, R.C., 1979, *Contested Terrain: The Transformation of the Workplace in the Twentieth Century* (New York: Basic Books).

Edwards, R.C., Reich, M. and Gordon, D.M. (eds), 1975, *Labor Market Segmentation* (Lexington, Mass.: D.C. Heath).

Elbaum, B. and Wilkinson, F., 1979, 'Industrial relations and uneven development: a comparative study of American and British steel industries', *Cambridge Journal of Economics*, **3**, 275-303.

Elbaum, B., Lazonick, W., Wilkinson, F. and Zeitlin, J., 1979, 'The labour process, market structure and Marxist theory', *Cambridge Journal of Economics*, **3**, 227-30.

Elger, T., 1979, 'Valorization and deskilling — a critique of Braverman', *Capital and Class*, **7**, 58-99.

Elsheikh, F. and Bain, G.S., 1980, 'Unionisation in Britain: an inter-establishment analysis based on survey data', *British Journal of Industrial Relations*, **18**, 169-78.

Ester, P., 1981, 'Environmental concern in The Netherlands', in T. O'Riordan and R.K. Turner (eds), *Progress in Resource Management and Environmental Planning*, Vol. 3 (Chichester: Wiley), 81-108.

Filion, P., 1987, 'Concepts of the inner city and recent trends in

Canada', *The Canadian Geographer*, **31**, 223-32.

Finn, D., 1987, *Training Without Jobs: New Deals and Broken Promises: From Raising the School Leaving Age to the Youth Training Scheme* (London: Macmillan).

Fishbein, M. and Ajzen, I., 1975, *Belief, Attitude, Intention, and Behavior: An Introduction to Theory and Research* (Reading, Mass.: Addison-Wesley Pub. Co.).

Flier, H. and van Kooten, G., 1981, *Stakingen: Statistiek en Dynamiek [Strikes: Statistics and Dynamics]* (Rotterdam: Erasmus University).

Ford, J., Robinson, F. and Sadler, D., 1986, *The Quiet Revolution: Social and Economic Change in Teesside 1965-1985* [A special report for BBC North-East] (Newcastle: University of Newcastle upon Tyne, Centre for Urban and Regional Development Studies).

Forester, T. (ed.), 1985, *The Information Technology Revolution* (Cambridge, Mass.: MIT Press).

Fothergill, S. and Gudgin, G., 1978, *The Influence of Industrial Structure on Regional Employment Change: A Shift-share Analysis of the UK Regions* (London: Centre of Environmental Studies, Working Paper 475).

Fredriksson, C.G. and Lindmark, L.G., 1979, 'From firms to systems of firms: a study of interregional dependence in a dynamic society', in F.E.I. Hamilton and G.J.R. Linge (eds), *Spatial Analysis, Industry and the Industrial Environment, Vol.1 Industrial Systems* (Chichester: Wiley), 155-86.

Freedman, M.K., 1976, *Labor Markets: Segments and Shelters* (Montclair, New Jersey: Allanheld, Osmun).

Friedman, A.L., 1977, *Industry and Labour: Class Struggle at Work and Monopoly Capitalism* (London: Macmillan).

Fuà, G., 1983, 'Rural industrialization in later developed countries: the case of northeast and central Italy', *Banca Nazionale del Lavoro Quarterly Review*, No. 147, 351-77.

Fuà, G. and Zacchia, C., (eds), 1983, *Industrializzazione senza Fratture [Industrialisation without Break]* (Bologna: Il Mulino).

Galbraith, J.K., 1967, *The New Industrial State* (London: Hamish Hamilton).

Garnsey, E., 1981, 'The rediscovery of the division of labor', *Theory and Society*, **10**, 337-58.

Garnsey, E., Rubery, J. and Wilkinson, F., 1985, 'Labour market structure and work-force divisions', in R. Deem and G.

Salaman (eds), *Work, Culture and Society* (Milton Keynes: Open University Press), 40-76.

Gibson, K.D. and Horvath, R.J., 1983, 'Global capital and the restructuring crisis in Australian manufacturing', *Economic Geography*, **59**, 178-94.

Giddens, A., 1979, *Central Problems in Social Theory: Action, Structure and Contradiction in Social Analysis* (Berkeley: University of California Press).

Giddens, A., 1981, *A Contemporary Critique of Historical Materialism. Vol. 1. Power, Property and the State* (Berkeley: University of California Press).

Glasson, J. and Porter, J., 1980, 'Power stations: their local socio-economic effects', *Town and Country Planning*, **49**(3), 84-7.

Glenn, E.N. and Feldberg, R.L., 1979, 'Proletarianizing clerical work', in A. Zimbalist (ed.), *Case Studies on the Labor Process* (New York: Monthly Review Press), 51-72.

Goldberg, M.A. and Mercer, J., 1986, *The Myth of the North American City: Continentalism Challenged* (Vancouver: University of British Columbia Press).

Goldstein, N., 1984, 'The new training initiative: a great leap backward', *Capital and Class*, **23**, 83-106.

Gordon, A., 1984, *Redundancy in the 1980s: The Take-up of Voluntary Schemes* (Brighton: University of Sussex, Institute of Manpower Studies).

Gordon, D.M., 1972, *Theories of Poverty and Underemployment: Orthodox, Radical, and Dual Labor Market Perspectives* (Lexington, Mass.: D.C. Heath).

Gordon, D.M., 1977, 'Class struggle and the stages of urban development', in D.C. Perry and A.J. Watkins (eds), *The Rise of the Sunbelt Cities* (Beverly Hills: Sage), 55-82.

Gorzelak, G., 1986, 'Quality of life: the regional perspective', in A. Kukliński (ed.), *Regional Studies in Poland: Experiences and Prospects, Studia Regionalia*, **1**, 172-96.

Goudsblom, J., 1968, *Dutch Society* (New York: Random House).

Graziani, A. (ed.), 1969, *Lo sviluppo di un'Economia Aperta* [*Development of an Open Economy*] (Naples: Edizioni Scientifiche Italiane).

Green, R.T. and Bruce, G.D., 1976, 'The assessment of community attitudes towards industrial development', *Growth and Change*, **7**(1), 28-33.

Griffiths, R.T., 1981, *The Economy and Politics of The Netherlands since 1945* (The Hague: Martinus Nijhoff).

Gudgin, G. and Fothergill, S., 1984, 'Geographical variation in the rate of formation of new manufacturing firms', *Regional Studies*, **18**, 203-6.

Habermas, J., 1984, *The Theory of Communicative Action. Vol. 1. Reason and the Rationalization of Society* (Boston: Beacon Press).

Hägerstrand, T., 1967, *Innovation Diffusion as a Spatial Process* (Chicago: University of Chicago Press).

Hägerstrand, T., 1970, 'What about people in regional science?', *Papers of the Regional Science Association*, **24**, 7-21.

Hägerstrand, T., 1973, 'The domain of human geography', in R.J. Chorley (ed.), *Directions in Geography* (London: Methuen), 67-87.

Hakim, C., 1987, 'Trends in the flexible workforce', *Employment Gazette*, **95**, 549-61.

Hamnett, C. and Randolph, B., 1986, 'The role of labour and housing markets in the production of geographical variations in social stratification', in K. Hoggart and E. Kofman (eds), *Politics, Geography and Social Stratification* (London: Croom Helm), 213-46.

Handy, C., 1985, *The Future of Work: What Jobs will there be? What will Life be Like? What Needs to be Done?* (Oxford: Basil Blackwell).

Hanson, S. and Johnston, I., 1985, 'Gender differences in work-trip length: explanations and implications', *Urban Geography*, **6**, 193-219.

Harrington, J.W., 1985, 'Corporate strategy, business strategy and activity location', *Geoforum*, **4**, 349-56.

Harrison, B., 1972, *Education Training and the Urban Ghetto* (Baltimore: Johns Hopkins Press).

Harvey, D., 1982, *The Limits to Capital* (Chicago: University of Chicago Press).

Herman, A., 1982, 'Conceptualizing control: domination and hegemony in the capitalist labour process', *The Insurgent Sociologist*, **11**(3), 7-22.

Hibbs, D.A., 1978, 'On the political economy of long-run trends in strike activity', *British Journal of Political Science*, **8**, 153-75.

Hirschman, A.O., 1970, *Exit, Voice, and Loyalty: Responses to Decline in Firms, Organizations and States* (Cambridge, Mass.: Harvard University Press).

Holmes, J., 1986, 'The organization and locational structure of production subcontracting', in A.J. Scott and M. Storper (eds),

Production, Work, Territory: the Geographical Anatomy of Industrial Capitalism (Boston: Allen and Unwin), 80-106.

Holmes, J., 1987a, 'The crisis of Fordism and the restructuring of the Canadian auto industry', in J. Holmes and C. Leys (eds), *Frontyard/Backyard: The Americas in the Global Crisis* (Toronto: Between the Lines Press), 95-129.

Holmes, J., 1987b, 'Technical change and the restructuring of the Canadian auto industry', in K. Chapman and G. Humphrys (eds), *Technical Change and Industrial Policy* (Oxford: Basil Blackwell), 121-56.

Holmes, J. and Leys, C., 1987, 'Introduction', in J. Holmes and C. Leys (eds), *Frontyard/Backyard: The Americas in the Global Crisis* (Toronto: Between the Lines Press), 3-22.

Howe, A. and O'Connor, K., 1982, 'Travel to work and labor force participation of men and women in an Australian metropolitan area', *Professional Geographer*, **34**, 50-64.

Hunt, A. and Hunt, T.L., 1985, *Human Resource Implications of Robotics* (Kalamazoo, Michigan: W.E. Upjohn Institute).

Ingham, G.K., 1974, *Strikes and Industrial Conflict: Britain and Scandinavia* (London: Macmillan).

Jackson, R.M., 1984, *The Formation of Craft Labor Markets* (Orlando: Academic Press).

Jaikumar, R., 1986, 'Postindustrial manufacturing', *Harvard Business Review*, **64**(6), 69-76.

Jałowiecki, B., 1982, 'Strategia uprzemysłowienia a proces urbanizacji. Studium socjologiczne [Industrialisation strategy and urbanisation process. A sociological analysis]', *Biuletyn Komitet Przestrzennego Zagospodarowania Kraju, Polska Akademia Nauk*, **119**, 9-118.

Jansen, A.C.M., de Smidt, M. and Wever, E., 1979, *Industrie en Ruimte [Industry and Space]* (Assen: Van Gorcum).

Jerczyński, M., 1977, 'Funkcje i typy funkcjonalne polskich miast [Functions and functional types of Polish towns]', in *Statystyczna charakterystyka miast. Funkcje dominujące [Statistical Characteristics of Towns. Dominant Functions]* (Warsaw: Główny Urząd Statystyczny), 20-117.

Jewtuchowicz, A., 1981, 'Wpływ zakładów przemysłowych na poprawe warunków bytowych ludności miejskiej [The influence of industrial plants on the improvement of living conditions of the urban population]', *Biuletyn Komitet Przestrzennego Zagospodarowania Kraju, Polska Akademia Nauk*, **115**, 95-166.

Johnson, J.H. and Zeigler, D.J., 1983, 'Distinguishing human responses to radiological emergencies', *Economic Geography*, **59**, 386-402.

Kahn, L., 1975, 'Unions and labor market segmentation', unpublished doctoral dissertation (Berkeley: University of California, Department of Economics).

Kaplinsky, R., 1984, *Automation: The Technology and Society* (London: Longman).

Kassenberg, A. and Rolewicz, C., 1985, 'Przestrzenna diagnoza ochrony środowiska w Polsce [Spatial diagnosis of the environmental protection in Poland]', *Studia, Komitet Przestrzennego Zagospodarowania Kraju, Polska Akademia Nauk*, **89**, 1-126.

Katz, H.C., 1984, 'The U.S. automobile collective bargaining system in transition', *British Journal of Industrial Relations*, **22**, 205-17.

Katz, H.C., 1985, *Shifting Gears: Changing Labor Relations in the U.S. Auto Industry* (Cambridge, Mass.: MIT Press).

Katz, H.C., 1986, 'Recent developments in US auto labour relations', in S. Tolliday and J. Zeitlin (eds), *The Automobile Industry and Its Workers: Between Fordism and Flexibility* (Oxford: Polity Press), 282-304.

Katz, H.C. and Sabel, C.F., 1985 'Industrial relations and industrial adjustment in the car industry', *Industrial Relations*, **24**, 295-315.

Keeble, D. and Wever, E., 1986, *New Firms and Regional Development in Europe* (London: Croom Helm).

Keeble, D., Owens, P.L. and Thompson, C., 1981, *The Influence of Peripheral Locations on the Relative Developments of Regions, Final Report* (Cambridge: University of Cambridge, Department of Geography).

Kelly, J., 1985, 'Management's redesign of work: labour process, labour markets and product markets', in D. Knights, H. Willmott and D. Collinson (eds), *Job Redesign: Critical Perspectives on the Labour Process* (Aldershot: Gower), 30-51.

Kerr, C., 1954, 'The Balkanization of labour markets', in E. Wight Bakke (ed.), *Labour Mobility and Economic Opportunity* (Cambridge, Mass.: MIT Technological Press), 92-110.

Kindleberger, C., 1964, *Economic Growth in France and Britain, 1851-1950* (Cambridge, Mass.: Harvard University Press).

King, A., 1986, 'Wheels of change?: labour and the organization of production of the automotive industry in Canada', unpublished M.A. dissertation (Toronto: University of Toronto, Department of Geography).

Knight, F.H., 1921, *Risk, Uncertainty and Profit* (Boston and New York: Houghton Mifflin).

Knox, P.L. and Cottam, M.B., 1981, 'A welfare approach to rural geography: contrasting perspectives on the quality of Highland life', *Transactions, Institute of British Geographers*, **6**, 433-50.

Kochan, T.A., Katz, H.C. and McKersie, R.B., 1986, *The Transformation of American Industrial Relations* (New York: Basic Books).

Korpi, W. and Shalev, M., 1979, 'Strikes, industrial relations and class conflict in capitalist societies', *British Journal of Sociology*, **30**, 164-87.

Kortus, B., 1985, 'Toward a more "humanistic-social" approach in Polish industrial geography', *Geographia Polonica*, **51**, 207-11.

Kortus, B., 1986a, 'An attempt to assess the role of industrialization and urbanization processes in the space economy of the Cracow voivodeship', in A. Kukliński (ed.), *Regional Studies in Poland: Experiences and Prospects, Studia Regionalia*, **1**, 225-60.

Kortus, B., 1986b. 'Spatial aspects of Polish crisis: spatial conflicts', *Folia Geographica, Series Geographia Oeconomica* (Kraków), **19**, 51-8.

Kortus, B., 1986c, 'The necessity of technological change in Poland: impacts and constraints', in K-H. Hottes, E. Wever and H-U. Weber (eds), *Technology and Industrial Change in Europe* (Bochum: Ruhr-Universität), 64-8.

Kozłowski, S., 1986, 'Poszukiwanie koncepcji ochrony i gospodarowania zasobami przyrody [Searching for a model of environmental protection and resource management]', *Studia, Komitet Przestrzennego Zagospodarowania Kraju, Polska Akademia Nauk*, **91**, 9-74.

Kraft, P., 1979, 'The industrialization of computer programming: from programming to "software production"', in A. Zimbalist (ed.), *Case Studies on the Labor Process* (New York: Monthly Review Press), 1-17.

Krannich, R.S. and Humphrey, C.R., 1983, 'Local mobilization and community growth: toward an assessment of the "growth machine" hypothesis', *Rural Sociology*, **48**, 60-81.

Krueger, A.O., 1963, 'The economics of discrimination', *Journal of Political Economy*, **71**, 481-6.

Krumme, G. and Hayter, R., 1975, 'Implications of corporate strategies and product cycle adjustments for regional employment changes', in L. Collins and D.F. Walker (eds), *Locational Dynamics of Manufacturing Activity* (New York: Wiley), 325-56.

Kukliński, A., 1976, 'Problemy przemysłu w systemie studiów regionalnych w Polsce [Problems of industry in the system of regional studies in Poland]', *Biuletyn Komitet Przestrzennego Zagospodarowania Kraju, Polska Akademia Nauk*, **93**, 100-8.

Kukliński, A., (ed.), 1986, *Regional Studies in Poland. Experiences and Prospects, Studia Regionalia*, **1**, 1-377.

Kukliński, A., 1987, 'Industrialization in Poland: experiences and prospects', (paper presented to the Japan-Poland Economic Geography Seminar, Tsuru University, Japan, March).

Labour Studies Group, 1985, 'Economic, social and political factors in the new labour market', in B. Roberts, R. Finnegan and D. Gallie (eds), *New Approaches to Economic Life: Economic Restructuring, Unemployment and the Social Division of Labour* (Manchester: Manchester University Press), 105-23.

Landau, Z., 1987, 'Etapy rozwoju Polski Ludowej [Development stages of Peoples Poland]', *Przegląd Historyczny*, **2**, 25-34.

Lane, T., 1982, 'The unions caught on an ebb tide', *Marxism Today*, September, 6-13.

Langlois, S., 1984, 'L'impact du double revenu sur la structure des besoins dans les ménages [The impact of double income on the structure of household needs]', *Recherches Sociographiques*, **25**, 211-65.

Lash, S. and Urry, J., 1987, *The End of Organized Capitalism* (Cambridge: Polity Press).

Lasuén, J.R., 1971, 'Multi-regional economic development: an open-system approach', in T. Hägerstrand and A. Kukliński (eds), *Information Systems for Regional Development — A Seminar* (Lund: Gleerup, Lund Studies in Geography, Series B, No. 37), 167-229.

Lazonick, W., 1979, 'Industrial relations and technical change: the case of the self-acting mule', *Cambridge Journal of Economics*, **3**, 231-62.

Leadbetter, C., 1988, 'Divisions of labour', *Marxism Today*, May, 19-23.

Lee, D., 1982, 'Beyond deskilling: skill, craft and class', in S.

References

Wood (ed.), *The Degradation of Work? Skill, Deskilling and the Labour Process* (London: Hutchinson), 146-62.

Lettieri, A., 1976, 'Factory and school', in A. Gorz (ed.), *The Division of Labour: The Labour Process and Class-struggle in Modern Capitalism* (Brighton: Harvester Press), 145-57.

Lever, W.F., 1985, 'Theory and methodology in industrial geography', in M. Pacione (ed.), *Progress in Industrial Geography* (London: Croom Helm), 10-39.

Lewis, W.A., 1954, 'Economic development with unlimited supplies of labour', *The Manchester School*, **22**, 139-91.

Ley, D., 1985, 'Work-residence relations for head office employees in an inflating housing market', *Urban Studies*, **22**, 21-38.

Ley, D., 1986, 'Alternative explanations for inner-city gentrification: a Canadian assessment', *Annals of the Association of American Geographers*, **76**, 521-35.

Linge, G.J.R., 1984, 'Industrialization and the household', *International Social Science Journal*, **36**, 319-39.

Lipietz, A., 1977, *Le Capital et son Espace [Capital and Its Space]* (Paris: F.Maspero).

Lissowska, M., 1987, 'Paryska konferencja na temat sterowania, cykliczności i kryzysów w krajach socjalistycznych [Conference in Paris on steering, cyclicity and crises in socialist countries]', *Gospodarka Planowa*, **1**, 44-7.

Littler, C. and Salaman, G., 1982, 'Bravermania and beyond: recent theories of the labour process', *Sociology*, **16**, 251-69.

Lloyd, P.E., 1988, *Fragmenting Markets and the Dynamic Restructuring of Production: Issues for Spatial Policy* (Manchester: University of Manchester, Department of Geography, North West Industry Research Unit Working Paper 21).

Lloyd, P.E. and Dicken, P., 1977, *Location in Space: A Theoretical Approach to Economic Geography* [2nd edn] (London: Harper & Row).

Lloyd, P.E. and Shutt, J., 1985, 'Recession and restructuring in the North West region 1975-82: the implications of recent events', in D. Massey and R. Meegan (eds), *Politics and Method: Contrasting Studies in Industrial Geography* (London: Methuen), 13-60.

Lodkowska, G., 1985, 'Przestrzenne zróżnicowanie poziomu i warunków życia ludności w Polsce w 1980 r. [Spatial differentiation of living standards and conditions in Poland in

1980]', *Przegląd Geograficzny*, **57**(3), 319-40.

Lojkine, J., 1976, *Stratégies des Grandes Entreprises et Politiques Urbaines [Big Firms' Strategies and Urban Policies]* (Paris: Centre d'Etude des Mouvements Sociaux).

London, B., Lee, B.A. and Lipton, S.G., 1986, 'The determinants of gentrification in the United States: a city-level analysis', *Urban Affairs Quarterly*, **21**, 369-87.

Lorenz, E., 1984, 'Labour supply and employment strategies of French and British shipbuilders' (paper presented to the International Working Party on Labour Market Segmentation, Budapest).

Loveridge, R. and Mok, A., 1976, 'Theories of labour market segmentation: Main Report', in *Programme of Research and Actions on the Development of the Labour Market* (Commission of the European Communities, Stud. 76/1).

Loveridge, R. and Mok, A., 1979, *Theories of Labour Market Segmentation* (The Hague: Martinus Nijhoff).

Lulofs, J.G., 1987, 'Vakbeweging tussen arbeidsmarkt en arbeidsorganisatie [Labour unions between labour market and labour organisation]', in A. Burtendam (ed.), *Arbeidsmarkt – Arbeidsorganisatie – Arbeidsverhoudingen [Labour Market – Labour Organisation – Labour Relations]* (Deventer: Kluwer), 153-78.

Luria, D.D., 1986, 'New labor-management models from Detroit?' *Harvard Business Review*, **64**(5), 22-32.

Lutz, V., 1962, *Italy: A Study in Economic Development* (London: Oxford University Press).

Mackenzie, S., 1987, 'Neglected spaces in peripheral places: homeworkers and the creation of a new economic centre', *Cahiers de Géographie du Québec*, **31**, 247-60.

Macpherson, C.B. (ed.), 1978, *Property: Mainstream and Critical Positions* (Toronto: University of Toronto Press).

Madden, J.F., 1981, 'Why women work closer to home', *Urban Studies*, **18**, 181-94.

Maguire, M., 1988, 'Work, locality and social control', *Work, Employment and Society*, **2**, 71-87.

Mahon, R., 1987, 'From Fordism to ?: new technologies, labour markets and unions', *Economic and Industrial Democracy*, **8**, 5-60.

Maik, W., 1986, 'Struktura funkcjonalna miast [Functional structure of towns]', in R. Domański and S. Kozarski (eds), *Województwo poznańskie. Zagadnienia geograficzne i społeczno-gospodarcze* [*Poznań voivodeship. Geographical and Socio-economic Issues*] (Warsaw-Poznań: Państwowe Wydawnictwo Naukowe), 242-6.

Mandel, E., 1975, *Late Capitalism* (London: New Left Books).

Manikowska, B., Matykowski, R. and Stryjakiewicz, T., 1985, 'Tendencje lokalizacyjne i struktura przestrzenna przedsiebiorstw polonijno-zagranicznych w Polsce [Location tendencies and spatial structure of foreign enterprises in Poland]', *Czasopismo Geograficzne*, 56(3-4), 365-77.

Manwaring, T. and Wood, S., 1985, 'The ghost in the labour process', in D. Knights, H. Willmott and D. Collinson (eds), *Job Redesign: Critical Perspectives on the Labour Process* (Aldershot: Gower), 171-96.

Marans, R.W. and Rodgers, W., 1975, 'Toward an understanding of community satisfaction', in A.H. Hawley and V.P. Rock (eds), *Metropolitan America in Contemporary Perspective* (New York: Halstead), 299-352.

Markusen, A.R., 1981, 'City spatial structure, women's household work, and national urban policy', in C.R. Stimpson, E. Dixler, M.J. Nelson and K.B. Yatrakis (eds), *Women and the American City* (Chicago: University of Chicago Press), 20-41.

Markusen, A.R., 1985, *Profit Cycles, Oligopoly, and Regional Development* (Cambridge, Mass.: MIT Press).

Martens, A., 1985, 'Vakbondsgroei en vakbondsmacht in België [Union growth and union power in Belgium]', *Tijdschrift voor Arbeidsvraagstukken*, 1(1), 35-41.

Maslow, A.H., 1970, *Motivation and Personality* (New York: Harper & Row).

Massey, D., 1983, 'Industrial restructuring as class restructuring: production decentralization and local uniqueness', *Regional Studies*, 17, 73-90.

Massey, D., 1984, *Spatial Divisions of Labour: Social Structures and the Geography of Production* (London: Macmillan).

Massey, D., 1986, 'The legacy lingers on: the impact of Britain's international role on its internal geography', in R. Martin and B. Rowthorn (eds), *The Geography of De-industrialisation* (London: Macmillan), 31-52.

Massey, D. and Meegan, R., 1978, 'Industrial restructuring versus the cities', *Urban Studies*, 15, 273-88.

Massey, D. and Meegan, R., 1982, *The Anatomy of Job Loss: The How, Why and Where of Employment Decline* (London: Methuen).

References

Matykowski, R., 1987, 'Struktura przestrzenna Gniezna i przemieszczenia jego mieszkańców [The spatial structure of Gniezno and the movement of its population]', unpublished doctoral dissertation (Poznań: Instytut Geografii Społeczno-Ekonomicznej i Planowania Przestrzennego, Adam Mickiewicz University).

Maurer, R.C. and Napier, T.L., 1981, 'Rural residents' perspectives of industrial development', *Rural Sociology*, **46**, 100-11.

Maurice, M., Sellier, F. and Silvestre, J.J., 1984, 'Rules, contexts and actors: observations based on a comparison between France and Germany', *British Journal of Industrial Relations*, **22**, 346-63.

McCall, J.J., 1970, 'Economics of information and job search', *The Quarterly Journal of Economics*, **84**, 113-26.

Michelson, G., 1985, 'La problematica dell'industrializzazione diffusa nelle scienze sociali italiane [The problems of diffused industrialisation in the Italian social sciences]', in R. Innocenti (ed.), *Piccola Città e Piccola Impresa: Urbanizzazione, Industrializzazione e Intervento Pubblico nelle Aree Perifreiche [Small Towns and Small Enterprises: Urbanisation, Industrialisation and Public Intervention in the Peripheral Areas]* (Milan: Angeli), 73-98.

Mok, A.L., 1985, 'Arbeidsverhoudingen in Nederland en België [Labour relations in The Netherlands and Belgium]', *Tijdschrift voor Arbeidsvraagstukken*, **1**(1), 4-17.

Moore, W.J. and Newman, R.J., 1975, 'On the prospects for American trade union growth: a cross-section analysis', *Review of Economics and Statistics*, **57**, 435-45.

Morris, L., 1987, 'Constraints on gender: the family wage, social security and the labour market: reflections on research in Hartlepool', *Work, Employment and Society*, **1**, 85-106.

Moulaert, F., 1987, 'An institutional revisit to the Storper-Walker theory of labour', *International Journal of Urban and Regional Research*, **11**, 309-30.

Murgatroyd, L. and Urry, J., 1984, 'The re-structuring of a local economy: the case of Lancaster', in D. Massey and J. Allen (eds), *Geography Matters! A Reader* (Cambridge: Cambridge University Press), 112-27.

Nelson, K., 1986, 'Labor demand, labor supply and the suburbanization of low-wage office work', in A.J. Scott and M. Storper (eds), *Production, Work, Territory: The Geographical*

Anatomy of Industrial Capitalism (Boston: Allen and Unwin), 149-71.

Newby, H., Bujra, J., Littlewood, P., Rees, G. and Rees, T.L., 1985, *Restructuring Capital: Recession and Reorganization in Industrial Society* [Explorations in Sociology 20] (London: Macmillan).

Nichols, T., 1986, *The British Worker Question: A New Look at Workers and Productivity in Manufacturing* (London: Routledge and Kegan Paul).

Norcliffe, G.B., 1984, 'Nonmetropolitan industrialization and the theory of production', *Urban Geography*, **5**, 25-42.

Nord, P., 1987, 'Labour, commerce and consumption: studies in market culture in nineteenth century France', *Radical History Review*, **37**, 82-92.

Oakey, R., 1984, *High Technology Small Firms: Innovation and Regional Development in Britain and the United States* (London: Frances Pinter).

Offe, C. (ed.), 1985, *Disorganized Capitalism: Contemporary Transformations of Work and Politics* (Cambridge: Polity Press).

Offe, C. and Berger, J., 1985, 'The future of the labour market', in C. Offe (ed.), *Disorganized Capitalism: Contemporary Transformations of Work and Politics* (Cambridge: Polity Press), 52-79.

Offe, C. and Hinrichs, K., 1985, 'The political economy of the labour market', in C. Offe (ed.), *Disorganized Capitalism: Contemporary Transformations of Work and Politics* (Cambridge: Polity Press), 10-51.

Oppenheimer, M., 1985, *White Collar Politics* (New York: Monthly Review Press).

Owen, S.J., 1987, 'Household production and economic efficiency: arguments against domestic specialization', *Work, Employment and Society*, **1**, 157-78.

Paci, M. (ed.), 1980, *Famiglia e Mercato del Lavoro in un Economia Periferica* [*Family and Labour Market in a Peripheral Economy*] (Milan: Angeli).

Paci, M., 1981, 'Struttura di classe e complessità sociale [Class structure and social complexity]', *Inchiesta*, **54**, 81-8.

Pacione, M., 1982, 'The use of objective and subjective measures of life quality in human geography', *Progress in Human Geography*, **6**, 495-514.

Palloix, C., 1975, *L'Internationalisation du Capital* [*The*

Internationalisation of Capital] (Paris: F.Maspero).

Palloix, C., 1976, 'The labour process: from Fordism to Neo-Fordism', in Conference of Socialist Economists, *The Labour Process and Class Strategies* (London: Stage One), 46-67.

Palmer, B., 1975, 'Class, conception and conflict: the thrust for efficiency, managerial views of labour and the working class rebellion, 1903-22', *Review of Radical Political Economics*, **7**(2), 31-49.

Parker, M., 1986, *Inside the Circle: A Union Guide to QWL* [Quality of Working Life] (Detroit: Labor Notes).

Peck, J.A., 1984, *A Dynamic Approach to the Study of Unemployment* (Manchester: Manchester University, Department of Geography, North West Industry Research Unit Working Paper 14).

Peck, J.A., 1988, 'The structure and segmentation of local labour markets: aspects of the geographical anatomy of youth employment in Great Britain', unpublished doctoral dissertation (Manchester: Manchester University, Department of Geography).

Peck, J.A. and Haughton, G.H., 1987, *Training and the Contemporary Reconstruction of Skill* (Manchester: Manchester University, Department of Geography, North West Industry Research Unit Working Paper 19).

Peck, J.A., Haughton, G.H. and Lloyd, P.E., 1987, *Skills in Flux: Inertia and Change in the Engineering Industry* (London: Economic and Social Research Council).

Perrons, D.C., 1981, 'The role of Ireland in the new international division of labour: a proposed framework for regional analysis', *Regional Studies*, **15**, 81-100.

Phillips, A. and Taylor, B., 1980, 'Sex and skill: notes towards a feminist economics', *Feminist Review*, **6**, 79-88.

Piore, M.J., 1968, 'The impact of the labour market upon the design and selection of productive techniques within the manufacturing plant', *The Quarterly Journal of Economics*, **82**, 602-20.

Piore, M.J., 1979, 'Dualism in the labour market: a response to uncertainty and flux: the case of France', *Revue Economique*, **19**, 26-48.

Piore, M.J. and Sabel, C.F., 1984, *The Second Industrial Divide: Possibilities for Prosperity* (New York: Basic Books).

Poland, *Rocznik Statystyczny, 1986* [*Statistical Yearbook, 1986*] (Warsaw: Główny Urząd Statystyczny).

References

Pratt, G. and Hanson, S., 1988, 'Gender, class and space', *Environment and Planning D: Society and Space*, **6**, 15-35.

Pred, A., 1985, 'Interpenetrating processes: human agency and the becoming of regional spatial and social structures', *Papers of the Regional Science Association*, **57**, 7-17.

Pyke, F., 1986, 'Labour flexibility and the use of time' [mimeo] (Manchester: Manchester University, Department of Geography, North West Industry Research Unit).

Pyke, F., 1987, 'Industrial networks and modes of co-operation in a British context' [mimeo] (Manchester: Manchester University, Department of Geography, North West Industry Research Unit).

Raffestin, C., 1980, *Pour une Géographie du Pouvoir* [*Towards a Geography of Power Relations*] (Paris: Litec).

Rainnie, A.F., 1984, 'Combined and uneven development in the clothing industry: the effects of competition on accumulation', *Capital and Class*, **22**, 141-56.

Reich, M., 1981, *Racial Inequality: A Political Economic Analysis* (Princeton: Princeton University Press).

Reid, D.M., 1981, 'Labor, management and the state in an industrial town: Decazeville, 1826-1914', unpublished doctoral dissertation (Stanford: Stanford University, Department of History).

Reijnaerts, W.H.J., 1983, 'Collectieve onderhandelingen [Collective bargaining]', in W.H.J. Reijnaerts (ed.), *Arbeidsverhoudingen, Theorie en Praktijk* [*Labour Relations, Theory and Practice*] (Leiden: Stenfert Kroese), 1-77.

Reijnaerts, W.H.J., 1985, 'Kantelende posities, arbeidsverhoudingen in een keertijd [Turning positions, labour market relations in changing times]', in *Bespiegelingen over de Toekomst van de Sociale Partners* [*Reflections About the Future of Social Partnerships*] (The Hague: OSA), 1-84.

Reynolds, L.G., 1978, *Labor Economics and Labor Relations* [7th edn] (Englewood Cliffs: Prentice-Hall).

Robertson, D. and Wareham, J., 1987, *Technological Change in the Auto Industry: CAW Technology Project* (Willowdale, Ontario: Canadian Auto Workers Union).

Robinson, F., 1987, *'It's Not Really Like That'* ... *Living With Unemployment in the North-East* [A special report for BBC North-East] (Newcastle: University of Newcastle upon Tyne, Centre for Urban and Regional Development Studies).

Rose, D., 1984, 'Rethinking gentrification: beyond the uneven development of Marxist urban theory', *Environment and Planning D: Society and Space*, **2**, 47-74.

Rose, D. and Villeneuve, P., 1988, 'Women workers and the inner city: some social implications of labour force restructuring in Montreal, 1971-1981', in C. Andrew and B. Moore-Milroy (eds), *Life Spaces: Gender, Households, Employment* (Vancouver: University of British Columbia Press).

Rose, J. and Jones, B., 1985, 'Management strategy and trade union response in the plant-level reorganization of work', in D. Knights, H. Willmott and D. Collinson (eds), *Job Redesign: Critical Perspectives on the Labour Process* (Aldershot: Gower), 81-106.

Ross, A.M. and Hartman, P.T., 1960, *Changing Patterns of Industrial Conflict* (New York: Wiley).

Ross, C.E., 1987, 'The division of labor at home', *Social Forces*, **65**, 816-33.

Rothwell, R. and Zegveld, W., 1985, *Reindustrialisation and Technology* (London: Longman).

Rubery, J., 1978, 'Structured labour markets, worker organisation and low pay', *Cambridge Journal of Economics*, **2**, 17-36.

Rubery, J. and Wilkinson, F., 1981, 'Outwork and segmented labour markets', in F. Wilkinson (ed.), *The Dynamics of Labour Market Segmentation* (London: Academic Press), 115-32.

Rutkowski, J., 1984, *Rozwój gospodarczy i poziom życia* [*Economic Development and Quality of Life*] (Warsaw: Główny Urząd Statystyczny).

Rutkowski, J., 1986, 'Społeczna efektywność rozwoju gospodarczego Polski w latach 1960-1981 [Social efficiency of economic development in Poland 1960-1981]', *Gospodarka Planowa*, **1**, 23-8.

Sabel, C., 1979, 'Ambiguities of class and the possibility of politics', in A.Liebich (ed.), *The Future of Socialism in Europe?* (Montreal: Interuniversity Centre for European Studies), 257-79.

Sabel, C., 1982, *Work and Politics: The Division of Labour in Industry* (Cambridge: Cambridge University Press).

Sabel C., and Zeitlin, J., 1985, 'Historical alternatives to mass production: politics, markets and technology in nineteenth-century industrialization', *Past and Present*, **108**, 133-76.

Salop, S.C., 1973, 'Systematic job search and unemployment', *The Review of Economic Studies*, **40**, 191-201.

Sawers, L. and Tabb, W.K. (eds), 1984, *Sunbelt — Snowbelt: Urban Development and Regional Restructuring* (New York: Oxford University Press).

Sayer, A., 1984, *Method in Social Science: A Realist Approach* (London: Hutchinson).

Schaefer, G.P., 1977, 'The urban hierarchy and urban area production function: a synthesis', *Urban Studies*, **14**, 315-26.

Scott, A.J., 1981, 'The spatial structure of metropolitan labor markets and the theory of intra-urban plant location', *Urban Geography*, **2**, 1-30.

Scott, A.J., 1986, 'Industrial organization and location: division of labor, the firm and spatial process', *Economic Geography*, **62**, 215-31.

Scott, A.J. and Storper, M., 1986a, 'The geographical anatomy of industrial capitalism: a summing up', in A.J. Scott and M. Storper (eds), *Production, Work Territory: The Geographical Anatomy of Industrial Capitalism* (Boston: Allen and Unwin), 301-11.

Scott, A.J. and Storper, M. (eds), 1986b, *Production, Work, Territory: The Geographical Anatomy of Industrial Capitalism* (Boston: Allen and Unwin).

Screpanti, E., 1987, 'Long cycles in strike activity', *British Journal of Industrial Relations*, **25**, 99-124.

Séguin, A-M. and Villeneuve, P., 1987, 'Du rapport hommes-femmes au centre de la Haute-Ville de Québec [Gender relations in Quebec's inner upper town]', *Cahiers de Géographie du Québec*, **31**, 189-204.

Shils, E., 1975, *Center and Periphery: Essays in Macrosociology* (Chicago: University of Chicago Press).

Shlay, A.B. and DiGregorio, D.A., 1985, 'Same city different worlds: examining gender- and work-based differences in perceptions of neighborhood desirability', *Urban Affairs Quarterly*, **21**, 66-86.

Shorter, E. and Tilly, C., 1974, *Strikes in France, 1830-1968* (London: Cambridge University Press).

Shutt, J. and Whittington, R., 1984, *Large Firm Strategies and the Rise of Small Units: the Illusion of Small Firm Job Generation* (Manchester: Manchester University, Department of Geography, North West Industry Research Unit Working Paper 15).

Shutt, J. and Whittington, R., 1987, 'Fragmentation strategies and the rise of small units: case studies from the North West', *Regional Studies*, **21**, 13-23.

References

Simpson, W., 1987, 'Workplace location, residential location, and urban commuting', *Urban Studies*, **24**, 119-28.

Singell, L.D. and Lillydahl, J.H., 1986, 'An empirical analysis of the commute to work patterns of males and females in two-earner households', *Urban Studies*, **23**, 119-29.

Smit, E. and Visser, J.C., 1986, 'Bedrijfssluiting en bedrijfsbezetting [Factory closure and factory occupation]', *Tijdschrift voor Arbeidsvraagstukken*, **2**(1), 13-25.

Smith, D. and Irwin, A., 1984, 'Public attitudes to technological risk: the contribution of survey data to public policy-making', *Transactions, Institute of British Geographers*, **9**, 419-26.

Sofranko, A.J. and Fliegel, F.C., 1984, 'Dissatisfaction with satisfaction', *Rural Sociology*, **49**, 353-73.

Soja, E., Morales, R. and Wolff, G., 1987, 'Industrial restructuring: an analysis of social and spatial change in Los Angeles', in R. Peet (ed.), *International Capitalism and Industrial Restructuring: A Critical Analysis* (Boston: Allen and Unwin), 145-76.

Soja, M., 1986, 'Functioning of the Lenin Steel Works in Kraków in the light of selected spatial links', *Zeszyty Naukowe Uniwersytetu Jagiellońskiego, Prace Geograficzne*, **66**, 61-92.

Spooner, D., 1981, Mining and *Regional Development* (Oxford: Oxford University Press).

Stark, D., 1980, 'Class struggle and the transformation of the labor process: a rational approach', *Theory and Society*, **9**, 89-130.

Staveley, M., 1987, 'Newfoundland: economy and society on the margin', in L.D. McCann (ed.), *Heartland and Hinterland: A Geography of Canada* (Scarborough: Prentice-Hall), 247-85.

Storper, M., 1985a, 'The spatial and temporal constitution of social action: a critical reading of Giddens', *Environment and Planning D: Society and Space*, **3**, 407-24.

Storper, M., 1985b, 'Oligopoly and the product cycle: essentialism in economic geography', *Economic Geography*, **61**, 260-82.

Storper, M. and Walker, R., 1983, 'The theory of labour and the theory of location', *International Journal of Urban and Regional Research*, **7**, 1-41.

Streeck, W., 1985a, *Industrial Relations and Industrial Change in the Motor Industry: An International View* (Coventry: University of Warwick, Industrial Relations Research Unit).

Streeck, W. (ed.), 1985b, *Industrial Relations and Technical Change in the British, Italian and German Automobile*

Industry: Three Case Studies (Berlin: International Institute of Management, Labour Market Policy Discussion Paper, 85-5).

Stryjakiewicz, T., 1987, 'Kierunki badawcze geografii przemysłu w Polsce [Research trends in industrial geography in Poland]', in Z. Zioło (ed.), *Geografia przemysłu w akademickim kształceniu nauczycieli [Industrial Geography in an Academic Training of Teachers]* (Kraków: Wyższa Szkoła Pedagogiczna), 22-45.

Stryjakiewicz, T., 1988, *Czynniki lokalizacji i funkcjonowania przemysłu rolno-spożywczego oraz jego struktura przestrzenna w regionie poznańskim [Factors of Location and Functioning of the Agricultural Processing Industry and its Spatial Structure in the Poznań Region]* (Poznań: Adam Mickiewicz University).

Szczepański, J., 1973, *Zmiany społeczeństwa polskiego w procesie uprzemysłowienia [Changes in Polish Society in the Process of Industrialisation]* (Warsaw: Instytut Wydawniczy Centralnej Rady Związków Zawodowych).

Taaffe, E.J., Morrill, R.L. and Gould, P.R., 1963, 'Transport expansion in underdeveloped countries: a comparative analysis', *Geographical Review*, **53**, 503-59.

Taylor, F. W., 1911, *The Principles of Scientific Management* (New York: Harper).

Taylor, M.J., 1987, 'Enterprise and the product-cycle model: conceptual ambiguities', in G.A. van der Knaap and E. Wever (eds), *New Technology and Regional Development* (London: Croom Helm), 75-93.

Taylor, M.J. and Thrift, N.J., 1982, 'Industrial linkage and the segmented economy: 1. Some theoretical proposals', *Environment and Planning A*, **14**, 1601-13.

The Netherlands, Centraal Bureau voor de Statistiek, 1985, *Statistiek van de Vakbeweging [Statistics of the Labour Unions]* (The Hague: CBS).

Thomas, R.J., 1985, *Participation and Control: New Trends in Labor Relations in the Auto Industry* (Ann Arbor: University of Michigan, Center for Research on Social Organization, Working Paper 315).

Thompson, E.P., 1978, *The Poverty of Theory, and Other Essays* (London: Merlin Press).

Thompson, J.G. and Blevins, A.L., 1983, 'Attitudes towards energy development in the Northern Great Plains', *Rural Sociology*, **48**, 148-58.

References

Thompson, P., 1983, *The Nature of Work: An Introduction to Debate on the Labour Process* (London: Macmillan).

Tinacci-Mossello, M., 1984, 'Laboro e risorse nell'organizzazione regionale [Labour and resources in the regional organisation]', *Rivista Geografica Italiana*, **91**, 371-95.

Tolliday, S. and Zeitlin, J., 1986, 'Introduction: between Fordism and flexibility', in S. Tolliday and J. Zeitlin (eds), *The Automobile Industry and Its Workers: Between Fordism and Flexibility* (Oxford: Polity Press), 1-26.

Törnqvist, G., 1970, *Contact Systems and Regional Development* (Lund: Gleerup, Lund Studies in Geography, Series B, No. 35).

Törnqvist, G., 1978, 'Swedish industry as a spatial system', in F.E.I. Hamilton (ed.), *Contemporary Industrialization* (London: Longman), 86-109.

Treu, M.C., 1983, 'Decentramento produttivo e capitale fisso sociale [Industrial decentralisation and fixed social capital]', in Instituto Regionale di Ricerca della Lombardia, *I Fattori Territoriali nello Sviluppo della Piccola e Media Impresa* [*Spatial Factors in the Development of Small and Medium Size Enterprise*] (Milan: Angeli), 87-170.

Tuppen, J., 1983, *The Economic Geography of France* (London: Croom Helm).

Turner, H.A., 1962, *Trade Union Growth, Structure and Policy: A Comparative Study of the Cotton Unions* (London: Allen and Unwin).

Urry, J., 1981, 'Localities, regions and social class', *International Journal of Urban and Regional Research*, **5**, 455-73.

Urry, J., 1982, 'Some themes in the analysis of the anatomy of contemporary capitalist societies', *Acta Sociologica*, **25**, 405-18.

van der Knaap, G.A., 1987, 'Labour market and spatial policy', *Tijdschrift voor Economische en Sociale Geografie*, **78**, 348-58.

van der Knaap, G.A. and Erkens, G., 1982, 'De stabiliteit van de regionale inkomens verdeling [The stability of regional income distributions]', *Geografisch Tijdschrift*, **16**, 114-28.

van der Knaap. G.A. and Louter, P., 1986, *De Middelgrote Stad* [*The Medium-size City*] (Rotterdam: Erasmus University, Economic Geography Institute).

van der Knaap, G.A. and van Geenhuizen, M., 1988, *A Longitudinal Analysis of the Growth of Firms* (Rotterdam:

Erasmus University, Economic Geography Institute).

van der Knaap, G.A., Linge, G.J.R. and Wever, E., 1987, 'Technology and industrial change: an overview', in G.A. van der Knaap and E. Wever (eds), *New Technology and Regional Development* (London: Croom Helm), 1-20.

van der Laan, L., 1987, 'Causal processes in spatial labour markets', *Tijdschrift voor Economische en Sociale Geografie*, **78**, 325-39.

van der Pligt, J., Eiser, J.R. and Spears, R., 1986, 'Attitudes toward nuclear energy. Familiarity and salience', *Environment and Behavior*, **18**, 75-93.

van Duijn, J.J., 1977, *Eb en Vloed, de Lange Golf in het Economisch Leven* [*Ebb and Flow, the Long Wave in Economic Life*], Inaugural lecture (Delft: Interfaculteit Bedrijfskunde).

van Duijn, J.J., 1979, *De Lange Golf in de Economie, kan Innovatie ons uit het dal Helpen* [*The Long Wave in Economics an Innovative Way to Come out of the Trough*] (Assen: Van Gorcum).

van Hoof, J., 1987, *De Arbeidsmarkt als Arena* [*The Labour Market as an Arena*] (Amsterdam: SUA).

van Kooten, G. and van der Laan, L., 1987. 'Ruimtelijke aspecten van het stakingsgedrag [Spatial aspects of strike behaviour]', *Maandschrift Economie*, **51**, 379-92.

van Liere, K.D. and Dunlap, R.E., 1980, 'The social bases of environmental concern: a review of hypotheses, explanations and empirical evidence', *Public Opinion Quarterly*, **44**, 181-97.

van Voorden, W., 1985, 'De verscheidenheid van flexibilisering van de arbeidsmarkt [The variety of the flexibilities of the labour market]', in *Pre-adviezen over de Flexibilisering van de Arbeidsmarkt* [*Report About the Flexibility of the Labour Market*] (The Hague: OSA), 37-49.

van Weenen, B., 1977, *De Gevolgen van Automatisering voor de Organistie* [*The Organisational Consequences of Automation*] (Tilburg: University Press).

Vernon, R., 1977, *Storm over the Multinationals: The Real Issues* (Cambridge, Mass.: Harvard University Press).

Villeneuve, P. and Rose, D., 1986, 'Force de travail et redéploiement industriel dans la région de Québec, 1971-1981 [Labour force and industrial restructuring in the Quebec city region, 1971-1981]', *Canadian Journal of Regional Science*, **9**,

183-205.

Villeneuve, P. and Rose, D., 1988, 'Gender and the separation between employment and home in Metropolitan Montreal, 1971-1981', *Urban Geography*, **9**, 155-79.

Villeneuve, P. and Viaud, G., 1987, 'Asymétrie occupationelle et localisation résidentielle des familles à double revenu à Montréal [Occupational asymmetry and residential location of double-earner families in Montreal]', *Recherche Sociographiques*, **28**, 371-91.

Vinay, P., 1985, 'Family life cycle and the informal economy in central Italy', *International Journal of Urban and Regional Research*, **9**, 82-98.

Visser, J., 1985, 'Vakbondsgroei en vakbondsmacht in West-Europa [Union growth and union power in West Europe]', *Tijdschrift vor Arbeidsvraagstukken*, **1**(1), 18-38.

Visser, J.C., 1986, 'Bedrijfsbezetting, het verleden van een nieuw actiemiddel [Factory occupation, the history of a new approach to action]', unpublished dissertation (Rotterdam: Erasmus University).

Walker, R. and Storper, M., 1981, 'Capital and industrial location', *Progress in Human Geography*, **5**, 473-509.

Walker, W.B., 1979, *Industrial Innovation and International Trading Performance* (Greenwich, Conn.: Jai Press).

Warde, A., 1985, 'Spatial change, politics and the division of labour', in D. Gregory and J. Urry (eds), *Social Relations and Spatial Structures* (London: Macmillan), 190-212.

Watts, H.D., 1981, *The Branch Plant Economy: A Study of External Control* (Harlow: Longman).

Webber, M.J., 1984, *Explanation, Prediction and Planning: The Lowry Model* (London: Pion).

Webber, M.J., 1986, 'Regional production and the production of regions: the case of Steeltown', in A.J. Scott and M. Storper (eds), *Production, Work and Territory: the Geographical Anatomy of Industrial Capitalism* (Boston: Allen and Unwin), 197-224.

Wells, D., 1986, *Soft Sell: QWL and the Productivity Race* (Ottawa: Canadian Centre for Policy Alternatives).

Wever, E., 1985, *Regionaal-economisch Perspectief* [*Regional Economic Perspective*] (Nijmegen: Katholieke Universiteit, Geografisch en Planologisch Instituut).

White, M., 1983, 'Long-term employment: labour market aspects', *Employment Gazette*, **91**, 437-43.

References

White, R., 1986, 'The old and the new: workplace organization and labour relations in the auto industry', *Atkinson Review of Canadian Studies*, **4**(1), 8-10.

Williams, K., Cutler, T., Williams, J. and Haslam, C., 1987, 'The end of mass production?', *Economy and Society*, **16**, 404-39.

Williamson, O.E., 1975, *Markets and Hierarchies: Analysis and Antitrust Implications: A Study in the Economics of Internal Organization* (New York: The Free Press).

Williamson, O.E., 1985, *The Economic Institutions of Capitalism: Firms, Markets, Relational Contracting* (New York: The Free Press).

Windolf, P., 1985, 'Industrial robots in the West German automotive industry', *Politics and Society*, **14**, 459-95.

Wójcik, P., (ed.), 1984, *Położenie klasy robotniczej w Polsce* [*The Situation of the Working Class in Poland*]: *Vol. 1, Work Conditions and Standard of Health* (Warsaw: Instytut Podstawowych Problemów Marksizmu-Leninizmu KC PZPR).

Wood, S., 1982, 'Introduction', in S. Wood (ed.), *The Degradation of Work? Skill, Deskilling and the Labour Process (London: Hutchinson), 11-22.*

Wood, S., 1986, 'The cooperative labour strategy in the US auto industry', *Economic and Industrial Democracy*, **7**, 415-47.

Zacholska, E., 1986, 'Zmiana powiązań przestrzennych przemyslu Gniezna w latach 1976-84 [Change of spatial links of the industry of Gniezno 1976-84]', unpublished masters dissertation (Poznań: Instytut Geografii Społeczno-Ekonomicznej i Planowania Przestrzennego, Adam Mickiewicz University).

Żechowski, Z.A., 1973, *Przemiany małych miast w procesie uprzemyslowienia* [*Transformations of Small Towns in the Process of Industrialisation*] (Warsaw: Państwowe Wydawnictwo Naukowe).

Zeitlin, J., 1979, 'Craft control and the division of labour: engineers and compositors in Britain, 1890-1930', *Cambridge Journal of Economics*, **3**, 263-74.

Zeitlin, J., 1981, 'Craft regulation and the division of labour: engineers and compositors in Britain, 1890-1914', unpublished doctoral dissertation (Coventry : University of Warwick, Department of History).

Zienkowski, L., 1987, *Walka o podział dochodów* [*A Struggle for the Division of Incomes*] (Warsaw: Głowny Urząd Statystyczny).

Index

American Motors
    Corporation (AMC) 100,
    102
'areas of ecological danger'
    (Poland) 47
attitudes to industry 50-66
Australia 147
Austria 148, 149, 154, 155
authority constraints 130,
    187
automated control systems 2
automated guided vehicles
    (AGVs) 92
automobile industry, North
    American 87-106

Basque country 17
Belgium 147
bio-technology 2, 10
'black' economy 16-17,
    173, 183
blue-collar jobs 140, 174,
    175, 178, 182
Brampton (Ontario) 98
Bromont (Canada) 169, 175-
    8, 181
Bulgaria 45
business cycles 146 (*see
    also* Kondratiev)

Canada 45, 73, 92, 94, 102,
    106, 169, 172
Canadian Auto Workers Union
    102, 104
capability constraints 130
capital-intensive industry 13, 80,
    163-4
capitalist mode of production
    108
centralisation of decision power
    11
centrally planned economies 10,
    39-49, 128
Chrysler Corporation 98, 100,
    102
'closed shop' system 146
collective bargaining 87, 145,
    154
collective labour agreement
    (CAO) 145
commuting, *see* journey to work
computer integrated manu-
    facturing (CIM) 93
computer numerically controlled
    (CNC) tools 92, 93, 96
conditions of work 5, 13, 46, 48,
    49, 95, 99, 106, 137
connective bargaining 100, 101,
    104-5

constraints:
  authority 130, 187
  binding 3
  capability 130
  space-time 130, 137
  steering 130
consumer organisations, as
  power groups 14
'contingent' labour 90
contract labour 90
coping strategies 19, 167-84
'core' workers 90
corporate coping strategies 169-72
cost of living 147
cost of living escalator (COLA) 100
cottage industries 173
craft:
  employment 113, 121, 124
  industries 173
  skills 109, 110, 122, 134
  trade unions 121
  traditional 1
  workers 113
cycles of investment (Poland) 42-4
cyclical growth patterns 8
Czechoslovakia 45

decentralisation of:
  collective bargaining 154
  decision power 11, 32
  production 32, 35, 67
deconcentration of industry 163
dehumanised labour 2
Denmark 147, 148, 149, 155
de-skilling 25, 108, 109, 110, 112, 117-18, 119, 127, 174, 182
diffusion of manufacturing 9
discrimination theory 22

disorganised capitalism 113
diversification of output 6
Drente 155, 164
dual structure labour markets 27-30
dynamic market theory 8, 9
Działoszyce 63

early retirement 95, 115, 131, 132
economic base theory 74
economic recession 7, 48, 156
education of workforce 4, 131, 178
efficiency of production 13, 104, 131, 136
'electronic' cottages 80
employment, craft 113, 121, 124
employment security 18, 85, 93, 104
Engineering Industry Training Board (UK) 124
environment:
  external (of firms) 5, 14
  household 5
  internal (of firms) 5, 14
  metropolitan 11, 67-86
  natural 46
  rural 11
  social 5, 11
  work 5, 6, 11, 46, 95
environmental pollution 47, 49, 51, 62, 64
environmental sensitivity 53, 61-3
ethnicity 24
European Economic Community 17, 156
'exit' and 'voice' 69, 144
external environments of firms 5, 14
external labour markets 13

factory occupations 151-4, 159, 162-3
Federal Republic of Germany 45, 144, 149, 151, 155
female workers (*see* gender, women)
firms:
  capital-intensive 13, 80, 163-4
  external environments 5, 14
  'family' 34
  growth paths 8
  high technology 11
  interaction with households 68
  internal environments 5, 14
  internal labour markets 13
  labour-intensive 13, 80, 163-4
  large 7, 10, 13, 32
  multi-plant 6, 9
  organisational structure 7, 8
  small 7, 9, 10, 13, 19, 31, 113, 117, 119, 120, 122, 125, 172
finished consumer goods 6
fixed social capital 35
flexibility of production 13, 87, 88, 90, 91, 93, 96, 102, 106, 113, 151, 153
flexible machine systems (FMS) 93
Ford Motor Company 100, 102
Fordist management system 2, 87-9, 96, 99, 102, 106, 112, 113, 122, 127,
France 45, 145, 154, 155
Friesland 155, 164

Gdańsk 40, 47
Gelderland 155, 164
gender 67-86
gender:
  relations 68, 71, 82
  roles 115, 122
  trade unions 148

urban centrality 73-9
General Motors Corporation 100, 102
gentrification 82, 84-5
German Democratic Republic 45
GM Job Evaluation Centre 98
GM Packard Division 104
GM Saturn Project 104
GM-Suzuki plant 104
GM-Toyota joint venture 103
GM truck plant 98
Gniezno 130, 131, 132, 135, 137, 138-9
governance structures 12, 13, 15, 68, 69, 70, 71-2, 85
government assistance 171, 182, 184
government policies 125
Groningen 164

handicapped workers 138
'hard' technology 89, 93, 96
health and safety 47, 48, 95
Heckscher-Ohlin theorem 80
hierarchy of needs theory 10, 11, 13, 175
horizontal mergers 9
households:
  as governance structures 81
  as power groups 14
  career orientated 80
  coping strategies 168-84
  decision making 68
  dual earner 72, 73, 80, 82, 83, 85
  externalisation of tasks 68
  home orientated 80, 83-4
  interactions with firms 68
  single breadwinner 81
  single parent 72
  skills 19, 109
  urban centrality 79-85

housing 40, 41, 44, 62, 64, 67
human capital theory 22
humanising labour 13
Hungary 45

income per capita 156
industrial districts 31, 34, 35
industrial parks 171-2
industrial periphery 32, 33-5
industry, urban community
    attitudes 57-63
informal economy 16-17, 173,
    183
informal working practices 32
information society 8
innovation cycle theory 1, 8, 9
institutional economics 12
inter-firm linkages 119, 126
internal environments of firms 5,
    14
internal labour markets 13, 90,
    96, 104, 118
internal training schemes 13
international division of labour
    36, 37, 169
international economic
    recession 7, 156
internationalisation of
    production 9, 19, 153
investment 42-4, 51
Italy 20, 30-2, 33-5, 45, 145, 154
    155

Jelenia Góra 47
job:
    content 95-9
    control focus 105, 107
    de-skilling 96
    off-season 172
    opportunities 9, 94, 158
    redesign of 87
    security 18, 85, 93, 104

job-search theory 22
journey to work 74-5, 81-2, 128,
    129, 134, 137, 140-2
just-in-time (JIT) production 92,
    93, 97, 98

Katowice voivodeship 44, 47
Keynes, J.M. 30
Kolbuszowa 58, 60
Kondratiev waves 1, 2, 3, 155-6,
    162
Kraków 47, 53, 54, 57, 59, 61,
    63

labour:
    activism 144-66 (*see also*
    unions)
    apprentices 124, 125
    'contingent' 89
    dehumanised 2
    demand for 51, 117-21, 123-4
    handicapped 138
    international division of 36,
        37, 169
    laws about 17
    low-skilled 9
    process theory 107-11
    productivity 13, 104, 131, 136
    relations 99-105
    reproduction of 26
    shortage of 123-4
    supply 121-3
labour force:
    education 13, 40, 136
    gender 40, 67, 137
    part-time 105,
    recruitment 98
    skills 40, 94, 97
    training 95, 98, 127
labour 'geography' 107
labour-intensive firms 13, 80,
    163-4

labour market areas 5, 112-16
labour markets:
  dual structure 27-30
  external 13
  internal 13, 90, 96, 104, 118
  local 112-16
  models of 20-38
  neo-institutionalist theory 23-7
  neo-Marxist theory 23-7
  primary 22, 28
  secondary 22, 28
  segmented 15, 27-30, 36-8
  specific 167-84
  state regulation 123
  theories 14, 15, 16, 23-7
labour unions, *see* unions
large firms 7, 10, 13, 32
large-scale mechanisation 119
lay-offs 171, 180
Lenin Steel Works (Kraków) 47,
  49
life expectancy 46
linkages, inter-firm 119, 126
local initiatives 172-3
local labour markets 112-16
local pay bargaining 122
location theory 12, 13
Łódź voivodeship 44
long-wave theory, *see*
  Kondratiev
Lowry model 74

Malaysia 16
marginal workers 32, 170
market-orientated services 164
markets 7, 9, 12
Marxist theory 16, 20, 23-7, 30,
  107, 110
mass consumption 88
mass production 9, 11, 90, 96,
  119
material networks 8

mergers of firms 6, 9
metropolitan environments 11,
  67-86
micro-electronics 2
Montreal 73, 75-8, 82-3, 178,
  180
mortality rates 46
multinational firms 25, 75, 179
multi-plant firms 8
multi-shift operations 97

neo-classical labour market
  theory 16, 20, 21-3
neo-corporative society 144,
  146-7
neo-Fordism 25
neo-institutionalist labour
  market theory 23-7
neo-Marxism 15, 23-7, 150, 152
networks 7, 8
Newfoundland 172
new technologies, skills needs
  95-9
North American auto industry
  87-106
North-Brabant 164
North-Holland 164
North West Region (UK) 119,
  120, 123
Norway 155
Nowy Sącz 45, 57, 59
numerical flexibility 91

Ontario (Canada) 98, 104
organisation of production 13,
organisation of workplace 10
organisational change 13
organisational structure of firms
  7, 8
organisations, social 18
organised labour, *see* unions
output, diversification of 6

out-sourcing 112
outwork 119
Overijssel 155, 164

participation in unions 136, 145, 146, 148, 149
pensioners, employment of 132
peripheral sector 32
peripheral small firms 120
peripheralisation of workers 119
physical networks 7
'poaching' skills 123, 124
Poland 39-47, 50-66, 128-43
pollution, environmental 47, 49, 51, 62, 64
population welfare standards 41
post-Fordism 25, 87-9, 99, 102
post-industrialist school 108
Poznań 130, 134, 136, 140
People's Republic of China 17
primary inputs 6, 7
primary labour markets 22, 28
process innovations 9, 10
producer services 7, 166
producers' equipment 9
product life cycle theory 8, 11, 12, 25
production:
    capitalist mode 108
    cycle 32, 35
    decentralisation of 32, 35
    efficiency 13
    flexibility 13
    internationalisation of 9, 19, 153
    scale 7, 9
    systems 1, 3, 87, 89
productivity 13, 104, 131, 136
programmable controllers 92
programmable systematic automation 93
property rights 85-6

quality circles (QCs) 93
quality of life 39-47, 50-66
Quality of Work Life (QWL) programmes 105
Quebec 169
quick tool and die change (QTD) methods 92, 93, 97

Radomysl 63
Randstad 154, 155, 166
regional formations 36
regional policy 45
reproduction of labour 26
reprogrammable machines 89
residential accommodation 44, 51, 52
re-skilling 174
retirement 95, 115, 131, 132
right to work 146
risk sharing 7
robots 92, 93, 96
Rumania 45
rural urbanisation 31
Rzeszów 58, 59, 60

San Francisco 75
scale of production 2, 7, 164
schools, as power groups 14
Schumpeter, J.A. 30
'scientific management' 2, 11, 13, 25, 108
secondary labour market 28
segmentation of production 13
segmented labour markets 15, 20, 22, 27-30, 36-8
segmented markets 12
semi-skilled workers 164
shift work 97, 137
Skawina 47, 63
skill:
    availability 11
    change 107-11

craft 109, 110, 122, 134
creation of 13, 125
depletion of 114
domestic 115
enhancement 13
gender 174
latent 113, 114, 116
levels 95-9
'poaching' 112-16, 123, 124
pool 112-16, 125, 126
requirements 87
shortages 127
under-utilisation 114, 115
utilisation 112, 114
Słomniki 63
Słupca Konin Industrial District 134
small firms 7, 9, 10, 11, 13, 19, 31, 113, 117, 119, 120, 122, 125, 172
social:
  benefits 129
  change 10
  environment 5
  expectations 40
  formations 36
  infrastructure 57, 61, 64
  needs 40
  organisations 18,
  security 17
'soft' production technologies 89, 96
South-Holland 155, 164
South Korea 17
space-time budgets 80
space-time constraints 130, 137
Spain 16-17
spatial division of labour 25
standard of living 50, 135
standardisation 2, 3, 9, 88
state regulation of labour market 123

statistical process control (SPC) techniques 92, 93, 96
steering constraints 130
strikes 16, 148-66, 182
subcontracting 7, 19, 67, 104, 112, 118, 119, 120
subsidies, government 171
suburbanisation 163
'sunrise' industries 174
'sunset' industries 174
Sweden 147, 148, 149, 155
Switzerland 155
system areas 31

Tarnów 57, 58, 60, 63
task demarcation 94
tasks, standardisation of 2
Taylorist principles 2, 3, 11, 13, 108
team forms of work 96, 105
technological change 1, 6, 10, 13, 18, 99-105
technology:
  automated control systems 2
  automated guided vehicles (AGVs) 92
  backward 47
  computer integrated manu-facturing (CIM) 93
  computer numerically con-trolled (CNC) tools 92, 93, 96
  flexible machine systems (FMS) 93
  'hard' process 93
  just-in-time (JIT) production 92, 93, 97, 98
  programmable controllers 92
  programmable systematic automation 93
  quick tool and die change (QTD) 92, 93

robots 92, 93, 96
'soft' 93
standardisation of 9
statistical process control
  (SPC) techniques 92, 93, 96
total quality control (TQC) 93
temporary labour 90
The Netherlands 16, 45, 145,
  148, 149, 151, 154, 155, 159
theory:
  arena labour market
    approaches 16
  behavioural labour market 16
  discrimination 22
  dual labour market 15, 16
  dynamic market 8, 9
  economic base 74
  hierarchy of needs 52, 57
  human capital 16, 22
  innovation cycle 1, 8, 9
  job-search 22
  labour market 14, 15, 16, 23-7
  labour queue 16
  long-wave, *see* Kondratiev
  institutional labour market 15
  Marxian labour market 16, 20
  neo-classical labour market 16,
    20, 21-3
  neo-classical location 13
  neo-institutionalist labour
    market 23-7
  product life cycle 8, 11, 12, 25
  segmented labour market 20,
    27-30
'Third' Italy 31
time budgets 116
'time-served' apprenticeships
  124
total quality control (TQC) 93
trade unions, *see* unions
transaction cost economics 12,
  68, 69, 70, 85, 86

under-employment 21
unemployment 5, 21, 147, 158,
  174
United Automobile Workers
  Union (UAW) 100, 104
United Kingdom 45, 115, 123,
  146, 147, 148, 149, 155
unionisation, spatial implications
  144-66
unions:
  activism 144-66
  annual improvement factor
    (AIF) 100
  banned 17
  collective bargaining 87, 145,
    154
  connective bargaining 100,
    101, 104-5
  cost of living escalator
    (COLA) 100
  craft 121
  gender 148
  job control focus agreements
    101
  'locals' 104
  militancy 121, 144-66, 182
  participation in 136, 145, 146,
    148, 149
  relationship with management
    14, 15, 69, 95, 99-105
  skill supply 121
  wage rule agreements 100-1
United States 18, 45, 73, 102,
  103, 106, 146, 147
Upper Silesia 47
urban centrality 73-9
urban environment 137
urbanised countryside 31
USSR 45
Utrecht 155, 164

Valleyfield 169, 176, 180-3

vertical mergers 9
vertically related products 34

wages 122, 129, 135-6
Wałbrzych 47
'whipsawing' 105
white-collar jobs 148, 149, 174,
    175, 178
Windsor 169, 176, 178-81
women:
  in paid labour force 68, 71, 72-
    3, 115, 121, 131, 134, 137,
    170, 173, 178
  maternity leave 138
  occupational mobility 79
work environment 5, 6, 11, 46,
    95
work group/teams 96
worker activism, *see* labour
  activism
workers:
  'core' 90
  craft 113
  half-time 132
  handicapped 138
  health 46
  low-skilled 9
  marginal 32, 170
  part-time 91, 112, 132
  'peripheral' 90, 119
  retired 132
  semi-skilled 110
  temporary 112
workforce:
  de-skilling 25
  educational qualifications 4,
    131
  skills 4, 10
working hours 137
working practices 99, 106
workplace management 10, 87
work-related illness 48

Youth Training Scheme (UK)
  125
Yugoslavia 45

Zeeland 155, 164